Apocalyptic Futures

Apocalyptic Futures

MARKED BODIES AND THE VIOLENCE
OF THE TEXT IN KAFKA, CONRAD,
AND COETZEE

Russell Samolsky

FORDHAM UNIVERSITY PRESS   *New York*   2011

ML | the modern language initiative

THIS BOOK IS MADE POSSIBLE BY A COLLABORATIVE GRANT FROM THE ANDREW W. MELLON FOUNDATION.

© 2011 Fordham University Press

All rights reserved. No part of this publication may be reproduced, stored in a retrieval system, or transmitted in any form or by any means—electronic, mechanical, photocopy, recording, or any other—except for brief quotations in printed reviews, without the prior permission of the publisher.

Fordham University Press has no responsibility for the persistence or accuracy of URLs for external or third-party Internet websites referred to in this publication and does not guarantee that any content on such websites is, or will remain, accurate or appropriate.

Fordham University Press also publishes its books in a variety of electronic formats. Some content that appears in print may not be available in electronic books.

Library of Congress Cataloging-in-Publication Data

Samolsky, Russell.
  Apocalyptic futures : marked bodies and the violence of the text in Kafka, Conrad, and Coetzee / Russell Samolsky. — 1st ed.
    p. cm.
  Includes bibliographical references and index.
  ISBN 978-0-8232-3479-0 (cloth : alk. paper)
  ISBN 978-0-8232-3480-6 (pbk.)
  1. Fiction—20th century—History and criticism. 2. Kafka, Franz, 1883–1924—Criticism and interpretation. 3. Conrad, Joseph, 1857–1924—Criticism and interpretation. 4. Coetzee, J. M., 1940—Criticism and interpretation. 5. Spiegelman, Art—Criticism and interpretation. 6. Ethics in literature. 7. Apocalyptic literature. 8. Prophecy in literature. 9. Violence in literature. 10. Mimesis in literature. I. Title. II. Title: Marked bodies and the violence of the text in Kafka, Conrad, and Coetzee. III. Title: Violence of the text in Kafka, Conrad, and Coetzee.
PN3347.S26 2011
809.3'04—dc23
                                2011032058

Printed in the United States of America

13 12 11   5 4 3 2 1

First edition

For Rita, with love and admiration

CONTENTS

List of Figures — viii
Acknowledgments — ix

Introduction: Writing Violence: Marked Bodies
and Retroactive Signs — 1

1. Metaleptic Machines: Kafka, Kabbalah, Shoah — 33
2. Apocalyptic Futures: *Heart of Darkness*, Embodiment,
   and African Genocide — 64
3. The Body in Ruins: Torture, Allegory, and Materiality
   in J. M. Coetzee's *Waiting for the Barbarians* — 123

Coda: The Time of Inscription: *Maus*
and the Apocalypse of Number — 177

Notes — 211
Index — 233

FIGURES

1. *The Thirteenth Book of the Dead*, in which the publisher reads his own fate inscribed on the body of the sumo-wrestler sent to assassinate him   21
2. Leonard's body tattooed with the injunction to kill. The license plate number that will establish John Gammell as his next victim is inscribed on his thigh   22
3. *Time* cover (August 1994)   75
4. *Maus*: Hitler did it!   184
5. *Maus*: Prisoner on the hell planet comic   187
6. *Maus*: Spiegelman at the drawing board   190
7. *Maus*: reading the number   198

ACKNOWLEDGMENTS

Work on this book began at the University of Colorado, Boulder. It has been a number of years in the making and the path from the inception of the project to its becoming a book has taken me through many twists and turns. Some valued friends and colleagues accompanied me along the way, and I want to express my gratitude to those who offered their help and to pass on my thanks to those who read this book in its various stages.

I want first of all to thank Richard Halpern for kindly reading and commenting on my work. His belief in the merit of my writing has always meant a great deal to me. Particular thanks are due to Sue Zemka not only for her readings and thoughts on the project but also for her intimate friendship. Eric White, Adeleke Adeeko, and Paul Gordon read and remarked on the earliest draft of this book. I wish also to acknowledge R. L. Widmann, who offered her support during my early years at the University of Colorado, and to thank Katheryn Rios for her friendship. For her sage advice on matters professional, I owe thanks to Katherine Eggert.

I would like further to acknowledge a number of people who have in their various ways played important parts in my life during the course of the composition of this book: Rohan Quince for early imparting an appreciation for the powers of literature. Our friendship has been long and abiding. Christopher Brown for his encouragement at a moment when it was needed. Dirk Aardsma, who followed and encouraged the progress of this book from its inception, and Erin Edwards, with whom I have shared many long conversations.

I wish also to express my appreciation to my parents, Tony and Lorraine Samolsky, as well as my brother and sisters. I hope this book will help to dispel some of the mystery of what I have been up to over the past few years.

A number of my colleagues at the University of California, Santa Barbara, have generously read the manuscript of *Apocalyptic Futures*. Special thanks are due to Alan Liu, Carl Gutiérrez-Jones, Bishnupriya Ghosh, and James Kearney for the work each has done on my behalf. I would also like to offer my appreciation to Michael G. Levine for his reading of the manuscript and particularly for his remarks on the long coda devoted to *Maus*. Eleanor Kaufman read and astutely appraised this book. My thanks to her. Thanks, too, to Sam Durrant (with whom I shared a panel presentation on Coetzee) for his appreciative words with regard to my work.

Profound thanks are due to J. Hillis Miller and Henry Sussman for their gracious readings and wise comments on the manuscript of this book, which has benefited from their sagacious remarks. I offer my warm thanks and gratitude to Helen Tartar, who has kindly shepherded this book into production.

Finally, I want especially to thank Michelle Wemple, to whom I owe a great deal not only for her editorial assistance in the early stages of this book but also for her unstinting generosity and love during some difficult times. This has not been forgotten. My deepest debt and gratitude go to Rita Raley, who twice rescued this project by urging me first to get it done and then to get it out. Without her love and unwavering support, I am not at all sure that this book would ever have seen the light of day. She has been with me all the way and I hope this book brings her happiness.

A considerably shorter version of Chapter 1, "Metaleptic Machines," was published in *Modern Judiasm* 19:2 (May 1999).

INTRODUCTION

Writing Violence

Marked Bodies and Retroactive Signs

There is no law that is not inscribed on bodies.
—MICHEL DE CERTEAU, *The Practice of Everyday Life*

Commenting on the emancipatory utopian possibilities in relation to a work and its temporality, Ernst Bloch writes in *The Principle of Hope*: "Every great work of art, above and beyond its manifest content, is carried out according to a *latency of the page to come*, or in other words, in the light of the content of a future which has not yet come into being, and indeed of some ultimate resolution as yet unknown."[1] In contrast to Bloch, for whom the latent, as-yet-unrealized possibilities of art open out onto the still-unknown but potentially redemptive future, Franz Kafka considered the relation of his work to that future in starkly opposite terms. Whereas for Bloch works of art are invested with liberatory powers and hope that keeps faith with a radically open and utopian future, for Kafka it was precisely his lack of hope in the future powers of his writings that convinced him that they must be destroyed. It will not surprise us, since we are speaking of Kafka, that paradoxically the impossibility of hope in his art was a symptom not of the failure of his writings, but precisely of their powers of forecast. On one particular occasion, Kafka, together with his young disciple Gustav Janouch, was looking at some of Picasso's cubist still lifes and a painting of a "rose-coloured woman with gigantic feet" when Janouch accused the painter of being a "willful distortionist." "I do not think so," Kafka countered. "He only registers the deformities which have not yet penetrated our consciousness. Art is a mirror, which goes 'fast', like a watch—sometimes."[2] When, sometime later, Kafka adamantly insisted that the private "spectre of horror" embodied in his writings should be "burned and destroyed," Janouch suggested that, like Picasso's, Kafka's art foresaw the future. Anguished, Kafka covered his eyes, "You are right, you are certainly right. . . . One must be silent, if one can't give any help. No one, through his own lack of hope, should make the condition of the patient worse. For that reason all my scribbling is to be destroyed."[3] Our universe, Kafka intimated, resolutely withholds from us any possibility of hope. When asked on another occasion by Max Brod if hope still resided outside our world, Kafka ironically replied: "Plenty of hope—for God—no end of hope—only not for us."[4]

Had he lived to see Walter Benjamin's last years, Kafka himself might have considered Benjamin as trapped in something like the latent page of a Kafka text to come. But unlike the Kafka who consigned the majority of his writings to oblivion, Benjamin worked desperately and tenaciously on behalf of the survival or living on of his texts. Writing to Adorno in 1938 with regard to the completion of "The Paris of the Second Empire in Baudelaire," Benjamin reported that work on the essay amounted to "a race against the war; and despite the fear that choked me, I experienced a feeling of triumph on the day I brought the 'flâneur'—which had been planned for almost fifteen years—safely under a roof (even if only the fragile one of a manuscript!)."[5] And writing in that brief sliver of time between his release from the internment camp and his suicide before the Spanish border, Benjamin famously implored Gershom Scholem that "[e]very line we succeed in publishing today—given the uncertainty of the future to which we consign it—is a victory wrested from the powers of darkness."[6] Like Bloch, Benjamin held out hope for the powers of a past text to condition a redemptive future. This was never more so than in the last major text of his life, the messianic theses of "On the Concept of History."[7]

Introduction

But what if Kafka was right? Without necessarily acceding to claims of Kafka's special foresight or of the occult powers of his art with respect to the future (I shall examine more of this in the chapter on Kafka), we might still ask: what if certain texts contain coiled within themselves a textual will to their incarnation in an apocalyptic future? Joseph Conrad once asserted that "life and the arts follow dark courses, and will not turn aside to the brilliant arc-lights of science."[8] And sounding like a proto-poststructuralist in his essay on the composition of *The Magic Mountain*, Thomas Mann claimed that "[i]t is possible for a work to have its own will and purpose, perhaps a far more ambitious one than the author's—and it is *good* that this should be so."[9] Mann means by this that a book should in some sense be allowed to summon itself into being, to body itself forth, and that it should extend and compel the author's ambition over its projected course. "For the ambition," Mann maintains, "should not be a personal one; it must not come *before* the work itself. The work must bring it forth and compel the task to completion."[10] But what if that "will and purpose" extends not only out to the parameters or boundaries of the text itself but to the domain and dominion of its future reception?

It is ambition of this kind that James Joyce has Stephen Dedalus attribute to Shakespeare's *Hamlet* in his lecture on Shakespeare in the library episode of *Ulysses*. Drawing on Mallarmé's proclamation of the play's "sumptuous and stagnant exaggeration of murder," Stephen extrapolates upon the declamation as he charges Shakespeare and Shakespeare's *Hamlet* with preserving the power of imperial apocalypse:

> A deathsman of the soul Robert Geene called him, Stephen said. Not for nothing was he a butcher's son, wielding the sledded poleaxe and spitting in his palms. Nine lives are taken off for his father's one. Our Father who art in purgatory. Khaki Hamlet's don't hesitate to shoot. The bloodboltered shambles in act five is forecast of the concentration camp sung by Mr Swinburne.[11]

Stephen's point seems to be not only that lives died in the composition of the play, that Hamnet's death allowed for Hamlet's birth, but that a colonizing textual violence lies at the heart of Shakespeare's literary economy. It is not simply that Shakespeare's art was put to colonizing purpose by imperial Britain, but, as I read it, that an apocalyptic power accrues to the field of *Hamlet's* future reception. In this sense, the "blood-boltered shambles in act five is forecast of the concentration camp" that took the lives of Boer woman and children. Joyce's meditation on the violent economy that attends the composition and reception of Shakespeare's text may well have been prompted by his premonition of a "scorching" force, as he puts it, that marked the composition and progress of his own text. "The progress of the book," he wrote after his composition of the "Sirens" chapter, "is in fact like the progress of some sandblast. As soon as I mention or include any person in it I hear of his or her death or departure or misfortune: and each successive episode dealing with some province of artistic culture (rhetoric or music or dialectic), leaves behind it a burnt up field."[12] The "burnt up field" left in the path of the book's progress certainly takes up apocalyptic rhetoric, but Joyce was also deadly serious or mindful of the lives consumed in the wake of his book. "In confirmation of what I said in my last letter," he wrote to his patron, "I enclose a cutting from a Dublin paper, just received announcing the death of one of the figures in the episode."[13]

In light of the examples of Joyce and Kafka's claims for the prophetically catastrophic powers of their texts, I propose to examine the possibility that certain modern works actually constitute a self-referential meditation on the ethics of their future destiny. Or to put this differently, that these texts may be imbued by their authors with an internal metacommentary that reflects not only on their untimeliness and powers of prolepsis but also on the fate of those bodies that may come to be absorbed into the field of their texts's future reception.

The impetus for this train of thought originated for me not only out of a consideration of particular literary works but also

Introduction 5

out of the historical and material context of the unfolding of the Rwandan genocide. I vividly recall watching one particular piece of television news footage that displayed a mass of mutilated corpses floating down one of Rwanda's rivers. Below the footage ran the caption, "Heart of Darkness." What immediately struck me was the effect these dead bodies had on transforming Conrad's *Heart of Darkness* from a novel that exposed the calamitous effects of a genocidal colonial violence upon the bodies of the African people of the late-nineteenth-century Congo into a text of late-twentieth-century African genocide. Was this simply a cynical misappropriation of Conrad's text by the Western mass media, I wondered, or was there some aspect of *Heart of Darkness* that worked to overcode these bodies, to incorporate them within the horizon of its field of reception? How might such a textual coming to power over these Rwandan bodies take place? It is, of course, easy to attribute an unthinking misappropriation to the mass media, but, as we shall see, even sophisticated intellectuals find themselves falling into the trap of coding the Rwandan genocide in particular, and African genocide in general, in terms of Conrad's text. Without acceding to the prophetic powers claimed by Joyce and Kafka, since I believe no writer however strong commands a strict foresight upon the future, was there some way, I wondered, in which a text may be written so as to metaleptically overcode these bodies in the accrual of an apocalyptic dimension? What exactly is the relation between the mutilated African bodies in Conrad's text and the mutilated black bodies of African genocide? Is it possible that Conrad invested his text with a metaleptic program or mechanism that marks the assimilation of these bodies as something more than arbitrary or retrospective? Or might this absorption of genocidal bodies into the ambit of the text's future reception be the result not of authorial intension but of a linguistic or textual "will to power" in Nietzsche's sense of a blind drive or force? In this case, how might Conrad have contended with this drive that was bound to wrest his text from its historical and ethical context in the accretion of ever greater powers? And what role might a Freudian *Nach-*

träglichkeit (belated projection or belated recognition) play in accounting for the way in which bodies may be pulled back into the orbit of a text that attaches to the abyssal trauma of genocide?

It is out of a pressing concern with these thoughts and questions that this book emerged. I found myself obliged to reconsider a whole tradition of eminent thinkers who granted Kafka's texts the singular prescience of forecasting the Jewish Holocaust. Is this just a vulgar misreading of Kafka, or is there some program constituted by his texts that orchestrates precisely this incorporation of apocalypse? In light of this, how might we regard the ethics of Kafka's insistence that his text be burned? As is well known, Kafka left instruction with Max Brod that his writings were to be eradicated and very late in his life at Kafka's behest Dora Diamant did indeed burn a number of his manuscripts. But what of those texts that Kafka grudgingly allowed to be published? What, for example, of his great story "In the Penal Colony"? What ethical responsibility does Kafka bear with regard to this program that he seemed so clearly to see operating in his texts? Might "In the Penal Colony," with its famous Harrow and needles that inscribe a sentence on the body of the condemned, be Kafka's commentary on the writing machine that programs a text's destiny? Janouch records once calling upon Kafka in his office just as a package arrived by mail. Opening the package, Kafka became visibly anxious as he recognized the green-and-gold volume as a proof copy of his *In the Penal Settlement*. "You should be very satisfied, Herr Doktor," Janouch remarked. Kafka demurred, "Publication of some scribble of mine always upsets me." Pressed by Janouch as to why he allowed his writings to be printed, Kafka first answered that it was so as not to disappoint friends like Brod who were convinced of their value as literature. But a moment later Kafka bethought himself of this half truth, "In fact," he went on, "I am so corrupt and shameless that I myself co-operate in publishing these things."[14] Is it possible, then, that part of what is at stake in Kafka's story is the very question of the right of a deadly piece of private writing to public literary existence? Or perhaps even the struggle of a story against an author who would out of ethical concern extinguish its very living on.

In his *Diary of a Bad Year*, J. M. Coetzee invents a kind of literary doppelgänger, JC, who reflects upon the untimeliness of his novel *Waiting for the Barbarians*. Commenting on the emergence of his novel out of the context of the police state of 1970s-era apartheid South Africa, in which the law was abrogated, and atrocities were justified in the name of the struggle against terrorism, JC remarks, "I used to think that the people who created these laws that effectively suspended the rule of law were moral barbarians. Now I know they were just pioneers, ahead of their time."[15] JC remarks here on the way in which the post-9/11 American security state duplicates the same state of exception in its operation of the Guantánamo camp, and how officially sanctioned torture at Abu Ghraib Prison and black sites in the name of homeland security iterate the security apparatus of late apartheid South Africa. What he had taken to be the death throes and vestiges of a residual colonialism turned out to be nothing less than a forerunner of the techniques that would be adopted and adapted to twenty-first century America. While we ought to guard against collapsing J. M. Coetzee into his fictional counterpart JC—who is five years older and occupies a different, though somewhat parallel, literary universe—it does seem to me that we can draw a correlation between this forecast and the way in which Coetzee's *Waiting for the Barbarians* has also revealed itself to be ahead of its time with regard to its undiminished powers to critique not only torture in the chambers of South Africa's apartheid prisons but also the torture inflicted in the dark chambers of Iraq's Abu Ghraib Prison. In an extraordinary claim made in his *Defence of Poetry*, Percy Bysshe Shelley maintains that the poet "not only beholds intensely the present as it is, and discovers those laws according to which present things ought to be ordered, but he beholds the future in the present, and his thoughts are the germs of the flower and the fruit of latest time."[16] In a striking image that resonates with Kafka's observation that art is the mirror that reflects the future back into the present, Shelley holds that poets are "the mirrors of the gigantic shadows which futurity casts upon the present."[17] In my chapter devoted to Coetzee's *Waiting for the Barbarians*, I shall examine how Coetzee's allegory functions as such a mirror, although my focus here will not be torture in the context of the American war on terror, but the revelations of state-sanctioned torture that emerged from the South African Truth and Reconciliation Commission (TRC). How, I shall ask, does Coetzee's text engage the ethical question of those tortured South African bodies fated to be drawn into the horizon of its reception to come? As with the Rwandan genocide, this chapter of my book had its inception in and grew out of witnessing the anguished testimonies televised and recorded during the course of the truth commission hearings.

In this regard *Apocalyptic Futures* looks back to the historical context of the mid- and late twentieth century and the reception of Kafka, Conrad, and Coetzee's texts. This is not simply to situate my book in closer historical proximity to the historical context out of which each author wrote, nor because the mechanisms or forces that I analyze are no longer currently operative—genocide in the Congo and the Darfur region of Sudan continue to be coded as the heart of darkness—but because by their sheer magnitude, the Jewish Holocaust, the Rwandan genocide in particular, and South African apartheid are the material histories which, like black holes, have to this point exerted the greatest influence upon the reception of these works. But dialectically, as we shall see, what I will also be concerned to demonstrate is the way in which these texts search out, "incarnate," or more properly "incorporate," themselves in the aftermath of these catastrophes, attaining thereby an apocalyptic legibility.

My project begins, then, with the recognition that future catastrophic events exert a profound influence upon the reception of a past text, and particularly in the case of a past text (past, that is, from the perspective of the apocalyptic event) that deploys an apocalyptic discourse. African genocide has accorded a ghastly apocalyptic afterlife to *Heart of Darkness* and the Jewish Holocaust has conferred a prophetic power on Kafka's corpus. My contention is that this accrual of apocalyptic powers is not simply due to retrospective apposition, but that these texts have encoded within them various mechanisms or programs by which they target apocalypses to come in the acquisition of a living on through a drive to power over bare life. This program comprises different mechanisms and dimensions, not all of which are consequent upon the agency or intention of the author. The fate of a text, we all know, slips from the hand of the author to a very uncertain reception, but it is my further claim that this aberrant textual drive to power over the political and ethical intent or design of the author constitutes part of the narrative unfolding or discourse of these texts themselves. These works are indeed, to recite Bloch, "carried out according to a *latency of the page to come*, or in other words, in light of the content of a future which has not yet come into being, and indeed of some ultimate resolution as yet unknown," but this "ultimate resolution" appears to resolve not into a messianic or utopian future but precisely into the dystopia of actual apocalypse.

But what of Bloch's hope for the redemptive powers of a text? Is the apocalyptic trajectory always absolutely determinative in deciding the reception of a text that is inhabited by apocalyptic discourse? Is it always a work's apocalyptic trajectory that is materialized or made manifest? How might such an apocalyptic program be disarmed or at least countered? Might Conrad's novel, for example, also be positioned to release an ethical or political counterreception? I have chosen the triune set of works "In the Penal Colony," *Heart of Darkness*, and *Waiting for the Barbarians* as the primary texts around which to situate my analysis not only because of the spectacular reception that has accrued to their textual fields but also because their use of the apocalyptic figure of the marked or mutilated body allows me to locate and look into part of the working of this program. Or to state this from a different perspective, one of the crucial questions that this project asks is this: what role does the marked body play in both allowing for and even soliciting an apocalyptic incorporation? This question will be taken up again in my long coda devoted to Art Spiegelman's graphic novel *Maus*. My concern with *Maus*, however, is not with marked bodies incorporated into the future field of the text, but with the way in which the Holocaust dead haunt the reception of *Maus I*, along with Spiegelman's self-referential commentary in *Maus II* on the guilt and ethical burden that threatens to consume his project. The word "incorporation" will inevitably call up Nicholas Abraham and Maria Torok's lexicon. The reader will quickly discern, however, that I am not using "incorporation" according to its psychoanalytic register but rather to demarcate how marked bodies are inscribed into the ambit of a text's reception. My book ends by invoking Benjamin's theses on history and the promise of a redemptive reading of the marked body that offers a tiny moment of hope in the face of apocalypse.

While the figure of the marked body is often invoked in literary theory, it has itself been far less frequently the subject of commentary. In fact, no project has provided a full reading of the history of this figure, or even of the history of this figure in the twentieth or twenty-first centuries; nor will I try to offer one in this book, but any treatment of this theme that pushes beyond a mere taxonomy does require some careful delimiting and theoretical framework. A full commentary on the history of this figure would begin with the history of mimesis itself, for at the dawn of Western writing the marked body appears to stand as ground and guarantor of identity and signification. God's marking Cain with the sign of the outcast is not presented as a moment that is subject to the ambiguities of interpretation. As the Bible records, "And the Lord set a mark upon Cain, lest any finding him should kill him"; the mark is given as legible and secure in its purpose of protecting Cain from death. Odysseus's scar and Jesus's wounds both confirm and confer identity and serve to function as ineradicable linguistic signs pressed into the body. Peter Brooks, in his *Body Work: Objects of Desire in Modern Narrative*, comments on these scenes of recognition:

> As in Aristotle's theory of tragedy—which is itself indebted to the Homeric poems—the moment of recognition is a dramatic climax, a coming into the open of hidden identities and latent possibilities. Here the recognition comes, as it

often does in Greek tragedies, through a mark on the body itself. It is the body marked in a significant moment of the person's past history that enables recognition—a scenario that will be replayed throughout literature, and given its most formulaic version in the notorious *croix de ma mère of melodrama*, the token affixed or engraved on the abandoned orphan which at last enables the establishment of identity. It is as if identity and its recognition, depended on the body having been marked with a special sign, which looks suspiciously like a linguistic signifier. The sign imprints the body, making it part of the signifying process. Signing or marking the body signifies its passage into writing, its becoming a literary body, and generally also a narrative body, in that the inscription of the sign depends on and produces a story. The signing of the body is an allegory of the body become a subject for literary narrative—a body entered into narrative.[18]

Brooks's generalized claim here for the relation between body and text adumbrates his more specific thesis of *Body Work* that "modern narratives appear to produce a semioticization of the body which is matched by a somatization of the story."[19] This claim features strongly in this book; my work, however, diverges from Brooks's in that his concern is almost exclusively with the intratextual representation of the body in eighteenth- and nineteenth-century narratives while my concern is with the relation between "intra" and "extra" textual bodies in the twentieth century. Aside from this, and apart from his more general conception of the inscribed body, there is also a further difference between our projects. Brooks's emphasis tends to be on the mark as fixed sign of identity and on the marked body as readable. He argues that "the bodily marking not only serves to recognize and identify, it also indicates the body's passage into the realm of the letter, into literature: the bodily mark is in some manner a 'character,' a hieroglyph, a sign that can eventually, at the right moment of the narrative, be read."[20] Certainly, this has been the predominant case through the course of literature; the body has stood, after all, as the foremost refuge, the first and the last ground of identity. But the mark, if readable, is never singular in this reading. The Talmud is full of midrashic exegesis on the mark of Cain, and the scar (wound, mark, sign) has always had to conceal, or guard against, the arrogation of a false identity or the ascription of a false meaning. Consider again the apparently secure case of Odysseus's recognition by the sign of the scar. The moment of recognition marks a break in the narrative, a pushing back to the story of Odysseus's being gored by the boar; the scar reopens the story, marking itself not only as marker but also as maker of identity. As Terence Cave has pointed out:

> The scar, then, is more than a sign by which Odysseus is recognized. It composes his identity by calling up retrospectively a fragment of narrative, since only narrative can compose identity as continuity once severance has occurred, and the scar here may well look like a sign of the wound, the hiatus, the severance constituted by Odysseus' wanderings.[21]

We may assign to the scar the same aspect of *polytropos* given to its bearer (in the first line of the poem Odysseus is named as *Polutropos* or man of many ways or figures); for the scar, like the stories it seals and conceals, may always break its surface, revealing once again what writers have always known, that the word is also a wound. If the ancient figure of the marked body lives on in its modern incarnations it is in the form of the inscribed body as falsely legible or even indecipherable, and it is this self-conscious emphasis of the severance of the signifying bond between wound and word as sign and signifier that demarcates its modern usage. It is precisely the instability of this mark and the capacity of this detachable signifier to migrate to different material contexts that lies at the heart of my project.

It is of course in Kafka's great story that the word is also literally a wound: "HONOR THY SUPERIORS!" is the sentence (in the double sense) that the prisoner is to have inscribed on his body. "BE JUST" is the ironic inscription the officer programs into the machine.[22] Despite the fact that this sentence's lethal legibility was to emerge in proportion to a violence imposed but

Introduction

whose legibility, in a mangled scene of man and machine, turns out to signify nothing but violence itself, Kafka's story stands as the foremost exemplum of the inscribed body in its strict sense in modern literature. Kafka's inscribed body is also emblematic, however, of the inscribed body in its more generalized sense. In his "Nietzsche, Genealogy, History," Michel Foucault, for example, speaks of the body as "the inscribed surface of events ... a volume in perpetual disintegration." The task of genealogy, he further argues, is "to expose a body totally imprinted by history and the process of history's destruction of the body."[23] Remarking on this particular sense of "inscription" in Foucault, Judith Butler writes:

> If the creation of values, that signifying practice of history, requires the destruction of the body, much as the instrument of torture in Kafka's *Penal Colony* destroys the body on which it writes, then there must be a body prior to that inscription, stable and self-identical, subject to and capable of that sacrificial destruction. In a sense for Foucault, as for Nietzsche, cultural values emerge as the result of an inscription *on* the body, where the body is understood as a medium, indeed, a blank page, an unusual one, to be sure, for it appears to bleed and suffer under the pressure of a writing instrument.[24]

However, Foucault's assumption of a blank body ontologically prior to its inscription leads Butler to point out the contradiction with Foucault's position on the constructed status of the body itself and with his claim that there is no body that is antecedent to the law or discursive power regimes. These contradictions lead Butler to ask "whether the understanding of the process of cultural construction on the model of 'inscription'—a logocentric move if ever there was one—entails that the 'constructed' or 'inscribed' body have an ontological status apart from that inscription, precisely the claim that Foucault wants to refute."[25] For Butler, then, Foucault's rhetoric appropriates a Kafkan force of inscription that works against or undermines his very claim for the discursively constructed body, and she further charges Foucault with having ultimate recourse to this prediscursive body as the site of resistance to the inscriptional powers of the discursive regimes of culture and history. If this supposition of a body prior and external to discursive practice is withdrawn or itself subjected to a genealogical critique, would it still, Butler asks, "be possible to give a Foucaultian account of the demarcation of bodies as such as a signifying practice?"[26] In briefly gesturing toward an answer to her question, Butler offers a prescription for the form such an account of the body as discursively constructed by cultural practice would take:

> What is clear is that inscription would be neither an act initiated by a reified history nor the performative accomplishment of a master historian who produces history as he writes it. The culturally constructed body would be the result of a diffuse and active structuring of the social field with no magical or ontotheological origins, structuralist distinctions, or fictions of bodies, subversive or otherwise, ontologically intact before the law.[27]

I do not share Butler's claim that in his story Kafka conceives of the body simply as a blank page awaiting its inscription; rather, it seems to me that Kafka conceives of bodies in "In the Penal Colony" precisely as always already juridically demarcated or acted upon. Of all writers, it is surely Kafka who teaches us that the body is never "ontologically intact *before the law*." The act of inscription in Kafka's text is already an act of inscribing over. What Kafka's text figures is not the inscription of the blank body but the superscription, in the strict sense, of a body already juridically inscribed in the generalized sense. This is not to dismiss Butler's critique but merely to point out that it seems to me to be wholly misplaced with regard to Kafka. My other objective in covering this ground, however, is not to try to offer a fuller answer to Butler's question with regard to Foucault, but to use her analysis to better situate my project. My concern is not with Foucault's genealogical account of history as a master inscriber of the body in the generalized sense, but rather with the admittedly smaller project of the way in which particular texts appropriate marked material bodies. More specifically, I wish to examine the ways in which marked textual bodies work to "incorporate" marked material bodies into the field of their texts. It is important here to delineate exactly what I am speaking of when I refer to marked textual and marked material bodies: by marked textual bodies, I refer to bodies, such as those in Kafka's story, that are literally inscribed with words, but I also mean mutilated bodies such as the staked skulls on the palisade surrounding Kurtz's hut, failed apotropaic devices that are expressly read as signs, as well as the scars left by torture such as those on the barbarian woman in Coetzee's novel that the Magistrate struggles to decipher. What links each of these instances is that the marked or mutilated body is expressly treated and read as a text or sign system. I refer to precisely the same range of markings when I speak of materially marked bodies, by which I mean bodies literally inscribed with numbers such as those in the Auschwitz concentration camp, or those mutilated in African genocides, or those scarred in South African torture chambers. I am speaking then not only of the discursive construction of bodies but also of bodies specifically marked in this more strict or literal sense. Indeed it is precisely because "the body" is always already culturally conditioned by constructions of race, gender, or ethnicity that it is susceptible to this further violent marking or differentiation. What I shall try to demonstrate, to offer one example, is the way in which the writing machine with its inscribed bodies in Kafka's story works to "write over" and thereby "incorporate" not blank bodies, but carceral bodies, Jewish bodies, already horribly inscribed (inscribed, that is, in the strict sense) with the violent writing instruments of the Auschwitz concentration camp.

If Butler is correct to assert that Foucault's presupposition of the body as surface and site of resistance to the act of inscription should itself be submitted to a geological critique, this does not entirely vitiate the ethical force of Foucault's analysis of the task of genealogy to "expose a body totally imprinted by history and the process of history's destruction of the body."²⁸ If the body is constituted through relations of power, and if the body has no existence outside the discursive powers of the law, this does not mean that we cannot differentiate between those forces within a "diffuse and active structuring of the social field," those forces, in other words, that both constitute and act upon this socially constituted body, marking it with the signs of violence. Still, my project might seem to fall prey to reinscribing the logocentric order of simply substituting a master text in place of Foucault's master history. I try to guard against this, however, by conceiving the text not as constituted by some monological apocalyptic drive but precisely by working to differentiate between the competing dialectical drives that orchestrate its future reception; and, similarly, my conception of "the body" is not of a plenum unmarked and unconditionally sufficient or present to itself. In this regard, I take cognizance of Jean-Luc Nancy's disruption of "the" body as a singular or essential entity unto itself in his assertion that "there is not 'the' body, there is not 'the touch,' there is not 'the' *res extensa*."²⁹ However, as Jacques Derrida points out in his reading of Nancy in *On Touching—Jean-Luc Nancy*, the "the" cannot be done away with or evaded as it ineluctably determines the very formulation that would dispense with it: "The definite or defining article is already engaged or required by the discourse that disputes it. It is with this limit that Nancy grapples, within this transaction, in this wrestling match of thinking."³⁰ I shall return to wrestle with precisely this problem of the articulation of "the" body and linguistic formulation as I again draw on Judith Butler (who also touches upon this) in an analysis of the body in *Barbarians*. Like Foucault, however, I will be deeply concerned to articulate an ethico-political analysis of the ways in which these marked bodies might be said to resist their textual appropriation.

Having now, I hope, clearly delineated what I intend by "marked bodies," I still need at the outset of this project to begin to address the role of language and the force of inscription in the discursive production of the body itself. The slipperiness of the term "inscribed body"—at times a catachresis, at others a literal entity—emerges in Butler's subtle and varied analysis. If Butler charges Foucault with having recourse to (or at times lapsing into) the fiction of a prediscursive body, she herself has taken up a position against the strong version of constructionism that holds to the notion of the body as linguistically composed. Such a notion sees the body as inseparable from the language that fabricates or figures it. The threat of the fate of such extreme linguisticism is illustrated by several characters in Coetzee's fiction: in *Foe*, for example, Susan Barton finds herself forced to insist against the story that she feels is consuming her substantial body, that "I am not a story, Mr. Foe . . . I am a substantial being with a substantial history in the world."[31] So, too, does Elizabeth Costello insist on the substance of her body against a fabricated world into which she finds herself trapped: "Not only is she *in* this body, this thing which not in a thousand years she could have dreamed up, so far beyond her powers would it be, she somehow *is* this body."[32] Faced with the threat of being reduced to or dissolved by the fabrications of language, both of these characters anchor themselves in the material substrate of their bodies. This is a position with which Butler would agree, for the body, she argues, is never reducible to language; it is always in some respect the other of language. But if she holds to a body that is itself not language, is Butler not then in danger of repeating Foucault's gesture of positing a purely prediscursive or extralinguistic body? It is here, however, that we need to grasp the subtlety of her analysis, for while Butler claims that if the body evades reduction to the flux of language, it is also given or knowable only through the coordinates of language. The body, then, cannot escape its implication in language; it cannot, that is, effect its utter severance from language, which governs its knowability and articulation. But if the body is somehow both linguistically produced and yet precisely that which is not language, what kind of entity is it? Butler's answer to this question is to claim that although our grammar allows us to pose this question, the very object of this questioning evades its grammatical capture: "The body escapes the terms of the question by which it is approached. And even to make such a formulaic claim, relying on 'The Body' as the subject-noun of the sentence, domesticates precisely what it seeks to unleash. Indeed, the grammar itself exposes the limits of its own mimetic conceit, asserting a reality that is necessarily distorted through the terms of the assertion, a reality that can only appear, as it were, through distortion."[33] We have reached an impasse here, I think, for the body can only be articulated by that which it is not, and the body can never escape its implication in the discourse that it both is but also is not. My project will not attempt to bridge this impasse, and I will not attempt to further address the question of the interrelation of the body and language at the purely ontological level of the constitution of the body itself. My concern is not with the body that is reducible to or dissolved in a flux of language, but with the way in which language or texts might be said to further act on bodies that have already been acted upon. It is with regard to my particular framing of this problem that I want to again take up Butler's posing of the question of this relation: "If language acts on the body in some way, if we want to speak, for instance, of a bodily inscription, as so much cultural theory does, it might be worth considering whether language literally acts on a body, and whether that body is an exterior surface for such action, or whether these are figures that we mobilize when we seek to establish the efficacy of language."[34]

I shall offer further thought on Butler's analysis of the relation of inscription to the body in my chapter on Coetzee's *Barbarians*, but for now I want to return to the body as the site and scene of inscription. There is, after all, a way in which under the rigors of philosophical scrutiny the particular material entity of the marked body itself seems to get written out of the realm of objective existence. This has of course not been the case in the realm of art, where the marked body still compels us to its insistent and fascinated exhibition. Far from philosophically undermining the conflation of script and body, a number of writers have insisted on the act of autoinscription as bodying forth a poetic identity. In *Finnegans Wake*, for example, Joyce has his artist Shem the Penman extract from "his unheavenly body a no uncertain quantity of obscene matter" and "with this double dye ... write over every square inch of the only foolscap available, his own body."[35] Unbeknownst to Joyce, in a newly discovered poem, Samuel Taylor Coleridge had already done Shem the Penman one better in this respect, when after running out of ink, Coleridge bites into his body, drawing his own blood out of his thumb to write his "An Autograph on an Autopergamene"—meaning "self-parchment"—which seems to have been written in blood on a shred of skin that had peeled off in the bath:

> Why, sure, such a wonder was never yet seen!
> An Autograph on an Autopergamene!
> A poet's own Name, and own Hand-writing both,
> And the Ink and the Parchment all of his own growth—
> The ink his own Blood and the Parchment his Skin—
> This from's Leg, and the other from's razor-snipt Chin.[36]

In both instances the author signs his own body in an act of artistic production in which the word literally takes on its own flesh. This does not mean that the body is lost in the signs of language or that the word is consumed in the materiality of the body—both word and body survive only through the preservation of their separate identities—but what lies behind the power of such acts of poetic inscription and identification is the way in which they demonstrate the indissociable implication of the body in the word and the word in the body.

This relation between word and body is made strikingly visible in two extraordinary, late-twentieth-century filmic renditions of the violence of inscription: Peter Greenaway's *The Pillow Book* (1996) and Christopher Nolan's *Memento* (2000). If the body in Kafka's text functioned as a page on which was incised the vengeance of the law, the inscribed body becomes itself an instrument of revenge in these two films, both of which take up Kafka's discourse on the lethal power of the letter over bodies. My purpose here is not to try to do justice to the sheer intricacy of this inversion in these films but to indicate how the body might be said to be "captured" by the act of inscription. For reasons already discussed, Butler asserts that "[a]lthough the body depends on language to be known, the body also exceeds every possible linguistic effort of capture."[37] But this of course depends on what exactly is meant by "capture." If "capture" is taken to mean that the body is reified out of existence and transmuted into language itself, then I think Butler is correct, but if "capture" is taken to mean the way in which language codes, acts upon, transfigures, and destines bodies, then I think things are surely different.

The Pillow Book, for example, offers us a story of the way in which inscribed bodies act on and in so doing "capture" or determine the destiny of other bodies.[38] The film engages us in intricate scenes of spectacular calligraphy performed upon bodies. What is on put on display here is not only the transfiguration of the human body into a work of art but instances in which the destiny of these bodies is literally scripted. *The Pillow Book* tells the story of a young girl indelibly marked by her parents' textual proclivities: her mother's reading to her from Sei Shonogan's *The Pillow Book* and her father's practice of calligraphically inscribing birthday greetings on her face. What results is a deep libidinal attachment to the commingling of calligraphy and flesh, a desire to write her own memoirs, and a drive to seek revenge upon the corrupt publisher who has blackmailed her father and appropriated the body of her lover. As Nagiko proceeds in her transformation from the inscribed girl to the inscribing woman, one of the crucial acts of inscription that she performs is to write over the body of her dead lover, Jerome, who is coincidently also the lover of the publisher. In mourning for his lover, the publisher has the body exhumed and the inscribed skin flayed and preserved as his own pillow book. In the reduction from body to book, the inscribed body is literally disembodied or flattened out. Necromantic scenes follow in which the publisher wraps the pillow book around his body, as if to bestow upon it an anamorphic embodiment. What is haunting about this book of skin, however, is not the threat that it might be given back its body, but that it does seem to preserve in its pages the register of the evacuated body of Jerome. The publisher's pillow book of inscribed skin, then,

Introduction   21

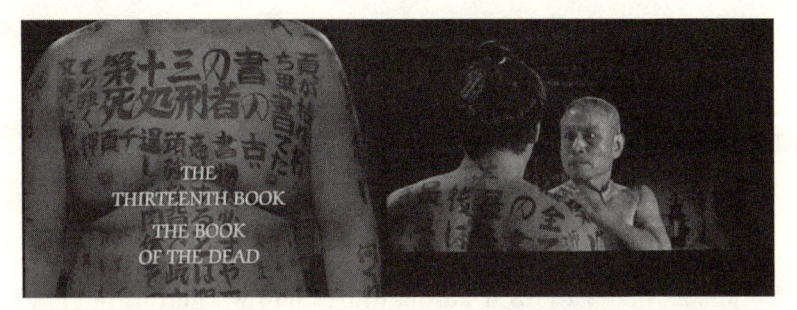

Figure 1. *The Thirteenth Book of the Dead*, in which the publisher reads his own fate inscribed on the body of the sumo-wrestler sent to assassinate him.

does not possess the anamorphic powers of embodiment but is haunted by an an-anamorphosis that would register not simply the failure of anamorphic embodiment, but an emptied out or deconstructed anamorphosis not sufficient or fully present to itself, but in which is still preserved the trace of the evacuated body. (The anamorphic properties of the skulls in *Heart of Darkness* and the postmodern flattening of the surface of the marked body in *Barbarians* will be featured in the chapters that follow.) The powers of writing to script the destiny of a body are made manifest in the scene in which the corrupt publisher reads his own fate inscribed on the body of an assassin who has been sent to kill him (figure 1). Now it might be objected that, although the publisher reads his fate in the Thirteenth Book written upon the body of the assassin, it is the assassin and not the letter itself that literally kills. This is true of course, but the mark of the slash across the throat of the publisher confers a performative felicity upon the book written on the body of the assassin. If it is not the script itself that does the killing, the death of the publisher's body still confers a strange kind of "life" upon the script written on the assassin's body, which is after all the Book of the Dead. The dead letter of this script acquires a "life" even as it takes a life, and the life of the letter is purchased by the death of the publisher's body.

If, unlike Kafka's writing machine, the script inscribed upon the body in *The Pillow Book* only proclaims but does not itself strictly speaking execute its sentence, in *Memento* we are brought even closer to the power of a script written on a body to indite (and indict) the fate of other bodies. *Memento* features the extraordinary scenario of Leonard Shelby, who is on an unrelenting mission to take his revenge upon the man who murdered his wife. What makes Leonard's case extraordinary is that during the attack in which his wife was murdered, Leonard himself suffers an injury to his head that leaves him with a form of amnesia in which he is unable to encode new memories. In order to overcome this deficiency, Leonard resorts to tattooing what he calls the "facts" of the case onto his body and he deploys these inscriptions to act in the place of memory and as a bridge to support the radically discontinuous temporality of his incremental self. Our belief that the "facts" tattooed on Leonard's body will lead Leonard to the murderer is wholly undermined when his version of events is contradicted by Teddy, who claims to be the police officer first sent to investigate the murder of Leonard's wife. According to Teddy, Leonard has already avenged his wife, and having killed his wife's killer he inscribes upon his body a "puzzle [he] won't ever solve."[39] This puzzle functions as a lack that can never be made complete, a lack that is emblematized by the empty patch of skin above Leonard's heart that still awaits its inscription, or that corresponds to the hole left in Leonard's memory that can never be made whole.

By thrusting us into its vertiginous temporality and contradictory narratives, *Memento* forces the viewer to experience some aspect of Leonard's condition but, as I read it, what is at stake in this film is not so much our taking on the task of duplicating Leonard as detective in our quest to solve its dilemmas, but rather our grasping the power of inscription to perform or destine its victim. What proves decisive in this film is Leonard's willingness to manipulate his condition in order to turn against those who have used him as he sets up his next kill by incising Teddy's license plate number onto his body. If the accuracy of the inscription to determine the identity of killer is to be doubted, its efficacy to perform the identity of "the killer" is not. As he makes

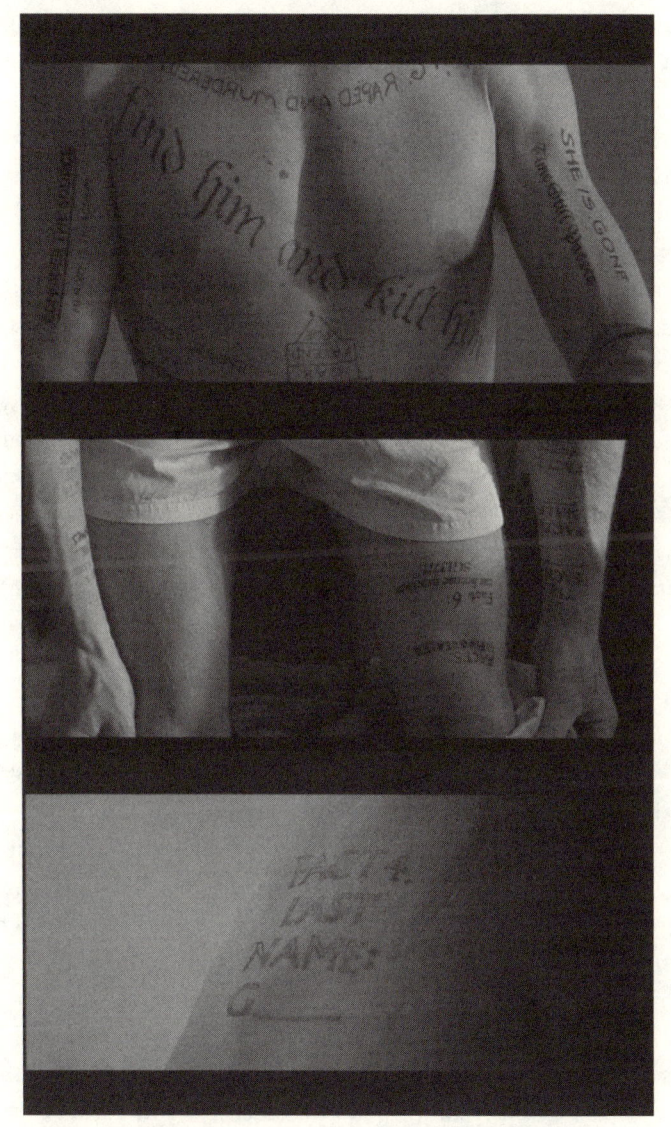

Figure 2. Leonard's body tattooed with the injunction to kill. The license plate number that will establish John Gammell as his next victim is inscribed on his thigh.

his decision to inscribe Teddy (also known as John Gammell) as the killer, Leonard says to himself, "You're a John G.? Fine, then you can be *my* John G."[40] We should read the italicized "*my*" according to a double register, for what Leonard means by this is not only that he will install Gammell as the murderer upon whom he must take his revenge, but that in making John G. *my* John G. he constitutes the possibility for the continuity of a self (for the "*my*") in his quest to kill Gammell. In other words, in his act of inscribing the exterior surface of his body, Leonard attempts to constitute the continuity of an interior self, a self that is purchased with the dead body of John G. (figure 2). Knowing that he will forget the moment in which he manipulates himself into inscribing Gammell as the murderer, Leonard attempts to infuse the inscription with a kind of stored agency, but an agency to which he can remain true only by paradoxically forgetting the falsity of its origin. The identity of the murderer is thus retroactively determined and inscribed.

But for all of Leonard's manipulation of his condition toward an agential inscription of a self, he too falls prey to what he inscribes. Is Leonard, that is, the agent of his inscription or is he determined by what he inscribes? No matter the extent of his manipulation of his "self," I would argue, Leonard is never able to position himself as outside his system of inscription; rather, he is always inscribed by what he inscribes. It is not only that his inscriptions determine their victims but also that they inscribe Leonard's very "self" in that he is propelled along by the force of inscription that determines his trajectory. In this regard, Leonard becomes the very embodiment of writing as a killing machine. This is made clear by the fact that Leonard cannot determine the veracity of his inscriptions and thus the authenticity of his revenge killings. And even in the case of Teddy, where Leonard seems to be able to program or target his next kill by means of inscription, he seems unable to halt the very signifying inscription upon which his very "self" depends. Leonard here is the very agent of inscription but also a surface upon which the machinal "agency" of inscription is itself inscribed. In this respect, he is emblematic of the way in which an author may both program a text as well as the ways in which a text functions like a writing machine, programming its future to come.

What, then, we might ask, will halt this fatal inscriptional drive? One possible answer, I suppose, is that, like the text that Kafka's Officer implores the Explorer to read, Leonard's body may become so overinscribed that his writing will become illegible. But the texts I examine suffer no such limitations. It is not enough, then, to claim, as Butler does, that the body "exceeds every possible linguistic effort of capture," for what we are given in *Memento* is precisely an instance of what it might mean to speak of a body as captured by a text. It is just such a metaleptic form of bodily capture that I have already determined to be at work in Kafka's story. In an article published well before the release of *Memento*, and which now constitutes an earlier version of my first chapter, I examined the way in which Kafka's text functions as its own writing machine retroactively inscribing its victims to come.[41] That *Memento* should so closely follow Kafka here is not entirely surprising, as the film is in some respects a rewriting of Kafka's great story. In a sense, what *Memento* does is to embody Kafka's writing machine in the person of Leonard who functions both as writing machine and textual surface and who marks his victims with lethal violence. *Memento* is itself one of those future artistic incarnations already partly programmed by Kafka's text. What my chapter on Kafka and the Shoah sets out to do is establish how Kafka's text may be said to capture the inscriptional machine of the concentration camp in a metaleptic inscription of the Jew as the target of Kafka's text. If *Memento* literalizes Kafka's story, examining ways in which the inscribed body may literally mark its victim, my chapter examines the subtle powers of Kafka's text to incorporate those inscribed dead bodies into the horizon of its reception. My focus, then, is not so much on the power of inscription to take life but on the textual overcoding and capture of those lives already taken.

Before concluding this introduction, I do want very briefly to point to some uncanny and unanticipated intersections of my project with Jacques Rancière's thought, which I encountered only after completing the chapters of this book. In *The Flesh of Words*, Rancière asserts that "[l]iterature lives only by the separation of words in relation to any body that might incarnate their power. It lives only by evading the incarnation that it incessantly puts into play."[42] In this regard, his approach to the question of the embodiment of the word may seem the inverse of my claim for apocalyptic texts' will to live on, or "take their flesh," by means of metaleptic incorporation. But I think it is more precise to say that Rancière's text gives us not so much the inverse, but rather the obverse of my project. As opposed to belles lettres, literature emerges for Rancière only around the beginning of the nineteenth century when the adequation between style and the social hierarchy to which it was bonded was undone. What resulted was a tension between this free-floating indifferent surface of words no longer tied to any social body and the "desire to replace the old expressive conventions with a direct relationship between the potential of words and the potential of bodies, where language would be the direct expression of a potential for being that was immanent in beings."[43] It is out of this generative contradiction, Rancière argues, that literature itself develops, along with a modern politics imbued in the letter.

What Rancière betokens by "politics of literature" is not the writers' engagement or social commitment to the struggles of their times, but the way in which literature frames what does or does not come to be seen and said. Literature is political in that it participates in what he calls the "distribution of the sensible," which amounts to the partition or framing of sensible data that establishes categories of perception in which the world is inscribed. Or as Rancière himself puts it, "The politics of literature thus means that literature as literature is involved in this partition of the visible and the sayable, in this intertwining of ways of being, doing and saying that frames a polemical common world."[44] Thus writing is by its nature actively political in that it conditions modalities of perception and being: "The syntagma 'politics of literature' means that literature 'does' politics as literature—that

Introduction

there is a specific link between politics as a definite way of doing and literature as a definite practice of writing."[45] A modern politics of the letter emanates out of the fall or lapse of the state that obtained between words and social hierarchies to which they were attached before the French Revolution. Words now passed from the age of rhetoric that conceived of power as the influence of one will upon another to a relationship between signs and other signs. This democratic equivalence of signs leads to a new partition of the sensible order, one in which the writer struggles to ground these indifferent signs in a new body.

> Literature as such displays a twofold politics, a twofold manner of re-configuring sensitive data. On the one hand, it displays the power of literariness, the power of the "mute" letter that upsets not only the hierarchies of the representational system but also any principle of adequation between a way of being and a way of speaking. On the other hand, it sets in motion another politics of the mute letter: the side-politics or metapolitics that substitutes the deciphering of the mute meaning written on the body of things for the democratic chattering of the letter.[46]

Rancière traces the different expressions of this conflict in Balzac, Rimbaud, and Mallarmé. In *The Village Rector*, to give one example, Rancière reads Balzac as struggling to resolve this contradiction. The story involves a book that enters the life of a working-class girl and the tragedy that ensues. Inducted into the ideal of pure, chaste, and romanticized love, the girl dreams of entering into such a union. She later enters into a loveless marriage with the town banker. Now a rich patron, she meets a poor but noble worker and falls deeply in love. Desperate to flee with her, the young worker robs and murders an old man. He is arrested, sentenced to death, and dies silently, never denouncing the woman for whom he committed his crime: "Thus the democratic availability of the 'dead letter' becomes a power of death." Later, a rich widow who retires to a country village, she is guided to her salvation by the country parson. The means of her salvation come not by way of an uplifting stream of words that touch her soul—this was, after all, precisely the cause of her demise—but, Rancière remarks, "[R]edemption must be written in another kind of writing, engraved in the flesh of real things."[47] The widow thus becomes a contractor who improves the lot of the small village by installing sluices and irrigation trenches that turn the barren land into green meadows. She engraves her repentance upon the land itself. This fable attests for Rancière precisely to the contradiction at the heart of literature: the unmoored circulation of the letter makes available to all a new and democratic partition of the sensible, but the need to ground this dangerous surplus in a new social body ultimately leads to a cancellation of the word in the realm of things. Literature is caught on the horns of a dilemma whose only solution is the end of writing itself. "The politics of writing," Rancière argues, "carries a contradiction that can be solved only by self-suppression."[48]

My own analysis sees this move to the cancellation of the word in its embodiment in the "flesh of real things" not as a utopian solution to the predicament that besets modern literature, but as the disastrous outcome of the text's apocalyptic drive becoming materialized and thus overwhelming its redemptive potential. Like Rancière, I, too, see the modern text (or at least some modern texts) as caught between the ungrounded circulation of words and the drive toward the embodiment of these words. In the works with which I am concerned, this dangerous ungroundedness of the word takes the form of the sign on the body becoming detached from its literary context and migrating to other embodied contexts. The apocalyptic text, as I see it, is staged upon the supposition that the embodiment of its apocalyptic drive results not in the self-cancellation of the text but in its living on in the accrual of ever greater powers of self-literalization. The ethico-political struggle with which the text is engaged is precisely the redemptive uncoupling of the text's word from the apocalyptic or tortured body toward which it strives. It is my contention, then, that Kafka's, Conrad's, and Coetzee's texts might ultimately be read as allegories of this dialectical struggle between this will to apocalyptic embodiment and the redemptive turn from this drive to the incarnation of the word. In this regard, the protagonist-antagonist pairings that generate these texts might also be thought of as allegorizing the antipodes of this struggle. Like Rancière, I, too, see literature as actively political and reiterate what his work teaches with respect to the crucial importance of the practice and politics of literary embodiment. It is my hope that this book will offer a further ethico-political treatment and intervention in the question of the political destiny of the text.

While *Apocalyptic Futures* is concerned with modern and contemporary apocalypse, it is important to note that the violence with which these modern works of art invest the marked body can be traced back to the biblical figure of the *inscripted* body. The biblical scene of writing is often a scene of violence, and this violence comes to its apotheosis in the apocalyptic books. The topos of God's lethal handwriting on the wall in the book of Daniel is typologically registered by the mark of the beast in the book of Revelation. In a certain sense, the inscribed bodies that I have been analyzing are each avatars of the biblical figure. The 666 of the book of Revelation was supposedly, at the time of its writing, a specific reference to the Roman emperor Nero and his persecution of the early Christians. Yet this 666 cannot be yoked to any strict and secure identification, and its numerical code is forever open to capture by an array of different regimes as is evidenced by the way in which the figure has been literalized in the accrual of an apocalyptic afterlife. The first Maxim machine gun, for example, could fire a symbolic 666 shots and was named the "devil's paint brush."[49] It was first used to devastating effect in the colonial battles of Africa and then in the First World War. The biblical apocalyptic has historically influenced even secular representations of the inscribed body, whose strong influence they cannot entirely escape. In my coda on *Maus*, however, we shall encounter one instance of how the practice of *gematria* or numerology within the privation of the camp was used to redemptive effect.

Apocalyptic Futures, then, sets out to examine how the marked body in Kafka, Conrad, and Coetzee is deployed according to the double register of "marked"—that is, in the sense both of "inscribed" and "targeted" but also of "targeting." Before launching into my specific analysis of each of these texts in the chapters that follow, I want to say a few more words about just how such a targeting might take place. My claim is that the marked body in these texts is invested with what we might call an "undeadness," and that in apocalyptic contexts these undead bodies have the effect of activating an undead potential in marked material bodies. Far from remaining dead or inert, these marked or mutilated intratextual bodies are invested with the power to exert an agitated fascination or are possessed of the uncanny temporality of spectral return. As the magistrate in *Barbarians* tells us, "It has been growing more and more clear to me that until the marks on this girl's body are deciphered and understood I cannot let go of her."[50] And far from proclaiming the death of the regime of the inscribing machine, an inscription on the grave stone of the Commandant of the penal colony reads, "There is a prophecy that after a certain number of years the Commandant will rise again and lead his adherents from this house to recover the colony. Have faith and wait!"[51] If, as I claim, these undead bodies are invested with the animating powers of exciting an undead incorporation of tortured bodies, it is not enough, then, to simply claim that the body evades its capture by the text or that it resists its reduction to language. It is incumbent upon my project to examine the ethical and political modes of resistance that the marked body might assume against this apocalypse of textual incorporation.

To this end, I shall undertake an analysis of Jacques Derrida's thought on the paradoxical logic of autoimmunity with regard to the living on of Kafka's undead story, "In the Penal Colony." While I acknowledge that Kafka's prophecy for his text's accrual of an untimely apocalyptic power has indeed been borne out, rather than acceding to Kafka's apocalyptic solution of burning his texts in order to prevent their future apocalyptic instantiation, I shall draw upon the way in which Kafka has influenced Walter Benjamin, Giorgio Agamben, and Eric Santner to a messianic thinking that I will summon in the hope of redeeming Conrad's *Heart of Darkness* from its incorporation of African apocalypse. What I hope to demonstrate, to again invoke Bloch, is the way in which Benjamin's messianic theses might redeem a past apocalyptic text for present and even future ethico-political purposes. In what may be considered a strange turn, I shall also deploy Paul de Man's posthumously published *Aesthetic Ideology*, which raises important questions concerning the politics of deconstruction and material practice, to examine the political consequences of the relation of de Man's concept of materiality to J. M. Coetzee's *Barbarians*. Here I will be concerned to show how the body in Coetzee's words "takes its power" in the historical context and aftermath of apartheid. My book, then, sets out to examine the marked body in relation to the antipodes of contemporary apocalyptic and messianic discourse. It will do so by attempting to think through this problem with regard to both the messianic tradition that we inherit from Benjamin as well as an apocalyptic politics as it is analyzed in the work of deconstruction.

My objective, however, is not to attempt to present a uniform philosophical or religious theory of the apocalyptic or the messianic. This is, rather, a work of literary analysis that draws on modern and contemporary discourses of the apocalyptic and the messianic in sometimes generalized as well as specific ways. *Apocalyptic Futures* thus sets out to articulate a new thinking and textual practice of the relation between reception and embodiment, but it is my hope that part of the significance of this book will also lie in the particular readings it offers of Kafka's, Conrad's, Coetzee's, and Spiegelman's canonical works. In reading these works as proleptic of future catastrophe, I attempt to look into the untimely powers held within these texts in order to subject them to a timely ethical and political critique. My concern is less to situate these works within their historical contexts than it is to examine the way in which these texts summon their specific future contexts. These apocalyptic works are never simply past, but rather release energies that both condition and are conditioned by future contexts. I propose, then, that part of the ethico-political work of criticism lies in unlocking or taking account of how a past text might have conditioned its ethical or political future—of how, in other words, it attains a particular apocalyptic legibility. In my reading of *Maus* that concludes this book, I shall attempt against the sheer weight of this apocalyptic legibility to counterpose a fragile Benjaminian *now*, or messianic, time.

Although my book inherits that element of apocalypticism in contemporary theory that runs from Foucault's "end of man" to Derrida's apocalyptic tone, my work is more specifically concerned with the apocalyptic in the narrow sense. In working to grasp the poststructural effects of the power of inscription in relation to the materiality of the body, my project constitutes part of what might be called the new or timely materialisms. In examining the circulation of a violent symbolic exchange between intra- and extralinguistic bodies in contemporary culture, this project presses up against some of the ultimate questions that can be asked of the fate of a text's reception, of the generative dialectic between words and wounds, and of the ethico-political role of criticism in disrupting such violent incorporations.

CHAPTER ONE

Metaleptic Machines

Kafka, Kabbalah, Shoah

We know that the Jews were prohibited from inquiring into the future.
—WALTER BENJAMIN, "On the Concept of History"

The future is already here within me. The only change will be to make visible the hidden wounds.
—FRANZ KAFKA, in Janouch, *Conversations with Kafka*

KAFKA AND SHOAH

Writing to his friend Gershom Scholem in June 1938, in a letter that would prove poignantly prophetic, Walter Benjamin claimed that Kafka's world was "the exact complement of his era which is preparing to do away with the inhabitants of this planet on a considerable scale. The experience which corresponds to that of Kafka, the private individual, will probably not become accessible to the masses until such time as they are being done away with."[1] Although he wrestled with the temptation of granting Kafka a prophetic eminence, Benjamin desisted. Kafka's "prescience" comes from a certain deep listening or auscultation of tradition and not from some farsightedness or prophetic vision:

> If one says that he perceived what was to come without perceiving what exists in the present, one should add that he perceived it essentially as an *individual* affected by it. His gestures of terror are given scope by the marvelous *margin* which the catastrophe will not grant us. But his experience was based solely on the tradition to which Kafka surrendered;

there was no far-sightedness or "prophetic vision." Kafka listened to tradition, and he who listens hard does not see.[2]

Despite Benjamin's disavowal, Holocaust literature has conferred upon Kafka a prophetic power, and we may assign Benjamin's letter as an inaugural moment in the association of Kafka with the prophetic and apocalyptic that will obtain through the course of the century. George Steiner, for example, has claimed that Kafka "heard the name Buchenwald in the word birchwood" and that he "prophesied the actual forms of the disaster of Western humanism."[3] Similarly, Bertold Brecht, despite his predilection for practical ideology and crude thinking, echoes Steiner by arguing that:

> We find in [Kafka] strange disguises prefiguring many things that were, at the time when his books appeared, plain to very few people. The fascist dictatorship was, so to speak, in the very bones of the bourgeois democracies, and Kafka described with wonderful imaginative power the future concentration camps, the future instability of the law, the future absolutism of the state *apparat*, the paralyzed, inadequately motivated, floundering lives of the many individual people; everything appeared as in a nightmare and with the confusion and inadequacy of nightmare.[4]

Brecht here sets up a haunting homology that links Kafka's nightmare vision with the nightmare world of the camps. Kafka's "strange disguises," in Brecht's reading, now disclose the horror they prefigured, the surreal and atrocious nightmare into which the world would wake.

More circumspect than both Steiner and Brecht, Theodor Adorno critiques the prevailing tendency of some critics to assimilate Kafka "into an established trend of thought while little attention is paid to those aspects of his work which resist such assimilation and which, precisely for this reason, require interpretation."[5] Occupying a space somewhere between Benjamin and Brecht, Adorno sees Kafka's art as unfolding a future out of the fragmented detritus of the present. For Adorno, Kafka does not

directly outline the image of the society to come—for in his
as in all great art, asceticism towards the future prevails—
but rather depicts it as a montage composed of waste-prod-
ucts which the new order, in the process of forming itself,
extracts from the perishing present. Instead of curing neu-
rosis, he seeks in it itself the healing force, that of knowledge: the wounds with which society brands the individual
are seen by the latter as ciphers of the social untruth, as the
negative of truth.[6]

Kafka, as my epigraph (which would also be an epitaph) inti-
mates, does indeed practice an "asceticism towards the future,"
one in which (as we shall see) the "wounds with which society brands the individual" will be seen not simply as "ciphers
of . . . the negative of truth," but as prophetic of the truth to
come. If Adorno will not grant Kafka a direct line to the future
image of society, he does cite favorably Klaus Mann's contention
"that there was a similarity between Kafka's world and that of
the Third Reich," and while he will not draw "direct political allusion," Adorno also asserts that "it is National Socialism, far
more than the hidden dominion of God, that his work cites." He
further adds that "it was not only Kafka's prophecy of terror and
torture that was fulfilled," but that in *The Castle* "the officials
wear a special uniform, as the SS did."[7] It is Holocaust analogies
like these (and they can be multiplied both in the work of Adorno
on Kafka as well as in many of Kafka's eminent commentators)
that Lawrence Langer sets out to critique in his 1986 essay "Kafka as Holocaust Prophet: A Dissenting View." "Someone must
have been spreading rumors about Franz Kafka," he writes, "for
without having done anything wrong, he was proclaimed one fine
morning the prophet of the Holocaust. But when rumor congeals
into willingly accepted critical truth, the time may have arrived
for an inquiry into its genesis and the sufficiency of its allega-
tions."[8] For Langer, Kafka's texts, with their dreamlike and ambiguous epistemologies, bear little resemblance to "the concrete
inhuman threats to existence that crowd the pages of Holocaust
literature," and the paradigm of the Holocaust is imposed upon

Kafka, not by any critical acuity or insight, but by critical fiat. Langer accuses Adorno, for example, of using "language to bludgeon the reader into accepting Kafka's prophetic role, even at the price of misrepresentation."[9]

Like Benjamin, Langer sees Kafka's uncanny art as a response to the events of his time, but unlike Benjamin, Langer discerns no deep continuity between tradition and the catastrophe of the future. Rather, he sees the "irrepressible thrust of retrospective vision, combined with a stubborn resolve to see the Holocaust as a necessary expression of cultural impulse that has been quivering for decades" as betraying "an urgent but misdirected modern need to find in past art (if not past history) 'logical' precedence for the unprecedented illogic of the Holocaust." The genesis of Kafka's imaginative world, for Langer, is derived from Kafka's "scrupulously observed inner plight" and the subsumption of the events surrounding him into the abyss of that plight. Although no continuity, prophetic or otherwise, obtains between Kafka's art and the event of the Holocaust, Langer does grant that "striking parallels certainly exist between Kafka's world and the world of Holocaust literature. But the alienated consciousness, Kafka's persistent theme, becomes 'physicalized,' as it were, in the latter period, where the problem is no longer a matter of finding counter measures to sustain perception, but the sheer necessity of maintaining physical existence."[10]

Langer has not been the only contemporary critic to challenge the attribution of a special foresight to Kafka; John Updike also sees Kafka as transmuting and extrapolating the quotidian of his experience:

> Kafka's reputation has been immeasurably enhanced by his seeming prophecy, in works so private and eccentric, of the atrocious regimes of Hitler and Stalin, with their mad assignments of guilt and farcical trials and institutionalized paranoia. But the seeds of such vast evil were present in the world of the Emperor Franz Josef, and Kafka was, we should not forget, a man of the world, for all his debilities. He attended the harsh German schools of Prague; he

Metaleptic Machines 37

> earned the degree of Doctor of Law; he had experience of merchandising through his father's business. . . . Out of his experience of paternal tyranny and decadent bureaucracy he projected nightmares that proved prophetic.[11]

In contradistinction to both Langer and Updike, Steiner has recently offered a recrudescence or reassertion of Kafka's prophetic power and prevision. Far from being the singular representation of an "inner plight" and "alienated consciousness," Kafka's art offers "a detailed clairvoyance" and actualization of augury:

> Kafka's "In the Penal Colony," his play on "vermin" and annihilation in "The Metamorphosis," were actualized shortly after his death. A concrete fulfillment of augury, of detailed clairvoyance, attaches to his seeming fantastications. Obscurely but unavoidedly, the question or mystery of responsibility nags. Is there some sense in which the previsions spelled out across Kafka's fictions and most especially in *The Trial* contributed to their enactment? Could prophecy so mercilessly articulate have been other than fulfilled? Kafka's Milena and his three sisters perished in the camps. The central European Jewish world which Kafka ironized and celebrated went to hideous extinction. The spiritual possibility exists that Franz Kafka experienced his prophetic powers as some visitation of guilt, that foresight stripped him naked.[12]

Such claims, then, can only strike Langer as a species of out-and-out mystification, another instance of linguistic bludgeoning that "illuminates the methodology by which Kafka has earned the reputation of prophet of the Holocaust. At this point, it is hardly necessary to remind ourselves how much of that reputation originates in Kafka's commentators, not in Kafka himself."[13] But despite the seeming cogency of Langer's critique and the large and implausible assertions of Steiner, according to Janouch, Steiner surprisingly has something like Kafka's sanction. We recall from the introduction that Kafka's young disciple once reminded him of his assertion that "art is a mirror which goes 'fast', like a watch—sometimes. . . . Perhaps your writing is . . . only a mirror of tomorrow," he added.[14] Distressed, Kafka reportedly covered his eyes and, swaying back and forth, softly replied, "You are right. You are certainly right. Probably that's why I cannot finish anything. I am afraid of the truth. But can one do otherwise? . . . One must be silent if one can't give any help. . . . For that reason all my scribbling is to be destroyed."[15] Janouch's testimony is tellingly evaded by Langer, or perhaps Langer simply regards Janouch's recorded conversations with Kafka as hearsay, or in light of Jaouch's hagiography, heresy. But when we consider Kafka's strict insistence that his writings be destroyed and that close to his death, in a purgative burning, he did indeed destroy that portion of his writings in his possession (Max Brod found ten large burnt notebooks that had formerly contained stories and parables among Kafka's belongings after his death), Kafka's gesture does grant Steiner's assertions a certain corroboration and gives his questions a certain urgency. But for those of us skeptical of Steiner's occulting of the letter of Kafka's text, some questions do indeed nag: how exactly does Kafka's "In the Penal Colony," for example, become actualized after his death, and how does a concrete fulfillment of augury, and detailed clairvoyance, attach to his seeming fabulations? Steiner does not give us any answer and the matter is not made any less obscure by Kafka's claims that his writing had given him an understanding of certain "clairvoyant states," or his daring diary confession of 1922 that he had aspired to create a new sacred scripture or kabbalah and that all such writing was "an assault on frontiers."[16] Steiner asks, "Is there some sense in which the previsions spelled out across Kafka's fictions . . . contributed to their enactment?" And "could prophecy so mercilessly articulate have been other than fulfilled?"[17] Walking in conversation with Janouch one day, Kafka stopped opposite the old synagogue of Prague. "The synagogue already lies below ground level," he said. "But men will go further. They will try to grind the synagogue to dust by destroying the Jews themselves."[18] Kafka died the slow death of the tubercular in 1924, but all three of his sisters (along with most of the Jewish population of the city) were to suffer suffocation

Metaleptic Machines

by gas only a few years later. My words are nooses, Kafka once remarked.[19]

In light of these claims, I suggest we require a much more sophisticated analysis of the relationship of the Kafkan text to the Holocaust. The current pro/contra Kafka-as-Holocaust-prophet debate is simply insufficient and undertheorized. After all, it cannot be purely by chance or coincidence (it is precisely this uncanny coincidence that requires theorizing), or simply the result of misreading or perversion, that the Kafkan text should attach so insistently to its critical figuration as predictive or prophetic.

This chapter, then, attempts to consider some of the questions advanced by Steiner. Specifically, I shall focus on these problems: What is the relationship of an apocalyptic or prophetic text to a future catastrophe or apocalyptic event? What role does the Kafkan text play in promoting precisely this accrual of prophetic and apocalyptic power? And to what extent can Kafka's text be said to anticipate the possibility for, or eventuality of, such a linkage? The first part of this chapter reads Kafka's claims to a new kabbalah in terms of Harold Bloom's *Kabbalah and Criticism*. I will try to show that, via the paradoxical temporality of revisionist reading, Kafka's texts do come to take on a kabbalistic eminence. Bloom's linkage of kabbalah and revisionism with a Nietzschean theory of causality leads to my second section. Here I will try to open Kafka to a Derridean reading of the text as programming machine coding in advance its future reception. My chapter then moves to a consideration of Kafka's "In the Penal Colony" and "A Hunger Artist" as exemplary texts, demonstrating that Kafka's work is already a meditation on many of these effects, including the death of the author as well as the ability of a text to attach to an event of apocalyptic proportions in order to "materialize" itself, thereby coding itself as performative and predictive. Taken together, then, these readings operate as a poststructuralist analysis of the structure of the performative to the prophetic in Kafka.

KAFKA AND KABBALAH

Commenting on Kafka, Gershom Scholem once observed that "[i]n substantial portions of his writing there is a kind of canonicity, that is to say, they are open to infinite interpretation; and many of them, especially the most impressive of them, constitute in themselves acts of interpretation."[20] Kafka's texts do indeed seem to contain their own exegesis, even if that exegesis is a stratagem for the evasion of exegesis or exegesis at least as foundational interpretation. In this sense they present an instance of their own thematic, or enactment of their own theme, both compelling and resisting interpretation. In Kafka's famous parable "Before the Law," for instance, the man from the country is denied access to the law just as the reader is denied access to the law of the text—in terms of a secure and singular grasp of the parable. As Robert Alter remarks, "The peculiar genius of Kafka's novels is to fuse narrative invention with exegesis, making the fiction a constant contemplation of its own perplexing meanings, with the perplexed protagonist repeatedly seen in the absurdity of his efforts of contemplation."[21] In a certain sense, then, like the detective hero of Alain Robbe-Grillet's novel *The Erasers*, who winds up committing the very murder he is sent to investigate, we as readers become the protagonists of Kafka's fiction. But it is important to understand that Kafka himself does not escape implication in the address of his own writing; he, too, is pulled in by its gravitational torque. In a diary entry for February 11, 1913, Kafka offers a diagnosis of "The Judgment," a crucial piece written early in his career in one tormented sitting on Yom Kippur night, and one that he considered a breakthrough in his writing. Prompted by reading the proofs of the story, which had been composed almost five months earlier, Kafka proposes to "write down all the relationships which have become clear to me in the story as far as I now remember them. This is necessary because the story came out of me like a real birth, covered with filth and slime and only I have the hand that can reach to the body itself, and the strength of desire to do so."[22] The story's ontology is one

Metaleptic Machines 41

of autonomous physical emergence, midwived by the guiding forceps of the pen. Upon its physical emergence after its strange and difficult delivery, the story compels scrutiny, and Kafka gives it canonical interpretation. Here is a hermeneutically loaded sample from his entry:

> Georg has the same number of letters as Franz. In Bendemann, 'mann' is a strengthening of 'Bende' to provide for all the as yet unforeseen possibilities in the story. But Bende has exactly the same number of letters as Kafka, and the vowel *e* occurs in the same places as does the vowel *a* in Kafka.
>   Frieda has as many letters as F. and the same initial, Brandenfeld has the same initial as B., and in the word 'Feld' a certain connexion [*sic*] in meaning, as well.[23]

Kafka's interpretive manner, his exorbitant theosophying of the letter, is resolutely kabbalistic. His text here borders on the sacrosanct, miming ancient Judaic modes of exegesis. As Robert Alter has noted, Kafka's method closely resembles Talmudic notarikon and gematria.[24] Every linguistic marker is made to register a submerged significance—a textual algebra in which words, names, letters, and spacing are open to manifold permutations, affording an open-ended arrangement of signification. An array "of unforeseen possibilities" will continue to make a cipher of the story, holding hidden secrets, even from the author from whom the text "came out." Composing a Talmudic textuality, the future interpretation of the Kafkan text is never closed and its borders never entirely delimited.

We gather, then, from this example that Scholem's bestowing upon the Kafkan text the canonical power to compel an infinite interpretation is already an effect of Kafkan exegesis. This receives further confirmation when, close to the end of his life and looking back on what his writing has meant, Kafka confesses that he has aspired to create a new sacred scripture. Meditating in his diary entry for January 16, 1922, "on something very like a breakdown" and on the solitude of his inner world, imposed by the "introspection" of his writing, Kafka encounters, as Harold

Bloom has pointed out,[25] something like the kabbalistic trope of the breaking of the vessels. His inner world in confrontation with his outer world leads to a fearful shattering: "What else can happen," he asks, "but that the two worlds split apart, and they do split apart in a fearful manner?" Kafka's autoanalysis here takes on a kabbalistic tone as he confirms when he moves to a reading of this introspective solitude:

> The solitude that for the most part has been forced on me, in part voluntarily sought by me—but what was this if not compulsion too?—is now losing all its ambiguity and approaches its denouement. Where is it leading? The strongest likelihood is that it may lead to madness; there is nothing more to say, the pursuit goes right through me and rends me asunder. Or I can—can I?—manage to keep my feet somewhat and be carried along in the wild pursuit. Where, then, shall I be brought? "Pursuit," indeed, is only a metaphor. I can also say, "assault on the last earthly frontier," an assault, moreover, launched from below, from mankind, and since this too is a metaphor, I can replace it by the metaphor of an assault from above, aimed at me from above.
>
> All such writing is an assault on the frontiers; if Zionism had not intervened, it might easily have developed into a new secret doctrine, a Kabbalah. There are intimations of this. Though of course it would require genius of an unimaginable kind to strike root again in the old centuries, or create the old centuries anew and not spend itself withal, but only then begin to flower forth.[26]

The act of writing here carries shattering force, an inner inscription or writerly spearing that "goes right through me and rends me asunder," a pursuit that amounts to an assault on being. Indeed, Kafka moves the metaphor from "pursuit" to "assault" and the tropic substitution carries with it an almost preternatural provenance, or "assault on the last earthly frontier," a subterranean assault carried out from below and in a further substitution—perhaps betokening a kind of revelation—an assault from above. This, then, is writing imbued with violent powers, a vio-

Metaleptic Machines 43

lence of the letter, a writing beyond volition, and a violation of future boundaries. This writing amounts to a revelatory "assault on frontiers," which, "if Zionism had not intervened, might easily have developed into a new secret doctrine, a Kabbalah." Kafka's remark concerning the intervention of Zionism is difficult to decode. Harold Bloom brilliantly offers it as a prevision of Scholem's magisterial reading of kabbalah as counterhistory. The very thing that Zionism formerly occluded, Zionism now releases:

> How are we to understand that curious statement about Zionism as the blocking agent that prevents Franz Kafka from becoming another Isaac Luria? Kafka darkly and immodestly writes: "There are intimations of this." Our teacher Gershom Scholem governs our interpretation here, of necessity. Those intimations belong to Kafka alone, or perhaps to a select few in his immediate circle. They cannot be conveyed to Jewry, even to its elite, because Zionism has taken the place of Messianic Kabbalah, including presumably the heretical Kabbalah of Nathan of Gaza, prophet of Sabbatai Zvi and of all his followers down to the blasphemous Jacob Frank. Kafka's influence upon Scholem is decisive here, for Kafka already has arrived at Scholem's central thesis of the link between the Kabbalah of Isaac Luria, the Messianism of the Sabbatarians and Frankists, and the political Zionism that gave rebirth to Israel.[27]

Astonishingly, in Bloom's gnomic formulation, Kafka stands as Scholem's great precursor, and becomes through the vessel of Scholem's strong misreading a new kabbalah:

> How much Kabbalah Kafka knew is not clear. Since he wrote a new Kabbalah, the question of Jewish Gnostic sources can be set aside. Indeed, by what seems a charming oddity (but I would call it yet another instance of Blake's insistence that forms of worship are chosen from poetic tales), our understanding of Kabbalah is Kafkan anyway, since Kafka profoundly influenced Gershom Scholem, and no one will be able to get beyond Scholem's creative or strong misreading of Kabbalah for decades to come. . . . A

> Kafkan facticity or contingency now governs our awareness of whatever in Jewish cultural tradition is other than normative.[28]

Intriguingly, a Kafkan contingency also governs Bloom's revisionary reading, or poetics of misprision. Concluding his brilliantly epigrammatic essay "Kafka and His Precursors," Jorge Luis Borges writes:

> The poem "Fears and Scruples" by Browning foretells Kafka's work, but our reading of Kafka perceptibly sharpens and deflects our reading of the poem. Browning did not read it as we do now. In the critics' vocabulary, the word "precursor" is indispensable, but it should be cleansed of all connotations of polemics or rivalry. The fact is that every writer *creates* his own precursors. His work modifies our conception of the past, as it will modify the future. In this correlation the identity or plurality of the men involved is unimportant.[29]

Borges, Kafka's most distinguished disciple, here stands as Bloom's great precursor, formulator of the ineluctable, if impersonal, paradigm of revisionary reading. Bloom's move is to return a Kafkan anxiety to this anxiety-evacuated paradigm, even as he infuses it with a Freudian or Oedipal rivalry. Bloom will vigorously affirm with Borges that the word "precursor" is indispensable to the critics' vocabulary, and that as "every writer creates his own precursors" his "work modifies our conception of the past, as it will modify the future." But he will argue that this process can never be cleansed "of all connotation of polemics and rivalry" since it is just this rivalry which is the originary engine in the production of poetry. Against Borges's canonical classicism, Bloom will counterpose a Kafkan and necessarily kabbalistic anxiety. This anxiety is necessarily kabbalistic, since for Bloom, kabbalah provides a formative model for all romantic (and postromantic) revisionism. This is so because romanticism, like kabbalah, is from the first a response to belatedness, thus both consequently share the same structural origins or formative processes. In Bloom's reading, then, kabbalah becomes a strong misprision of the orthodox or rabbinically normative canon. He interprets this misprision as an opening up of the Judaic canon to the Jewish agony of the exilic condition. What is particularly instructive about kabbalah for Bloom is that it uncovers "the normative structure of images, of tropes, and psychic defenses, in many central revisionary texts, including many poems of the last three centuries."[30] What kabbalah reveals most especially is that "the initial trope or image in any new poem is closely related to the hidden presence of the new poem in its precursor poem." This is to say that in some sense the latter poem inheres, or is already present in, its precursor poem. But paradoxically this presence is denoted precisely by an absence. "A poem," Bloom tells us, "is a deep misprision of a previous poem when we recognize the latter poem as being absent rather than present on the surface of the earlier poem, and yet still being in the earlier poem, implicit or hidden in it, not yet manifest, and yet there."[31] The Kafkan text inheres in kabbalah in precisely this way; it is implicit in it, darkly alluded to, but not quite manifest, and yet there, a further darkening and opening up tradition to the catastrophe of exile and to the linguistics of exile. Commenting on the predicament of the German Jewish writer, Kafka proceeds to a disquieting analysis:

> Most young Jews who began to write German wanted to leave Jewishness behind them, and their fathers approved of this, but vaguely (this vagueness was what was so outrageous to them). But with their posterior legs they were still glued to their fathers' Jewishness and with their waving anterior legs they found no new ground. The ensuing despair became their inspiration. . . . The product of their despair became their inspiration. . . . The product of their despair could not be German literature, though outwardly it seemed to be so. They existed among three impossibilities, which I just happen to call linguistic impossibilities. . . . These are: the impossibility of not writing, the impossibility of writing German, the impossibility of writing differently. One might also add a fourth impossibility, the impossibility of writing.[32]

Faced with the powerful blocking agent of exile and most particularly linguistic exile, Kafka forges a new kabbalah, a writing on the impossibility of writing, and a writing on the impossibility of writing German, itself written precisely in a meticulously limpid and gleaming German, but a German exiled upon uninterpretability. Like Moses Cordovero and Isaac Luria before him, Kafka turns the despair of exile into a negative inspiration, opening and revising the canon in accordance with his own catastrophic vision.

The revisionary use of catastrophe is nowhere better illustrated than in the starkly ironic Kafkan parable "Leopards in the Temple": "Leopards break into the temple and drink the sacrificial chalices dry; this occurs repeatedly, again and again: finally it can be reckoned on beforehand and becomes part of the ceremony."[33] Susan Handelman cites this piece as an uncanny description of the Jewish heretic hermeneutic. She sees in it an allegory of exile and Jewish modes of accommodation:

> In exile, a broken people try to heal themselves through ever more complicated figuration, opening, troping of their Sacred Text, trying somehow to make the facts of their historical catastrophe agree with the exalted promises of their Sacred Book. And this can be accomplished only through feats of subtle interpretive reversal: somehow the leopards have entered the Temple and must be accommodated without being allowed to triumph. Excessive troping, transgressive interpretation, Kabbalistic inversion, and displacement all appear under the guise of extension and application of the Sacred Book, part of its unfolding interpretation.[34]

This is an acute and articulate reading, but the parable is also open, I think, to another or further sense. Handelman's "subtle interpretive reversal" resembles a Nietzschean and kabbalistic theory of causality, which Bloom explicates as follows:

> The error we call a "cause," Nietzsche says, is merely "a capacity to produce events that has been super-added to the events," which means that any interpretation by causality

Metaleptic Machines 47

is a deception. Cordovero and Nietzsche are both talking about language, but what Nietzsche sees as a constraint put upon us, by language, is for Cordovero a supernatural gift rendered us through language.[35]

Kafka's parable functions by, or articulates precisely, this substitution of effect for cause: the ineluctable intrusion of the leopards into the temple is incorporated into the ritual as if by design. We might read this parable, I think, as Kafka's subtle commentary on the destiny of his own writing (or what would have been his own writing) in relation to future catastrophe. The Holocaust, like the leopard, gets superadded or intruded into his writing, but that writing comes to be seen as prefiguring precisely this intrusion; it is sutured into its structure, in a fusion of *topos* and text. Kafka's text provides a prevision of the Holocaust and this prevision contains within it its future enactment. Kafka's text opens out onto the catastrophe of the Holocaust and this catastrophe confers upon it a kabbalistically transgressive and mystical force, an assault on frontiers. It is this capacity of the Kafkan text to incorporate catastrophe and then modulate it, via a kabbalistic causality, as part of the text's deployed design that transforms Kafka into an avatar of Luria and Cordovero. Paradoxically it is precisely the massive cataclysm of the Shoah that powerfully confers on Kafka a new kabbalah.

INSCRIPTIONAL MACHINES

By the dim light cast by Kafka's kabbalistic parable, we might see Langer's charging critics with "an irrepressible thrust of retrospective vision" not so much as a critical perversion or recursive torquing of Kafka's texts, but as the result of Kafka's somehow coding in advance the future reception of his texts. But it remains to be asked just how such coding might take place; after all, not every text is granted such prophetic powers. Martin Jay, for example, has argued against any strict severance of the history of a text's "misinterpretations" from a preserved and pristine original:

> The history of a text's effects may well be more a chronicle of successive misunderstandings than perfect reproductions, that "map of misreadings" suggested by Harold Bloom, but the potential for the specific distortions that do occur can be understood as latent in the original text. Thus, while it may be questionable to saddle Marx with responsibility for the Gulag Archipelago or blame Nietzsche for Auschwitz, it is nonetheless true that their writings could be misread as justifications for these horrors in a way that, say, those of John Stuart Mill or Alexis de Tocqueville could not.[36]

But beyond insisting on the latent role of the text, Jay does not pursue the difficult question of what exactly it is in Nietzsche or Marx that makes available such misreadings or conversely, what it is in Mill or de Tocqueville that resists such stray appropriations. Less hermeneutically cautious, and more strongly insistent on the role of the text in foreshadowing the future, George Steiner goes much further, charging the Hebrew Bible with precise powers of prescription and performance:

> Rigorously viewed, the fate of Judaism is a postscript to the penalty clauses in God's contract (that fine print, again). It is a sequence of demonstrative footnotes, of marginalia, to the text of God's (non-)reply to Job and to the texts of the prophets. Everything is there, spelt out from the start. The rest has been unbearable fulfillment. No other nation, no other culture on this earth has been so prescribed. No other men have had to bear like witness to the cognate meanings of *prescription* and of *proscription*, which signify denunciation, ostracism and a written designation for death.[37]

The Hebrew Bible then, and more particularly its prophetic books, is programmatic, spelling out in apocalyptic utterance the entire course Judaic history will take. The prophet Amos's text, for example, is performative—a programmed code slowly playing out its prophetic proclamations. "The entire Zionist dream and purpose," Steiner tells us, "the manner of miracle in which these have been realized, are 'programmed' in . . . Amos's script."

Metaleptic Machines

And in our time, as if connected by apocalyptic umbilical cord to the prophetic line, Kafka, too, has scripted the future. "As no other speaker or scribe after the prophets," Steiner asserts, "Kafka *knew*. In him as in them, imagination was second sight and invention a pedantic notation of clairvoyance."[38] But for Steiner it is precisely here, on this question of clairvoyance, where commentary is most required that it most fails; commentary evades, he argues, the question that should haunt it most:

> The notion that the night-vision of the Jew has, somehow, in some secret measure, brought on itself the torments foreseen, is irrational, but haunting none the less.
>
> It is compelling in our reading of Kafka. The practices of literary criticism and study are more or less helpless before *The Trial* and *The Castle* with their minutely faithful prevision of the clerical inhumanities of life in our time. Explication, reference to stylistic means or literary context, merely trivialize Kafka's blueprint of the concentration-camp world, of coming obscenities of intimacy between torturer and victim, as these are spelt out, in October 1914, in "In the Penal Colony." Or consider Kafka's use of the word "vermin" in "The Metamorphosis" of 1912 in precisely the sense and connotations that would be given to it by the Nazis a generation later. In Kafka's writings there is a revealed literalism *avant la lettre* which renders almost wholly worthless the spate of commentaries which they have provoked. Even the masterly exchange on Kafka's meaning in the Walter Benjamin–Gershom Scholem letters, which may, together with Mandelstam's essay on reading Dante, be the best that the arts of modern literary criticsm have to show, avoid the urgent conundrum of the prophetic.[39]

Steiner himself has little by way of explication to add to the "urgent conundrum of the prophetic." He argues that "though the psychological mechanism remains obscure, the fact is a commonplace: prophecies are, to a degree, self-fulfilling. The stronger the prophecy the more often it is proclaimed, the greater its initial thrust toward realization. In his dread history the Jew would seem to have been intent to certify the accuracy of the road mapped for him by the Prophets."⁴⁰ While not inaccurate, Steiner's assertion that prophecies are to a certain degree self-fulfilling offers little insight into the programmatic workings of the prophetic text. Again many questions press: How precisely are Kafka's texts granted the power of foresight? By what mechanism do Kafka's writings become a "revealed literalism *avant la lettre*"? And by what means do Kafka's words program a material future?

One way into these questions might be found in Derrida's analysis of the problem of the extent and manner in which an author may be held responsible for future readings of his or her work.⁴¹ Derrida refers this question on the politics of reading to the appropriation of Nietzsche's texts in the service of Nazi ideology. Must we claim, Derrida asks in his *The Ear of the Other,* that Nietzsche's texts were seized and subjected to malign misreadings that wrenched them out of context and delivered his writings over to the service of Nazi ideology? Or is it not also incumbent upon us to consider whether Nietzsche's texts were particularly open to just such practices, that they did in some way prefigure or offer themselves up to the politics placed upon them by Nazi ideologues? Derrida does not himself try to ultimately decide this question, for such a decision will always be caught within the flow of contrary currents of evidence. It would clearly be the most irresponsible of readings that ipso facto held Nietzsche directly liable for the way in which his texts were propagandized by the Nazi state. But such exculpatory arguments, which simply aver that Nietzsche's writings have been perverted and polluted by Nazi reading practices, ignore Nietzsche's pronouncement on the untimely quality of his writings, whose full meaning and usage awaits future strong readers. Nietzsche's doctrine of eternal return, for example, is especially open to "untimeliness." "By definition," Derrida tells us, "it cannot let itself be heard or understood in the present: it is untimely, differant, anachronistic. Yet, since this news repeats an affirmation, since it affirms the return, the rebeginning, a certain kind of reproduction that preserves whatever comes back, then its very logic must give rise to a magisterial institution."⁴² In regard to Nietzsche, this "magiste-

Metaleptic Machines 51

rial institution" has come to take on a future form, whose aspect is ominously prefigured in a philosophy that at once beckons to and also decidedly disavows the uses to which it will later be put. It is not sufficient, then, to say that meanings were imputed to Nietzsche or that he did not intend this reading and to simply hold with claims of misappropriation or misreading since it is not just any text that can be so misappropriated or that so readily allows for just such misreading. Derrida insists that it cannot be wholly by chance or simply due to misreading that Nietzsche's texts took on their bad faith and uses during the Nazi period. In fact, it is their very appeal as an instrument of this ideology that requires us to ask "why the only program of indoctrination which has ever been able to take full advantage of Nietzsche's teachings has been that of the Nazis." Further, Derrida tells us, "the future of the Nietzsche text is not closed. But if, within the still open contours of an era, the only politics calling itself—proclaiming itself—Nietzschean will have been a Nazi one, then this is necessarily significant and must be questioned in all its consequences."[43] Of course, Nazi misappropriations of Nietzsche's texts have been strongly contested and devastatingly critiqued and indeed, remaining cognizant of this history, we must be always vigilant against any future giving over or surrender of Nietzsche's writings to an authoritarian politics. So it would appear, and I would argue, that the Nazi usage of Nietzsche is a "mimetic inversion and perversion" of his writings, one that preys on his texts by a cunning use and extraction of quotation that manages to fold back upon, simulate, and dissemble Nietzsche's text. But, as Derrida points out, it is still necessary to account for the "possibility of this mimetic inversion and perversion":

> If one refuses the distinction between unconscious and deliberate programs as an absolute criterion, if one no longer considers only intent—whether conscious or not—when reading a text, then the law that makes the perverting simplification possible must lie in the structure of the text "remaining.". . . Even if the intention of one of the signatories or shareholders in the huge "Nietzsche Corporation" had

nothing to do with it, it cannot be entirely fortuitous that the discourse bearing his name in society, in accordance with civil laws and editorial norms, has served as a legitimating reference for ideologues. There is nothing absolutely contingent about the fact that the only political regimen to have *effectively* brandished his name as a major and official banner was Nazi.[44]

There is something, then, in the Nietzschean text inviting this appropriation by the Nazis. It is not so much that his writings are replete with latent ideologies that might be called forth by the future executors of Nietzsche's corpus; rather, we should think in terms of a textual machine that somehow programs in advance the structural possibilities for a radically divergent ethics of reading. Commenting on the fact that the "'same' utterance can signify precisely the opposite, correspond to its own inverted meaning, to the reactive inversion of that which it mimes," Derrida asks what it is about Nietzschean utterance that makes it so available for Nazi deployment. In working toward a generalized answer, he advances the proposition of a textual programming machine:

> The question that poses itself for us might take this form: Must there not be some powerful utterance-producing machine that programs the movements of the two opposing forces at once, and which couples, conjugates, or marries them in a given set, as life (does) death? . . . Neither of the two antagonistic forces can break with this powerful programming machine: it is their *destination*; they draw their points of origin and their resources from it; in it, they exchange utterances that are allowed to pass through the machine and into each other, carried along by family resemblances, however incompatible they may sometimes appear.[45]

This radical duality, Derrida tells us, is no accident but part of "the destinational structure of all so-called post-Hegelian texts." But it is not enough only to decipher this textual programming machine; this decipherment must also amount to a "political intervention" in the "rewriting of the text and its destination": "The 'programming machine' that interests me here does not call only for decipherment but also for transformation—that is a practical rewriting according to a theory-practice relationship which, if possible, would no longer be part of the program."[46] Perhaps it was Kafka's perception of the impossibility of his transforming this program that decided him on destroying his texts. Perhaps this is what he meant by "one must be silent if one cannot give any help."[47] Certainly Kafka is implicated in the same machinal program that Derrida finds so forcefully operating in Nietzsche. His texts, too, are caught up in the same post-Hegelian destinational structure. That is, like Nietzsche's proclamation of "untimeliness" and his holding his text open to the strong spirits of the future to come, Kafka also offers his text as "an assault on frontiers." He, too, makes claims on a certain farsightedness and grants his writings the power of a future violence.

Despite the startling, intricate, and imbricated analysis played out in *The Ear of the Other*, Derrida's project here lies more in the delimiting and conceptual teasing out of the notion of a textual "programming machine" than in a full-blown decipherment of the constitution and mechanics of this program. This "programming machine," Derrida tells us, requires "decipherment" and as a consequence of the theoretical work still to be done, many aspects of this program appear somewhat opaque. What is clear is that Derrida's work here, together with his work on iterability and speech acts in "Limited Inc." and "Signature, Event, Context," marks one of the strongest theoretical attempts to delimit and demarcate the role of a text in the coding of its future reception. Perhaps some part of the future of theory will lie in the further untying of these intricate textual weaves and effects. For my part, I shall return to Derrida and iterability in my analysis of an uncanny temporality that conditions the skulls of *Heart of Darkness*.

In the interests of beginning to flesh out a further analysis of these effects, I wish to broach another means by which a text might be said to formulate its future: one that offers a structural explanation for Steiner's seemingly outrageous claim that Kafka's texts were literalized a generation after his death, and one that speaks to the power of a text to incorporate material bodies into its textual field.

Kafka's writings, as the self-referential parable of the leopard makes clear, are not merely constative acts of narration but hold a performative power.[48] Like the leopards breaking into the temple and becoming part of the ceremonial ritual, Kafka's writings both provisionally program in advance their future reception, and then via the hidden mechanism of enforced retrospection, program that programming as inevitable and not provisional or contingent. In a sense, then, the complex coding machine at work in Kafka's writing is composed of several versions of the performative. The first comports with the poststructuralist sense of the performative in which the future effects of performative enactment cannot be strictly predicted; unlike, for example, God's command in Genesis, "Let there be light," which cannot but succeed, and is strictly predictable, the performative in the poststructuralist sense is infused with a strong element of chance and a differential structure. It always performs something in the world, but that something cannot be strictly foretold. The ruse by which Kafka's prophetic fiction works is to seem to transform the performative in the poststructural sense into a strict performative—one in which there is a certain inevitability that the action denoted by the speech act will absolutely succeed.

It is not, then, only that Kafka's works lie in wait for a future catastrophic event to which they attach their own catastrophic pronouncements, but, as with Derrida's reading of Nietzsche, they constitute a program that makes their prophetic link to the Holocaust less than absolutely contingent. As in the parable of the leopard, Kafka's work contains, I think, its own internal metacommentary on this programming in advance of its own future reception, and to begin concluding this chapter, since the story is so often invoked as testament to Kafka's clairvoyance, I wish briefly to analyze this process in "In the Penal Colony."

At the same time that Freud was developing his conception of the psyche through the metaphor of a writing machine, and prefiguring Derrida, de Man, Deleuze, and the twentieth- century troping of the text as programming machine, Kafka advanced his own lethal version. "In the Penal Colony" concerns a writing machine that inscribes a "judicial" sentence directly onto the body of the condemned. This machine itself is programmed by an intricate and labyrinthine text handed down by the old Commandant, originator of this machine and its spectacular scriptual punishments, to the new officer, the last of his adherents. The officer is concerned to persuade an eminent explorer of the value of the machine and the perpetuation of its tradition, which is being phased out by the new Commandant of the penal colony. The officer puts the text on display, urging the explorer to decipher it:

> "Read it," said the officer. "I can't," said the explorer. "Yet it's clear enough," said the officer. "It's very ingenious," said the explorer evasively, "but I can't make it out." "Yes," said the officer with a laugh, putting the paper away again, "it's no calligraphy for school children. It needs to be studied closely. I'm quite sure that in the end you would understand it too. Of course, the script can't be a simple one; it's not supposed to kill a man straight off, but only after an interval of, on an average, twelve hours; the turning point is reckoned to come at the sixth hour. So there have to be lots and lots of flourishes around the actual script; the script itself runs around the body only in a narrow girdle; the rest of the body is reserved for the embellishments.[49]

Writing here functions as the ultimate in the representation of performative scriptural power, in both its resonances. (The embellishments may well be Kafka's ironic reading of the tradition of Judaic commentary forming a hedge around Torah—the prisoner, after all, will have "honor thy superiors" inscribed on his body, an inscription that echoes the ten commandments.) We have then a materiality of inscription, a writing on a body in which the letter literally kills—the violence of writing materialized. This writing becomes truly performative when it is linked to the inscribed bodies of the Holocaust victims who also had their sentences inscribed on their bodies. The text thus affixes to a materialized text in order to realize itself as prophetic and performative—an apocalyptic machine. This, then, becomes a text about the coding powers of textual machines that enacts itself, thus becoming a text about the coding powers of a text programming its own materialization. This very process of the retrospective assigning of prophetic power via the attachment of a text to its future material referent is already deeply coded in Kafka's story itself. As Benjamin tells us, "in 'The Penal Colony' those in power use an archaic apparatus which engraves letters with curlicues on the backs of guilty men, multiplying the stabs and piling up the ornaments to the point where the back of the guilty man becomes clairvoyant and is able to decipher the writing from which he must derive the nature of his unknown guilt."[50] Guilt or meaning, then, arrives retroactively, but it arrives, too, in the form of a prophecy; as Benjamin says, "the back of the guilty man becomes clairvoyant." This clairvoyant coding is given greater force when we consider that "In the Penal Colony" strongly marks itself as a prophetic text. Entering an enigmatic teahouse that gives the explorer "the impression of a historic tradition of some kind" and in which "he feels the power of past days," the explorer is led to a gravestone:

> There was an inscription on it in very small letters, the explorer had to kneel down to read it. This was what it said: "Here rests the old Commandant. His adherents, who now must be nameless, have dug this grave and set up this stone. There is a prophecy that after a certain number of years the Commandant will rise again and lead his adherents from this house to recover the colony. Have faith and wait!" (167)

As with the sentence proclaimed upon the back of the guilty man, the inscription here is also difficult to read. The explorer must kneel down as if pulled by the weight of the stone and the smallness of the text to an attitude of prayer, but the inscription is legible and its prophetic linkage with the Holocaust resonates with uncanny strength.

Metaleptic Machines 57

But Kafka's most painful and poignant attempt to speak to the power of a text to perform its own future must surely be his use of his own body as future material referent for his "A Hunger Artist." Written after Kafka had contracted tuberculosis, this story tells of a hunger artist whose prodigious feast of fasting decline from spectacular public reverence into a bleak neglect. He dies one day unnoticed, his body atrophied from one final fast. The story, enacting its own theme, runs down, atrophying its prose, miming in its textual body the hunger artist's body, which is wasting away. Two years later, himself almost dead, Kafka was engrossed in the galley proofs of "A Hunger Artist." As Ernst Pawel, Kafka's biographer, records:

> The throat lesions made speaking as well as swallowing progressively more difficult. Urged to spare his vocal cords as much as possible, Kafka began to communicate with his "little family" by means of written notes.... They document the courage... with which Kafka faced his death: "To think that I was once able to manage a big sip of water.". . .
>
> Kafka, by then quite unable to eat, was wasting away, dying of starvation—and immersed in the galley proofs of *A Hunger Artist*. Fate lacked the subtle touch of Kafka's art.[51]

But then again, maybe this was Kafka's subtle art prophesying fate. In an intricate and excruciating irony, Kafka's text becomes prophetically performative by attaching to his atrophied and starved body. It materializes itself precisely on the wasting away of its author. It inscribes itself on his body, even as it is a text about wasting away, which itself wastes away in the diminution of its prose. In a strange echo of the parable of the leopard, the hunger artist is replaced by a powerful panther whose "noble body, furnished almost to the bursting point with all that it needed, seemed to carry freedom around with it too, somewhere in his jaws it seemed to lurk; and the joy of life streamed with such ardent passion from his throat that for the onlookers it was not easy to stand the shock of it."[52]

As J. Hillis Miller claims, the very efficacy of any performative is always, in some sense, the death of the author.[53] But it was Kafka's great power to write himself into a state of clairvoyance. For both Bloom and Derrida, then (though in different ways), texts have the power to code in advance their future reception. Kafka already knew this, and predictably, he anticipated them both. Commenting on Kafka's *The Trial*, Pawel echoes Langer in denying Kafka the prophetic; he, too, sees Kafka's uncanny fiction as emerging from a deep mining of a tormented interiority:

> A preview of the fate of millions, of a century in which doomsday came to be an everyday event. Yet prophecy was the last thing on his mind, and not only because every café already had its prophet and every prophet his café. Kafka's gift was insight rather than foresight, the obsessive self-scrutiny that drove him on relentlessly beyond the self into the murky depths inaccessible to reason, where truth dissolved into a nexus of ambiguities and the irrational gave birth to an inexorable logic of its own—the syllogism of paranoia.[54]

The future destiny of Kafka's texts does give way to an "inexorable logic" of their own, but it is a logic in which the anxiety of insight becomes a kind of terrifying foresight. The Shoah is after all precisely a trauma in the Freudian sense, in that it generates its own retroactive antecedents. It is as if Kafka had the "preparatory anxiety" that should have cushioned the event; thus Kafka foresees the event, even as the event itself solicits a precursor. If Kafka had no powers of occulted prophecy, his texts nonetheless already function as inscriptional machines, prophetically writing their future to come.

"BE JUST!" is the juridical injunction that the officer deliberately programs into the machine—the embellished injunction that he sets to be exquisitely incised on his back (161). In the course of executing its last sentence the apparatus breaks down, and "no sign was visible of the promised redemption; what the others had found in the machine the officer had not found; the lips were firmly pressed together, the eyes were open, with the same expression as in life, the look was calm and convinced, through the forehead went the point

Metaleptic Machines

of a great iron spike" (166). In denying the officer the sadomasochistic pleasures of exquisite torture and the promised enlightenment, and in dismantling its intricate inscriptional apparatus, the machine does indeed ironically perform the officer's command that it "BE JUST." The exquisite vibrations of the needles of the Harrow are transformed into the thrust through the forehead of the single great iron spike, the metal remnant of the machine. But for all the macabre imagery of the staked head, what is truly grotesque is that even when it appears so utterly dead there is actually something undead about the officer. His eyes are wide open and he wears the same expression as in life. His look bespeaks a conviction that remains unchanged. Like the prophecy of the Commandant that will rise again, the undeadness of the officer seems to betoken a traumatism that can never be killed off once and for all.

Indeed in his giving himself up to the Harrow, in his sacrificial immolation before the regime of the machine, the officer enacts the contradictory double logic of autoimmunity in which the body forms antigens to fight off foreign invaders, but then turns its immune system against itself. In his suicidal autoimmunity the officer submits himself to the machine in an act of self-sacrifice that is designed to stave off the death of the tradition of the old Commandant. In effect, although he may think that he is deciding to make the ultimate sacrifice, his substitution of himself for the condemned man, his submission of himself to the machine is already programmed by the automatism of the logic of autoimmunity. Or perhaps this is exactly what the officer already understands as he offers his exorbitant fealty to the regime of the scriptural machine. In any event, the officer's immolation runs precisely according to the machinal logic of autoimmunity as Derrida theorizes it:

> This excess above and beyond the living, whose life has absolute value by being worth more than life, more than itself—this, in short, is what opens the space of death that is linked to the automaton . . . to technics, the machine, the prosthesis: in a word, to dimensions of auto-immune and

self-sacrificial supplementarity, to this death-drive that is silently at work in every community, every *auto-co-immunity*, constituting it as such in its iterability, its heritage, its spectral tradition.[55]

Whether he knows it or not, it is precisely this autoimmunitary response that the officer puts on display before the explorer. It is this implacable machinal logic that works through the officer and that is made manifest in the spectral undeadness of the spiked head, which is already taking its place in the lineage of relentless commitment to the undead spectral tradition of the old Commandant, of whom it is said that he, together with his adherents, his *community*, will rise again to recover the colony.

Speaking in the context of September 11, the suicide bombing of the World Trade Center towers, and the subsequent war on terror, Derrida remarks that "[i]t is the future that determines the unappropriability of the event, not the present or the past. Or at least, if it is the present or the past, it is only insofar as it bears on its body the terrible sign of what might or perhaps will take place, which will be *worse than anything that has ever taken place*."[56] What Derrida means by this is that the traumatism of terror is never over, that it cannot be worked through and put to rest because it always has the possibility of reconstituting itself around the threat of what is still to come, of that compulsion to repetition that will not be halted, of a certain undeadness that attends the specter of terror. Is this not what is truly terrifying about Kafka's story? For it is not only the officer who is caught in the implacable working of the logic of autoimmunity but the scriptural machine itself. In carrying out the officer's order, "BE JUST," the apparatus attacks itself—it destroys itself, dismantling the intricate machinery of its Designer. But the machine too is caught in the paradoxical logic of autoimmunity in that attacking itself gives rise to its spectral living on. It is not the death of the machine that constitutes the future reception of this story, but its capture by the inscriptional apparatus of the camps. Kafkan irony proves insufficient to the materializing of the machinal autoimmune logic of the Nazi apocalyptic. It is not the death's head, but the undead

Metaleptic Machines

spiked head, the fusion of the officer and the scriptural machine, that bears on its body the "terrible sign of what might or perhaps will take place, which will be *worse than anything that has ever taken place.*"

The working of this autoimmune or suicidal logic was no less clear to Kafka than it was to Derrida. So we are left to ask: does Kafka not place himself in the same position before the machine of his text as the explorer before the apparatus of scriptural torture? In allowing for the publication of this text, does he not also allow for its spectral incarnation? I mentioned in the introduction that what might be at stake in Kafka's story is the right of a dangerous piece of private writing to public literary existence and that Kafka's story might be interpreted as an allegory of the struggle of a story against its author, who would for ethical reasons extinguish its very literary existence. It is in coming up against this possibility, I think, that we encounter the full mastery of Kafka's irony. It may seem, upon first thought, that in threatening to burn his manuscript of his story machine, Kafka occupies the opposite position to the officer who works only on behalf of the perpetuation of the scriptural machine. But in burning his manuscript does Kafka himself not risk succumbing to the same autoimmune response as the officer? Does he not, that is, risk protecting himself only by attacking himself or that which emerges from himself (we recall here Kafka's trope of writing as giving birth)? Yet despite all his disavowals, in facilitating the publication of his text does he not inevitably court its spectral incarnation? Kafka, it appears, is inescapably trapped in the double logic of autoimmunity, and he would be faced with this dilemma as soon as his text emerged, even if only into the space of a private literary existence. It is perhaps part of Kafka's abyssal irony that we cannot decide if this is simply the effect of an autoimmune logic working through Kafka's story or if this is Kafka's cunning ploy to leave himself with no properly ethical option of erasing his text. Such a reading may strike some as supersubtle, but it is perfectly in keeping with Kafka's own autoanalysis of literary responsibility as well as his evasion of our considerable efforts at interpretation.

What options are we left with, then, for countering this programming machine or for the ethico-political redemption of the text's apocalyptic future? Perhaps the beginnings of such a countering already lie in this very undecidability at the heart of this textual machine with which Kafka leaves us. For is there still not one further analysis of Kafka's defensiveness available to us? In binding himself to the double logic of autoimmunity, in writing himself into an ethical corner, in blocking the ethical foreclosure of his text, does Kafka not risk all? Does Kafka, that is, not risk his text against the very destiny he foresees? Might we not see his writing of a text that troubles the possibility of his ethical erasure as Kafka's act of faith in the chance of text, in a text against which he has given himself no chance, or a text that is already taking its chances against the machinal destiny that he foresees? "No faith, therefore, nor future," Derrida tells us, "without everything technical, automatic, machine-like supposed by iterability. In this sense, the technical is the possibility of faith, indeed its very chance. A chance that entails the greatest risk, even the menace of *radical evil*. Otherwise, that of which it is the chance would not be faith but rather programme or proof, predictability or providence, pure knowledge and pure know-how, which is to say annulment of the future."[57] Might we not see in Kafka's composing a text that deploys the double logic of autoimmunity against its author his desperate keeping faith with the radical hope that this text will come to constitute the possibility of a future event against the machinal destiny that it also (as we have seen) encodes? Kafka's story anticipates and illustrates Derrida's contention that "[i]nstead of opposing them, as is almost always done, they ought to be thought together, as *one and the same possibility*: the machine-like and faith, and the same holds for the machinal and all the values entailed in the sacrosanct."[58] It was Kafka's great gambit to deploy the double logic of autoimmunity to guarantee his text life, to grant it immunity from the extinguishing fire, even if he could not do so from the apocalypse to come.

This was the price Kafka would have to pay for indemnifying

his text from his autoimmune impulse to consign it to oblivion. It was Kafka's ethical act to write a text that would turn against him, offering itself immunity by means of the double logic of its own inscribed autoimmunity. In doing so, Kafka writes a text that refuses its erasure from the future to come. If Kafka knew that this future would manifest itself in the apocalyptic, he must also have known that, in Derrida's words, there is "[n]o to-come without some sort of *iterability*, at least in the form of a covenant with oneself and *confirmation* of the originary *yes*. No to-come without some sort of messianic memory and promise, of a messianicity older than all religion, more originary than all messianism."[59]

If Kafka could not indemnify his texts against the coming apocalypse, his texts that have survived their consignment to oblivion have left us with a messianic tradition that was destined to condition the discursive future, and it is to this tradition that I will turn in an attempt to offer a redemptive reading of *Heart of Darkness*.

CHAPTER TWO

Apocalyptic Futures

Heart of Darkness, *Embodiment, and African Genocide*

The mind of man is capable of anything—because everything is in it, all the past as well as all the future.
—JOSEPH CONRAD, *Heart of Darkness*

Conrad's *Heart of Darkness* becomes *Apocalypse Now*. In the early days of the Vietnam conflict CIA agents set up their Ops in remote outposts, requisitioned private armies, overawed the superstitious natives and achieved the status of white Gods. So the context of 19th century colonialism was briefly duplicated. That is what writing is about: time travel.
—WILLIAM BURROUGHS, *The Adding Machine*

HEART OF DARKNESS AND AFRICAN GENOCIDE

In May 1994, I witnessed a televised scene of carnage from Rwanda. Panning out first to display a wilderness of dense foliage, the camera angle soon narrowed to reveal a mass of machete-mutilated bodies floating in macabre and ghastly procession down a tributary of the great Congo River. Along the bottom frame of the picture ran the caption "Heart of Darkness." The connection between caption and scene appears, at first, eerily apposite: after all, was this not the heart of Africa, site of the famously "unspeakable rites" witnessed and recorded by Marlow a hundred or so years previously? Could we not see in the bloated bodies floating across the "blood-dimmed tides" of Rwanda's rivers the figure of Marlow's speared helmsman grotesquely multiplied and horribly materialized in the pullulating violence? Given this resonance, the "heart of darkness" the caption seemed to indicate was making an uncanny return from its place as a generalized metaphor for evil back to the origin of its inception.

And yet to consider this more critically, Joseph Conrad's text portrays, in its critique of colonialism, a violence imposed upon the Africans of the Congo by the colonial powers of Europe. The televised news clip would repress this aspect of the novella, and thereby transform *Heart of Darkness* from a text concerning the "horror," Kurtz, and "all Europe" that contributed to its making into a text of primitive violence imposed by Africans upon Africans. Conrad's text has thus been covertly twisted and violently displaced to support the very racism it set out politically to combat in the first place, for if the primitive savagery of the Rwandan massacres is made to stand in for the unspeakable rites of the heart of darkness, Kurtz and the colonialist machinery responsible for this violence are tendentiously excised. The strategy behind the news broadcast's conflation of the Heart of Darkness with the primitive savagery of the Rwandan genocide is to materialize by rendering visible the unspeakable horror and unspeakable rites so tantalizingly registered in the text.[1] As Jean Baudrillard has claimed, "all media live off the presumption of catastrophe and off the succulent imminence of death," and here was horror great enough to live up to that suggested by the text and even filmically to match the powerful spectacle of that other rendition of *Heart of Darkness*: *Apocalypse Now*.[2]

It is, however, not only in Rwanda that African civil war is figured in terms of Conrad's *Heart of Darkness*. Like the breeding darkness burgeoning within the text of *Heart of Darkness* itself, the metaphor has spread to trace the history and code the representation of African massacre through the first decade of the twenty-first century. Reporting on the civil violence in Sierra Leone, *Time* magazine entitled its report on "a gruesome rebel offensive [that] has turned Sierra Leone into a bloody hell hole" the "Heart of Darkness."[3] As if to fill in the picture, voodoo, cannibalism, mutilation and amputation by panga seem retroactively to bring to life the tenebrous horrors of *Heart of Darkness* in a feature by the *London Times* entitled "In the Heart of Darkness." Relaying the history of Sierra Leone's civil war through the story of warlord Foday Sankoh, the *Times* asserts: "In just four years Sankoh had taken a grip on the Heart of Darkness and distorted traditional animistic belief into a voodoo that made the muggy air which hangs over Sierra Leone's interior seem misty with rot, blood and terror."[4] The feature goes on to cite the tradition of secret societies whose participants meet at night wearing masks symbolic of ancestors and fetishes whose spirits are sent as guides. The *Times* points out that according to myth these rituals would, very rarely, turn to blood sacrifices, which would extend to include the killing of a human being. "Human body parts," the *Times* continues, "are much prized in witchcraft all over Africa for their potency.... But in Sierra Leone no anthropologist had ever proved the existence of human sacrifice, much less the cannibalism that was said to follow." There was no proof, that is, until the revolution, fought by boy soldiers, erupted, bringing with it ritualistic mutilation and cannibalism. "The belief that eating the body of a vanquished warrior gives great strength is an ancient one," the *Times* notes. "Sankoh appears to have encouraged this horrific idea, and if there was going to be any cannibalism, there would be no bystanders at the rituals. One former rebel explained that it became easier after a while, and people would fight over what they thought were the 'best bits.'"

The shadowy invocation of Conrad's text by the London *Times*, its ghostly shades feeding off the spilled blood of Sierra Leone's dark rites, is brought into stronger relief when we recall that Kurtz presided over secret rites and that critical speculation names these rites as human sacrifice and cannibalism. The effect of the continuous figuring of African genocide as the "heart of darkness" by the mass media is to set up an oscillating homology that simultaneously projects these massacres onto *Heart of Darkness*, feeding mutilated bodies into the dark folds of its obscure rites, while also, in a retroactive fusion of topos and text, mapping *Heart of Darkness* onto African genocide and thereby coding it for a Western audience.

Apocalyptic Futures

The circularity of this homology is made more haunting with the return of the "heart of darkness" to the Congo around the turn of the end of the twentieth century. "It's déjà vu in the heart of darkness," according to the *Glasgow Herald*.[5] "A rebel army is closing in on Kinshasa, dilapidated capital of the Democratic Republic of the Congo." Commenting on the civil war in the Congo, which began as a direct result of the Rwandan genocide, and whose evil legacy has spread to incorporate a good part of sub-Saharan Africa, the *Herald* declares: "Congolese wars tend to be endless reruns of ancient tribal conflicts. The only difference now is that automatic weapons have replaced spears and pangas as the arbiters of political change." The "heart of darkness" is in endless rerun, as the headline of the piece has it: "Africa's Dark Heart [Is] in Crisis Again." For the mass media then, the "Heart of Darkness" is caught in a scene of repetition, the African genocide of the 1890s bleeding into the African genocide of the 1990s. What is elided in this confluence is precisely the memory of colonial atrocity. In 1800, Africa's tropical interior was unmapped terra incognita. The epic exploits of Sir James Bruce, John Hanning Speke, Sir Richard Burton, and Sir Henry Morton Stanley opened up Africa to the imaginary of empire. By 1885 the colonial powers had carved up Africa among themselves, and through the course of the 1890s, the move from the hunt for ivory to the enforced collection of wild rubber led to decimation on an apocalyptic scale. The publication of *Red Rubber* by E. D. Morel in 1906 documented that the worst atrocities had been committed to meet the burgeoning demand for rubber so required by the incipient automobile industry. As a result of its insulating qualities for electrical circuitry and use in motorcar production, rubber became the most crucial of imperial commodities. The demand for rubber ignited a series of genocidal cataclysms that changed the ecological face of tropical Africa and the Amazon forever. In the years between the beginning of the decade of the 1890s and the beginning of the First World War, when rubber was still tapped from tropical forests, contemporary historians estimate that the genocidal policies of the rubber agents of King

Leopold of Belgium culminated in the deaths of over ten million people, or a little more than half the population of the Congo state. What is written out of media accounts, then, is not only the history of European imperialism in Africa but the role this history has played in promoting future genocides.[6]

Certainly, the reception or reading of Conrad's text has been influenced by African genocide as massacred bodies are entered into its extended textual field. The question this chapter poses at the outset is this: is this reading simply a crude misinterpretation and misguided imposition by the mass media, and can we exculpate Conrad's text on these grounds, or is there something in *Heart of Darkness* itself promoting precisely this accrual of primitive apocalyptic power?[7] This question is given further significance when we come to understand that even critically sophisticated texts that deal in African genocide, however acutely aware of postcolonial discourse, do not escape the influence of *Heart of Darkness*'s long shadow. In his *Exterminate All the Brutes*, for example, Sven Lindqvist records his visits to historical sites of European genocide in Africa, while at the same time journeying through a litany of historical and literary sources that takes us literally up to the moment of Conrad's writing what was to register as one of the more famous and terribly prophetic utterances for the twentieth century: "exterminate all the brutes." The result is a somber book in which Lindqvist not only situates *Heart of Darkness* within the often-forgotten history of the European extermination of the African but also arrives at a confirmation of Hannah Arendt's thesis, formulated in *The Origins of Totalitarianism*, that it was European imperialism in Africa that made possible totalitarianism's later genocides in Europe. Lindqvist does not attempt to retrace Conrad's journey up the Congo, but travels in the deserts of the Sudan and Sahara, through an evacuated "heart of darkness" in reconnaissance with the ghosts of former genocides. He describes his book as follows:

> This is a story, not a contribution to historical research. It is the story of a man traveling by bus through the Saharan

desert and, at the same time, traveling by computer through the concept of extermination. In small, sand-ridden desert hotels, his study closes in on one sentence in Joseph Conrad's *Heart of Darkness*: "Exterminate all the brutes."

Why did Kurtz end his report on the civilizing task of the white man in Africa with these words? What did they mean to Conrad and his contemporaries? Why did Conrad make them stand out as a summary of all the high-flown rhetoric on Europe's responsibilities to peoples of other continents?[8]

In proffering his account as a kind of detective story and odyssey back into the heart of darkness and in locating his search for the origins of European genocide within the lacunae of Conrad's text, Lindqvist clearly figures himself as an avatar of Marlow returned for a further excavation of the source and history (as well as extrapolation of the future consequences) of the events that came together to constitute *Heart of Darkness*.

If Lindqvist figures himself as an avatar of Marlow returned to the past, Phillip Gourevitch, in his harrowing recounting of the Rwandan genocide, portrays himself as an avatar of Marlow projected into the present. As a writer for the *New Yorker*, following the killings of 1994 and struggling to apprehend against the limits imposed on the imagination by genocide (what Jean-François Lyotard has called the "sublime" in relation to the Holocaust), Gourevitch speaks of the paradoxical necessity of having to imagine what was in fact very real. On deciding to report from Rwanda in 1995, Gourevitch tells us:

> I was repeatedly reminded of the moment near the end of Conrad's *Heart of Darkness*, when the narrator Marlow is back in Europe, and his aunt, finding him depleted, fusses over his health. "It was not my strength that needed nursing," Marlow says, "it was my imagination that wanted soothing." I took Marlow's condition on returning from Africa as my point of departure. I wanted to know how Rwandans understood what had happened in their country, and how they were getting on in the aftermath. The word

"genocide" and the images of the nameless and numberless dead left too much to the imagination.[9]

It is doubtful that Gourevitch's imagination was much soothed by what he reveals in *We Wish to Inform You That Tomorrow We Will Be Killed with Our Families*, his meticulous scrutiny of the Rwandan carnage. Even the most exacting depiction of what Hutu Power termed the "Final Solution" will stall against the limits imposed by holocaust upon the imagination. How to comprehend the rising, across an entire nation, of neighbor against neighbor and father against child in the killing by machete of hundreds of thousands in fewer than one hundred days? But the undefined mass slaughter does give way to the anguished testimony of the victim; perpetrators of atrocity are named and their stories told so that fewer can now take refuge in the anonymity of collective genocide. Shifting into the ironic voice of Marlow, Gourevitch invites us to a closer look:

> Perhaps, in examining this extremity with me, you hope for some understanding, some insight, some flicker of self-knowledge—a moral, or a lesson, or a clue about how to behave in this world: some such information. I don't discount the possibility, but when it comes to genocide, you already know the difference between right and wrong. The best reason I have for looking closely into Rwanda's stories is that ignoring them makes me even more uncomfortable about existence and my place in it. The horror, as horror, interests me only insofar as a precise memory of the offense is necessary to understand its legacy.[10]

Marlow's modernist irony is governed here by Gourevitch's postmodernist cynicism. Conrad's nineteenth-century plumbing of the metaphysical depths of "The Horror" is placed under pressure of dissolution, and Kurtz's celebrated traumatic iteration of "The Horror!, The Horror!" is collapsed, in a gesture of deflation, into itself simply as "the horror as horror." But in taking on the aspect of a postmodern Marlow, even as he abjures the role of Virgil guiding us through the African inferno, Gourevitch still signals unmis-

Apocalyptic Futures 71

takably that the Western representation of African genocide goes unavoidably by way of Conrad's *Heart of Darkness*.

In light of this strong conjunction several questions press: What role do Conrad's lexical strategies play in programming this conjunction and to what extent can Conrad's text be said to anticipate the possibility for, or eventuality of, such a linkage? What are the textual mechanisms by which the genocidal bodies of the African apocalypse get incorporated into the textual reception of *Heart of Darkness*? What should be the ethical function of criticism in cases of such radically evil incorporation, and how might such a program of "materialization" be arrested, or if it does not prove possible, at least countered? This chapter approaches an answer to these questions by first examining the critical reception of *Heart of Darkness* as an apocalyptic text. The problem of the incorporation of a bodily catastrophe into an extended textual field in the accrual of apocalyptic power will then be taken up. In confronting these questions, this chapter further engages the difficult problem of the relation of an apocalyptic text to a future apocalyptic event, and in doing so proposes a consideration of how an apocalyptic text in general, and how *Heart of Darkness* in particular, may code its future reception. As promised at the end of my chapter on Kafka, I conclude this chapter by reading *Heart of Darkness* in relation to a contemporary discourse on messianism that can in many respects be traced back to Kafka's texts themselves. If Kafka could not indemnify his texts from the coming apocalypse, I attempt to deploy the messianic tradition that originates in the texts that survived him against *Heart of Darkness*'s drive to apocalyptic incorporation. As we shall see, what I ultimately hope to register is an ethical critique that opens an oppressed past to a redemptive future.

THE GENEALOGY OF APOCALYPSE

Looking back on *Heart of Darkness* near the close of the twentieth century, Cedric Watts proclaimed that "[i]t has proved to be 'ahead of its time': an exceptionally proleptic text."[11] What put *Heart of Darkness* ahead of its time was the fateful convergence of its intricate interior textuality, what Watts calls "its suggestive density and ambiguity—the layered narrations, ironic meanings, symbolic suggestions; its radical paradoxicality; and its designed opacities," with the irreducible exteriority of twentieth-century apocalypse.[12] While *Heart of Darkness*'s style proved especially responsive both to the New Criticism, with its focus on ambiguity, irony, and patterns of imagery and to what would later come to be known as modernism, "it also seemed, prophetically, to sum up areas of experience that gained new prominence in light of historical events in the twentieth century."[13] Striking a similarly prophetic note, Ian Watt also sees Conrad as imbuing Kurtz with an apocalyptic foreknowledge. Concerned to expose the generative conflict that operates as the ideological engine of *Heart of Darkness*, Watt argues in his seminal *Conrad in the Nineteenth Century* that "[the] summa emerges from the conflict between Marlow, in whom Conrad the seaman presents his lingering wish to endorse the standard values of the Victorian ethic, and Kurtz, in whom Conrad the seer expresses his forebodings that the accelerating changes in the scientific, political, and spiritual view of the world during the last decades of the old century were preparing unsuspected terrors for the new."[14] According to Watt, *Heart of Darkness* represents Conrad's closest approach to an ideological summation—certainly the twentieth and twenty-first centuries have borne out Conrad the seer—and it is surely the Kurtzian line that Conrad's critical reception has followed. Indeed, recent readings have pushed further the conjunction of *Heart of Darkness* with future apocalypse, thereby amplifying Watt and Watts on Conrad's prescience.

Stereoscopically juxtaposing the 1890s with the 1990s, Kirby Farrell's *Post-traumatic Culture* finds in Conrad's text a precursor to the Nazi economy of extermination. "Colonialism in the novel," he asserts, "is nothing less than a precursor of the Nazi war machine, fueled by racism, greed, and a fear of the incomprehensible darkness that can be assuaged by feeding on the vitality of others. Kurtz's remote camp even suggests the death camps in its obsession with hoarding the precious body parts of slain elephants and, impaled on stakes, men."[15] While Farrell detects in *Heart of Darkness* a "premonition of Hitler" and the slave economies of the twentieth century,[16] Jonathan Schell, the author of the *Fate of the Earth*, goes much further to find in Conrad's text not only the future voice of Hitler but a detailed augury of nuclear holocaust. In an essay entitled "The Unfinished Twentieth Century" written at the inception of the new millennium, Schell warns that the violent history of the past century will not have been written until the question of the elimination or proliferation of nuclear weapons has been decided. The writing of that history, according to Schell, begins with Conrad's *Heart of Darkness*, a text that gives us "a topographic map, clairvoyant in its specificity of the moral landscape of the twentieth century."[17] Schell is able to read the text through the scope of apocalyptic forecast because, he claims, Conrad witnessed the European experiment in Africa and was thus able to foresee that the new century was about to open on the manifold potentialities for evil. Schell sees in *Heart of Darkness* a foreshadowing of the Vietnam War, but it is in its augury of nuclear annihilation that the text achieves its apocalyptic apotheosis: "The most remarkable and telling augury of *Heart of Darkness*, however, was the glimpse that Conrad, vaulting ahead in prophecy to 1945, provided of the destination toward which all these preposterous and terrifying tendencies somehow were heading; namely, the threat that, with the help of the Kurtzes of the world, the human species might one day get ready to wipe itself off the face of the earth."[18]

While the majority of *Heart of Darkness*'s apocalyptic critics regard the story as prophetic of future cataclysm, J. Hillis Miller reads *Heart of Darkness* as a textual apocalypse. Miller is not principally concerned with *Heart of Darkness*'s powers of forecast but instead offers an analysis of the text in relation to the genre of apocalypse. Defining apocalypse as a narrative unveiling oriented toward the future, Miller moves to an interpretation of *Heart of Darkness*'s figure for the unfolding or elucidation of its own narrative unveiling, "the glow [which] brings out a haze in the likeness of one of those misty halos that sometimes are made visible by a spectral illumination of moonshine."[19] Opening up this figure to an extraordinary rhetorical reading, Miller demonstrates that *Heart of Darkness* is posited on the impossibility of granting the revelations it tries to proffer, since every moment of unveiling or shedding of light is met by a subsequent veiling or sealing up by the welling of darkness.[20] James Berger, writing for *Postmodern Culture*, echoes Miller in his reading of *Heart of Darkness* as a text whose proffered revelation offers only more darkness in place of a clarifying light. The traditional apocalypse would not only be a cataclysm of enormous proportions, but it would also serve a classificatory and purgative purpose. The apocalyptic revelation would not simply be an unveiling of truth from falsehood and evil but a radical purgation and expulsion of the last terms. Falsehood and evil would literally be obliterated, driven from memory, by the extinguishing light of revelation. In contradistinction to the postmodern apocalypse, which would be the apocalypse of simulation, the unveiling of whose surface would reveal only another simulacral surface (as in the endless peeling away of screen after fiery screen in some computer-generated Armageddon), the "anti-religious apocalypse of the *doppelgänger* is the apocalypse of modernity."[21] But it is a modernity beneath whose fractured surface moral distinctions decompose, as in the archetypal apocalypse of Kurtz, which was ushered into modernist literature by *Heart of Darkness* itself.

To this critical genealogy of *Heart of Darkness* as an apocalyptic text, this chapter will add the reading of *Heart of Darkness* as mediating, and, at times, incorporating African genocide. The modernist apocalypse of *Heart of Darkness* attaches, as we have seen, to the postcolonial apocalypse of African genocide, but it remains to be asked just how this postcolonial apocalypse gets absorbed into the textual apocalypse of *Heart of Darkness*. While literary criticism has accorded *Heart of Darkness* prophetic powers, and Miller and Berger have theorized its place within the genre of apocalypse, I wish to address the question of the per-

Apocalyptic Futures

Figure 3. *Time* cover (August 1994).

formative aspect of *Heart of Darkness* as apocalypse. That is, in what ways might *Heart of Darkness* be said to enact or embody its apocalyptic dimension?

In August 1994, approaching the end of the Rwandan genocide, the cover of *Time* magazine displayed a photograph composed of the corpse-strewn bodies of children folded into what appears at first as a rolled-out quilt of waste (figure 3). Surrounding this litter of corpses is a receding phalanx of Rwandan refugees and at the bottom corner of the photograph a child stands staring at the slain children piled beneath him. Spread across this quilt of corpses in bold yellow letters is written: "This is the beginning of the final days. This is the apocalypse."

The words are not those of a *Time* magazine correspondent or commentator. They are the words of an African resident of the Congo surveying the scene of trampled refugees at the Rwandan border. It might well have appeared to the Rwandans, the most Catholic of the African nations, that the seventh seal of the book of the book of Revelation had been opened, but to Western readers of the African apocalypse, the seal peels away to reveal the textual edges of *Heart of Darkness*.

DELAYED DECODINGS

In his well-known denunciation of *Heart of Darkness* for its obscurity, F. R. Leavis, in *The Great Tradition*, accuses Conrad of relying on an "adjectival insistence." Although he admires certain passages in the tale and considers *Heart of Darkness* a great accomplishment, Leavis charges Conrad with the deployment of superfluous abstraction in order to magnify a resonance of horror. For Leavis, Conrad does well when he sticks to the "concrete presentment" of scene and incident:

> It is a matter of such things as the heads on posts—a direct significant glimpse... in short, of the charge generated in a variety of highly specific evocations. The stalking of the moribund Kurtz, a skeleton crawling through the long grass on all fours as he makes his bolt towards the fires and the tom-toms, is a triumphant climax in the suggestion of strange and horrible perversions. But Conrad isn't satisfied with these means; he feels that there is, or ought to be, some horror, some significance he has yet to bring out. So we have an adjectival insistence and worse than supererogatory insistence on 'unspeakable rites,' 'unspeakable secrets,' 'monstrous passions,' 'inconceivable mystery,' and so on.[22]

The effect of this piling up of adjectives, as far as Leavis is concerned, is to overburden the story with an element of abstraction that cannot be sustained in the absence of particular referents. In his desire to supply a "thrilled sense of the unspeakable potentialities of the human soul," Leavis suggests Conrad falls into the rhetorical trap of "borrowing the arts of the magazine writer... in order to impose on his readers and on himself, for thrilled response, a 'significance' that is merely an emotional insistence on the presence of what he can't produce."[23] Ironically, in the case of African genocide, it is the journalists and magazine writers who, in their captions to the visceral graphics, now offer the "concrete presentment of incident, setting and image" that Leavis insists on—the photographs and televisual footage supply the presence of what Conrad could not produce—and the adjectival insistence that "betrays the absence" is augmented by and anchored both in this exhilarated display of savage killings and in the spectacle of ritualistic violence inscribed on the mutilated plenum of the African bodies. Here genocidal corpses bleed into Conrad's corpus.

While Leavis finds aesthetic fault with Conrad's epiphenomenal and free-floating descriptives, postcolonial critics have subjected Conrad's adjectival insistence to a political analysis. In a prescient assessment of the politics and destiny of Conrad's lexicon, Chinua Achebe asserted:

> The eagle-eyed English critic F.R. Leavis drew attention long ago to Conrad's "adjectival insistence upon inexpressible and incomprehensible mystery." That insistence must not be dismissed lightly, as many Conrad critics have tended to do, as a mere stylistic flaw; for it raises serious questions of artistic good faith. When a writer while pretending to record scenes, incidents and their impact is in reality engaged in inducing hypnotic stupor in his readers through a bombardment of emotive words and other forms of trickery much more has to be at stake than stylistic felicity.[24]

Far from simply providing for an enthralled response, these signifiers are conflated with Africa and come to stand in for the African. That the Rwandan killings should attach to *Heart of Darkness*, then, presumably comes as no surprise to such critics of Conrad's racism as Chinua Achebe and Frances B. Singh. If the mass media are able to appropriate *Heart of Darkness* as mediating and classificatory rubric, they would argue, this is not because of some mystified misreading on their part, but rather, that the media are only appropriating those racialist prototypes already present in Conrad's text to begin with.

Indeed, the very fact of this appropriation would provide a corroborating instance for Frances B. Singh's assertion that *Heart of Darkness*

> carries suggestions that the evil which the title refers to is to be associated with Africans, their customs, and their rites.

Marlow talks, for example, of their "unspeakable rites" and the "satanic litany" of Kurtz's followers. Furthermore he uses words like *brutal, monstrous, vengeful, implacable, inscrutable, evil, accursed, hopeless, dark*, and *pitiless* so constantly in talking about Africa that the people of Africa begin to be tinged by the qualities that these words connote.[25]

To a certain extent this is true. To be sure, Conrad's playing into primitivism, his depiction of the African as having "faces like grotesque masks" with the "white(s) of their eyeballs glistening" from afar, and upon closer inspection as "a whirl of black limbs, a mass of hands clapping, of feet stamping, of bodies swaying, of eyes rolling under the droop of motionless foliage . . . on the edge of a black and incomprehensible frenzy," certainly goes toward facilitating this association.[26] Moreover, Conrad critiques imperialism by demonstrating that European designs and actions fall into a primitive African savagery and fetishism. The measure of evil in Conrad's story thus becomes "going native," and if *Heart of Darkness* exposes the corruption behind European imperialism, this is caused by its failure to provide a bulwark against an Africa defined as evil because it is the source of dark temptations. In conflating African genocide with *Heart of Darkness*, the media, then, are only repeating a move already located in Conrad's text.

The problem of this conjunction, however, is far more complex, since to account for the grafting of the Rwandan killings onto the body of *Heart of Darkness* (as one of its episodes) on purely this basis would require the wholesale repression of Conrad's anti-imperialist critique. We would still have to explain how Conrad's critique can come to be so readily erased and nullified. But even at the linguistic level, the politics of both Conrad's "adjectival insistence" and his linguistic strategies are far from clear. In his adept reading of *Heart of Darkness* in *Culture and Imperialism*, Edward Said, for example, comments on the use of precisely these techniques as a linguistic protodeconstruction of colonialism:

Conrad's way of demonstrating this discrepancy between the orthodox and his own views of empire is to keep drawing attention to how ideas and values are constructed (and deconstructed) through dislocations in the narrator's language. . . . Marlow, for example, is never straightforward. He alternates between garrulity and stunning eloquence, and rarely resists making peculiar things seem more peculiar by surprisingly misstating them, or rendering them vague and contradictory. . . . By accentuating the discrepancy between the official "idea" of empire and the remarkably disorienting actuality of Africa, Marlow unsettles the reader's sense not only of the very idea of empire, but of something more basic, reality itself. For if Conrad can show that all human activity depends on controlling a radically unstable reality to which words approximate only by will or convention, the same is true of empire, of venerating the idea, and so forth.[27]

Also commenting on the political reading of Leavis's accusation of "adjectival insistence," Valentine Cunningham remarks: "It is interesting, albeit astonishing, to see this accusation adapted in the simple-minded anti-racist polemic of Frances B. Singh."[28] For Cunningham this is utterly to miss Conrad's point, for if *Heart of Darkness* engages an adjectival insistence this has nothing to do with a racist depiction of the African but powerfully registers Africa as an epistemological failure. "When what's experienced is inscrutable," Cunningham asserts, "it is also unspeakable. Marlow's negative rhetoric composes itself into two large, and necessarily connected, groups—a set of words to do with the failure of conception, epistemology, hermeneutics, which inevitably generate a vocabulary of defeated narration."[29] Conrad's adjectives, then, only record the traces of Marlow's failed attempts at a narrative navigation of the impenetrable obscurity and opacity of Africa.

I do not so much offer this countervailing and conflicting analysis of the politics of Conrad's adjectival insistence (and it can be multiplied) in order to intercede on behalf of one side or the other, but rather to argue for a generative contradiction or split that operates a dialectical mechanism at the heart of Conrad's lexical coding. Further, I claim that we have to radically extend our understanding of Conrad's impressionism (beyond the politics of linguistic primitivism) in order to fully comprehend what is at stake in the incorporation of the killing fields of Africa into the textual field of *Heart of Darkness*. In his virtuoso reading of Conrad in *The Political Unconscious*, Frederic Jameson establishes the role Conrad's discordant politics play in orchestrating a series of contradictory commentaries. "The discontinuities objectively present in Conrad's narratives," he maintains, "have, as with few other modern writers, projected a bewildering variety of competing and incommensurable interpretive opinions."[30] Following Jameson, Patrick Brantlinger has pointed out that any attempt to fix *Heart of Darkness* at either the purely imperialist (and therefore racist) or anti-imperialist pole is bound to founder on the immanent contradiction on which Conrad's text is founded. In the epilogue to his *Rule of Darkness: British Literature and Imperialism, 1830–1914*, Brantlinger examines the intersection of anti-imperialism, racism, and impressionism in Conrad's text. According to his analysis, the imbrication of these contradictory tendencies results in a text that manifestly and forcefully critiques European racism and imperialism, yet formulates this critique in a manner that itself falls into both imperialism and racism. For Brantlinger, then, Conrad's "impressionism" functions as the "fragile skein of discourse that expresses—or disguises—this 'schizophrenic'—contradiction as an apparently harmonious whole."[31] In coming to this position Brantlinger is preceded by Jameson, whose analysis he first draws on and then applies to *Heart of Darkness*:

> In *The Political Unconscious*, Fredric Jameson argues that Conrad's stories . . . betray a symptomatic split between a modernist "will to style," leading to an elaborate but essentially hollow "impressionism," and the reified, mass culture tendencies of romance conventions. In a fairly obvious way, *Heart of Darkness* betrays the same split, moving in one direction toward the "misty halos" and "moonshine" of a style

that seeks to be its own meaning, apart from any "kernel" or center or embarrassingly clear content, but also grounding itself in another direction in the conventions of Gothic romance with their devalued mass culture status—conventions that were readily adapted to the heroic adventure themes of imperialist propaganda. This split almost corresponds to the contradiction of an anti-imperialist novel which is also racist. In the direction of high style, the story acquires several serious purposes, apparently including its critique of empire. In the direction of reified mass culture, it falls into the stereotypic patterns of race-thinking common to the entire tradition of the imperialist adventure story or quest romance.[32]

If Brantlinger draws on Jameson in the formulation of his own paradoxical reading of *Heart of Darkness* as an anti-imperialist text that gets caught in the trap of its own imperialism, he also disavows Jameson's split and the opposition that it sets up. Brantlinger's main disagreement with Jameson's analysis is his contention that Conrad's "will to style," his impressionism, does not escape implication in the racist conventions of the gothic romance that Conrad seeks to shape into high art. Since the imperial gothic undergirds Conrad's impressionism and provides much of its material, it is not entirely possible to extract the one from the other—from the first, Conrad's novel is caught up in the racist paradigms of its gothic urtext. This convergence then threatens to subsume or "derealize" *Heart of Darkness*'s critique of empire within its own more strictly aesthetic project. For Brantlinger, the diffusion of Conrad's political critique within the mists of his impressionism results in a text that has fallen prey to a fetishism of the aesthetic. (This moment can only reverberate with irony given the text's breaking of idols and ironic stance toward all forms of fetishism.) Conrad's refusal, in fact, to wrest the text from the ambiguities upon which it is structured and the undecidability that its impressionism sustains leaves the novel, in Brantlinger's view, open to charges of hermetic aestheticism and self-consumption. He accuses *Heart of Darkness* of a "deliberate ambiguity and refusal of moral and political judgment at the heart of an impressionism and a will to style that seem to be ends in themselves, providing finely crafted artifacts and stories with contours smoothed, polished, like carefully sculpted bits of ivory—art itself as the ultimate commodity, object of rarefied aesthetic worship and consumption."[33]

While I agree with Brantlinger that Conrad's impressionism does tend to "derealize" or subsume *Heart of Darkness*'s political critique of empire, I do not believe that it resolves into a rarefied aestheticism. On the contrary, I will contend that coiled within Conrad's "modernist will to style"—his impressionism—is a modernist drive to power. Far from collapsing into a reified aestheticism, the split that Jameson discerns in Conrad's work becomes reactivated by a textual drive to material power, and *Heart of Darkness*'s impressionism is not simply consumed as an end in itself, or as an "object of rarefied aesthetic worship and consumption." But in a precise reversal of Brantlinger's position, I will claim that *Heart of Darkness*'s impressionism contains within itself its own powers of consumption in the absorption of a primitive apocalyptic power. In what follows, I shall attempt to justify and establish the consequences of this claim. I shall not attempt to collapse the immanent contradictions of the text but in a further exploration of the political oppositions of this split, I shall pursue this justification by subjecting *Heart of Darkness* to a rigorous analysis in terms of its future reception. More specifically, I will give a further critical turn to the analysis of *Heart of Darkness*'s impressionism and imperialism by claiming that much critical insight into this question can be gained by considering the issue from the perspective of the text's future reception.

Within the bifurcation of the impressionist will to style and the romance conventions of the imperial adventure story, Jameson also detects the nascent origins of what will come to be known as contemporary mass culture. "In Conrad," he maintains, "we can sense the emergence not merely of what will be called contemporary modernism . . . but also, still tangibly juxtaposed with it, what will variously be called popular culture or mass culture, the commercialized cultural discourse of what, in late capitalism, is often described as a media society."[34] If Conrad deploys the conventions and techniques of mass culture and inaugurates its modern emergence, this is surely significant in relation to the late-twentieth-century mass media appropriation of *Heart of Darkness* in their portrayal of African genocide. But this significance, I think, goes beyond Conrad's stationing his text on the contours of the imperial gothic, which the media then revive almost a century later. If the media attach to the mass cultural pole of Conrad's text, refracting through the moonshine of his impressionism their own satellite imaging equivalent, then this relationship is, in some part, necessarily dialectical and programmed by Conrad's text itself. But there is more to *Heart of Darkness*'s programming of its future reception than its dialectical relationship with the mass media. What is at issue here is the very functioning of *Heart of Darkness*'s impressionism in the performance of its material future. From a rather different critical perspective, this investigation will lead to a theoretical examination of Achebe's assertion that the text engages in "forms of trickery" and "that much more has to be at stake [in *Heart of Darkness*'s impressionism] than stylistic felicity."[35] What is at stake in this instance, I would like to suggest, is *Heart of Darkness*'s anticipation and programming in advance of the incorporation of African genocide into its textual field. What I propose is an antinomian reading of the play of Conrad's lexical resources and narrative maneuvers as a type of textual programming mechanism designed to co-opt future events as material attachments in a "filling in" or "fleshing out" of *Heart of Darkness* in what amounts to a radical embodiment of the text. The mechanism of this incorporation might be explained by means of the antithetical device of "hollowing out" and "filling in" that the text puts into play—a device, I shall endeavor to show, that involves not only the intratextual bodies of *Heart of Darkness*, but that is also positioned to take in the extratextual (extralinguistic) bodies of African genocide.[36]

Valentine Cunningham charges theory with a dissolution of the real, and in urging a breakout from the prison house of language, he calls for a return to history, not, however to the textualized history of the New Historicism, but to what he calls the "historico-worldly Other beyond the text, out there in the extralinguistic, heterologic zones of that which is not merely verbal."[37] Endlessly setting up the straw man of a purely rhetorical deconstruction that he proceeds to cut down with the empiricist scythe of "the stuff of history," Cunningham invokes *Heart of Darkness* as the counterexample of a paradoxically self-emptying text that also insists on the adamantine reserve of its material history. Cunningham agrees with Brantlinger on the question of the evacuative powers of Conrad's impressionism. "As far as expectations of skeptical (post)modernist criticism go," he asserts, "it would be hard to find a more succinct set of occasions than *Heart of Darkness*.... It is the busiest of refusing, skeptical, self-emptying texts. It steadily inducts the reader into negativity, blankness, crypticity, the hermetic."[38] But rather than erasing Conrad's political critique, his impressionism, as far as Cunningham is concerned, sustains it:

> The *vides* of this text are full of political and moral accusation. The hollowness at the heart of *Heart of Darkness* is by no means limited to a process of narrative self-emptying. The metatextual writing subject is also a colonial one.... Kurtz's writing is done at the behest of a colonial agency. At the centre of the labyrinth of the Belgian head offices 'squats a heavy writing-desk'. Colonizing means writing, and writing—whatever else it might mean—spells colonizing. The ink stains on the Belgian clerk's jacket sleeves come to look like the proleptic emblems of the whole enterprise's moral stains Marlow would soon encounter out in the field.[39]

This much is true, but it is far from the whole story since, as I also hope to show, the hollowed-out aspects of Conrad's impressionism are proleptic of even more than Marlow's encounter "out in the field" of the late-nineteenth-century colonial Congo, swallowed as this is by its late-twentieth-century neocolonialialist encounters with the hyperinflated boundaries of the textual field of

Heart of Darkness's imperial impressionism. While a great deal has been said about the political effects of the self-emptying aspects of the text's dialectic, far less analysis has been devoted to the political effects of its antithetical powers of fulfillment. Also, to my knowledge, this dialectic has not been extended to an analysis of the political effects of its capacity for corporeal capture or radical embodiment.

In a certain sense and in one of its aspects, this program begins as a hypertrophied extension of the trope of "filling in," of which the text consciously makes use. It is surely not insignificant that this is a featured element of both the content and prose of the novella. As a child, Marlow, we remember, pondered over the many blank spaces of the atlas, but now they have been filled in; they had become "a place of darkness":

> At that time there were many blank spaces on the earth and when I saw one that looked particularly inviting on a map. . . . I would put my finger on it and say: When I grow up I will go there. . . . But there was one yet—the biggest—the most blank, so to speak—that I had a hankering after. True, by this time it was not a blank space anymore. It had got filled since my boyhood with rivers and lakes and names. It had ceased to be a blank space of delightful mystery—a white patch for a boy to dream gloriously over. It had become a place of darkness. (8)

And Marlow's narrative will fill in some of that darkness. Indeed, the figure of Kurtz comes to us and to Marlow's interlocutors largely through a process of foreshadowing and adumbration—a steady, if not very sure, filling in. Equally, at the syntactic level, Conrad's prose works through a process of filling in, or "delayed decoding" as Ian Watt has felicitously termed it. What Watt means by delayed decoding is that a gap is established in Conrad's text between the recording of a sense impression and the interpretation or the assigning of meaning to that impression: "This narrative device may be termed delayed decoding, since it combines the forward temporal progression of the mind, as it receives messages from the outside world, with the much slower reflexive process of making out their meaning."[40]

Indeed, from the beginning, as we have seen, *Heart of Darkness* is caught up in a dialectic of "filling in" and "hollowing out." In his advance toward Kurtz, Marlow passes through a set of "paths, paths everywhere; a stamped-in network of paths spreading over the empty land" (19). Marlow's description of the paths as "stamped-in" refers to the beating down of the grass and thickets by the action of feet and sticks. But "stamped-in" is also very much in keeping with Marlow's recourse to graphic metaphors to take account of his encounter with the African landscape. He finds himself constantly called upon to decipher the signs of the land. Navigating his way upriver, he tells us, for example, that "I had to discern, mostly by inspiration, the signs of hidden banks; I watched for sunken stones" (34). Marlow's reading of such signs, as critics have noted, recalls Jacques Derrida's grammatological interpretation of the path as writing before the letter, a pretertextuality prior to speech but no less coded by a differential spacing and the violence of that spacing.[41] For Derrida the question of this "arche-writing" is the question of the genealogy of the path as signifying structure, the question of the road, and the question of access to the possibility of the road map. But Marlow's encounter with the path and the road also opens onto the contemporary scene of colonialist devastation. The network of paths has been evacuated, leaving Marlow to survey the vast solitude of desolated space, and on his way into the African hinterland, he passes by a demonstrative instance of the violence of the road as colonialist incursion. He comes across a uniformed white man "camping on the path" escorted by an armed guard of Zanzibaris who "was looking after the upkeep of the road, he declared. Can't say I saw any road or any upkeep, unless the body of a middle-aged negro, with a bullet-hole in the forehead upon which I absolutely stumbled three miles farther on may be considered as a permanent improvement" (20). Meditating on Conrad's skillful unification of these two modes of violence, textual and material, Cunningham acutely notes: "Those emblematic textual holes are also bullet holes. The network of erasures, the figures of meanings, traces, are also demolished homes, communities, lives."[42] As illustrative as this conjunction is of the dialectic of embodiment and disembodiment that subtends the text, it also forces open a signifying trail of skulls that winds its way through the textual jungle of *Heart of Darkness*. A tracking of these signifying skulls will allow for a further tracing of a Derridean violence of the letter in the text.

The violent trail of the colonial passage is everywhere inscribed, on the land in the form of "scar[s] in the hillside," in the figure of the half-erased roadway, and not least on the body of the colonized (16). If the road traced by the opening figures the differential violence of the graphic, the black body, too, is discerned and inscribed violently as another text. The violence of the graphic trace is also the violent trace of the bullet hole. As Homi Bhabha has declared, "the exercise of colonialist authority requires the production of differentiations, individuations, identity effects through which discriminatory practices can map out subject populations that are tarred with the visible and transparent mark of power."[43] And bodies tarred with the visible and transparent marks of power in *Heart of Darkness* become symbolic signifiers open to mysterious and talismanic rites of reading. While the bullet hole in the forehead of the middle-aged Negro ironically recalls the "reading" of Marlow's skull by the Belgian phrenologist, it also adumbrates, as part of this densely imbricated sequence, the mutilated heads on the gapped palisade and another spectacular rite of the reading of bodily signs. Our first sight of these severed heads is given in a specular moment by a brief look through Marlow's glass as he is steaming downriver in approach of Kurtz's inner station: "There was no enclosure or fence of any kind, but there had been one apparently, for near the house half a dozen slim posts remained in a row, roughly trimmed, and with their upper ends ornamented with round curved balls" (52). Several pages later this moment unfolds into another scene of delayed decoding in which Marlow realizes the error he has made, for the ornaments turn out to be heads shrunken and staked, failed apotropaic devices, turned to face the dying Kurtz:

> Now I had suddenly a nearer view and its first result was to make me throw my head back as if before a blow. Then I went carefully from post to post with my glass, and I saw my mistake. These round knobs were not ornamental but symbolic; they were expressive and puzzling, striking and disturbing—food for thought and also for vultures if there had been any looking down from the sky; but at all events for such ants as were industrious enough to ascend the pole. They would have been even more impressive, those heads on the stakes, if their faces had not been turned to the house. Only one, the first I had made out, was facing my way. I was not so shocked as you may think. The start back I had given was really nothing but a movement of surprise. I had expected to see a knob of wood there, you know. I returned deliberately to the first I had seen—and there it was black, dried, sunken, with closed eyelids—a head that seemed to sleep at the top of that pole, and with the shrunken dry lips showing a narrow white line of teeth, was smiling too, smiling continuously at some endless and jocose dream of that eternal slumber. (57)

Despite Leavis's claim for their "concrete presentment," these severed heads are open to manifold readings. The scene of the skulls, in fact, leaves itself open to some critical unpacking. The first thing Marlow tells us after recognizing his mistake is that the heads are not ornamental, by which he means decorative, as the round knobs might simply be, but "symbolic" (57). Far from offering up an obvious meaning, the skulls mysteriously beckon to him for decipherment. Marlow's reading of the heads, it turns out, negotiates a split between their material or literal and symbolic registers—a split that accords well with and plays into the previously discussed division between the gothic and the impressionistic in *Heart of Darkness*. On the one hand, in terms of their grotesque display as bodily signs, Marlow finds the heads "expressive" and "striking" (57). On the other hand, in terms of their figural or symbolic significance, the heads confront him as "puzzling" and "disturbing" (57). This split between the figural and material register of the heads is made more distinct in Marlow's further division of their possible consumption as "food for thought and also for vultures" (57). This distinction between the material and the figural is given another turn when we realize that the heads themselves are literally turned or "troped" and that they function here according to three aspects of the trope: figure, turn, and defense. As Harold Bloom instructs us, "It is worth noting that the root-meaning of our word 'defense' is 'to strike or hurt,' and that of 'gun' and 'defense' are from the same root, just as it is interesting to remember that *tropos* meaning originally 'turn, way, manner' appears also in the name *Atropos* and in the word 'entropy'. The trope-as-defense or ratio between ignorance and identification might be called at once a warding-off by turning and yet also a way of striking or manner of hurting."[44]

The second thing Marlow tells us about the heads is that they were turned away from his approach toward the house. The heads, we remember, were, according to Marlow's harlequin informant, those of "rebels," and their display invokes Michel Foucault's reading of spectacular punishment as the law of the sovereign inscribed on the body of the condemned, here transposed from the scaffolds of Europe to the sharpened stakes of colonial Africa. We might surmise that the heads originally guarded the approach to Kurtz's camp and that all, except for the first that Marlow had seen, have been turned to face the dying Kurtz, failing, as do all charms in the heart of darkness, in their apotropaic function of warding off or turning away death. The moment belongs to Atropos, whose name means she who cannot be turned, the last of the three fates of Greek mythology, and the one who cuts the thread of life.[45] It is well known that Marlow has already encountered the two fates Klotho and Lakhesis, whose figures he has seen in the two knitters of black wool before the door of the trading company in the "whited sepulchre" of Brussels, moments before he is to have his own head measured by the company doctor (9). Even the etymological link between "trope" and "entropy" will, as we shall later see, link *Heart of Darkness* and *Waiting for the Barbarians*; and as Marlow moves from ignorance to identification of the heads the defensive function of the trope as a warding off by turning also becomes a way of striking.[46] His first action upon making out the mutilated head is to throw back his own head "as if before a blow" (57). What has struck Marlow is not only the shock of perceiving the severed head through his glass but its rearing up at him. From the distance of the riverbank, Marlow has been surveying an opening in the jungle that contains Kurtz's dilapidated station house; finding no sign of life he marks the ruined roof and mud wall just visible above the tall grass. "And then," he tells us, "I made a brusque movement and one of the remaining posts of that vanished fence leaped up in the field of my glass. You remember I told you I had been struck at the distance by certain attempts at ornamentation, rather remarkable in the ruinous aspect of the place. Now I had suddenly a nearer view and its first result was to make me throw my head back as if before a blow" (57). Marlow's shifting of the angle of his glass has the anamorphic effect of raising up and manifesting before him the formerly obscured image of the severed head. In its foregrounding of the visual field, the magnifying powers of Marlow's binoculars function like the curved mirror that erects in its reflection the anamorphic skull in Hans Holbein's *The Ambassadors*. In its raising or bringing into three dimensions the flattened skull, anamorphosis in Holbein's painting performs much like embodiment in *Heart of Darkness*. Jacques Lacan's seminar on Holbein's painting will help us further grasp the relation between the mutilated heads and the mutilated bodies of African genocide.

Lacan turns to Holbein's portrait of *The Ambassadors* in order to illustrate his theory of the gaze. "In the scopic field," he maintains, "the gaze is outside, I am looked at, I am a picture."[47] The relationship between the viewer and the object viewed is here reversed. Superseding Walter Benjamin's concept of the "aura," in which the art object looks back at its observer, objects in Lacan's theory install the conditions of their own perception. It is their gaze that absorbs the subject's scopic field.[48] The anamorphic set of staked heads bears comparison with Lacan's reading of *The Ambassadors*. It is important to consider that the heads are only visible to Marlow through the magnifying powers of the binoculars, and the severed head that springs into his field of vision blocks out the remaining scene. Marlow's encounter with the ghostly gaze that looks back and captures is only foreshadowed by his encounter with the blinded gaze of the severed head. "It is precisely in seeking the gaze in each of its points that you will see it disappear," Lacan tells us,[49] and after looking into the drooped eyelids of the shrunken head, Marlow puts down his glass, "and the head that had appeared near enough to be spoken to seemed at once to have leaped away from [him] into inaccessible distance" (58). The head that appears near enough to be spoken to evokes what Paul de Man calls "the latent threat that inhabits prosopopeia, namely that by making the death speak, the symmetrical structure of the trope implies, by the same token that the living are struck dumb, frozen in their own death."[50]

It is not the deadened gaze of the severed skull that traps Marlow but the possibility of speaking with the voice of its killer. Shortly after the shock of discerning the severed head, Marlow encounters the deadly voice of Kurtz. The moment occurs when Marlow cuts off the escaping Kurtz who is crawling back to the beating drums and fires of his camp. He rises before Marlow, "unsteady, long, pale, indistinct like a vapour" (65). What follows is Marlow wrestling with the voice of a wraith that threatens to absorb him and empty him out into the very aspect of disembodiment Marlow perceives on his first view of Kurtz. Looking at Kurtz through his binoculars as he is carried on a stretcher, Marlow thinks of him as an "atrocious phantom" and "apparition" (59). He is fearful at that moment that Kurtz will call out to his followers, the "streams of human beings—of naked human beings—with spears in their hands, with bows, with shields, with wild glances and savage movements," to attack the boat (59). Watching Kurtz as he is borne toward the steamer, Marlow describes him as looking seven feet long and with his covering having fallen off, his "body emerged from it pitiful and appalling as from a winding-sheet. I could see the cage of his ribs all astir, the bones of his arm waving. It was as though an animated image of death carved out of old ivory had been shaking its hand with menaces at a motionless crowd of men made of dark and glittering bronze" (59). Here the disembodied Kurtz, "animated image of death" (reembodied in old ivory), holds in his voice the power to command the vital and animated black bodies of the Congo (59). (It is to this moment of the savage African horde, after all, that the media attach in their troping of African genocide as the "heart of darkness.") And Kurtz here is linked to the wilderness with its dark powers of projecting and absorbing African bodies. It is at the moment of his emergence that the stream of Africans was "poured into the clearing by the dark faced and pensive forest" and at the moment of his disappearance into the steamer Marlow notices the "crowd of savages was vanishing without any perceptible movement of retreat, as if the forest that had ejected these beings so suddenly had drawn them in again as the breath is drawn in a long aspiration" (59).

If the gaze and voice threaten to strip Marlow of his body and bestow upon him the godlike powers of the disembodied Kurtz, then this dialectic threatens to extend to the text of *Heart of Darkness* itself. In a third component of my exegesis of the scene of the skulls, Marlow, we remember, expects to see a row of wooden knobs but is confronted instead by the embodiment of the severed heads. Marlow's mistake here also foreshadows his later figuring of Kurtz's skull as ivory. The ornamental round knobs get transposed as "the lofty frontal bone of Mr. Kurtz," which "the wilderness had patted . . . on the head, and behold it was like a ball—an ivory ball; it had caressed him . . . got into his veins, consumed his flesh, and sealed his soul to its own by the inconceivable ceremonies of some devilish initiation" (48). The dying, emaciated, disembodied Kurtz here gets filled in by the wilderness. He is transmogrified and interred in the very commodity for which, as it turns out, he has sacrificed his life. But if Kurtz gets petrified or embodied in ivory (the ivory has, after all, consumed his flesh), he also gets "hollowed" out into discourse, into voice and into text. Kurtz is continually described by Marlow as "discoursing"; we are told that Marlow presciently perceives him as a voice: he "presented himself as a voice" (47), "he was very little more than a voice" (48), a disembodied voice that has torn itself loose from the earth (as Kurtz has "kicked himself loose of the earth" [66]). This disembodied voice of Kurtz merges with Marlow's voice in a telling of the tale that emanates from the pitch darkness as a "narrative that seemed to shape itself without human lips" (27). If Kurtz is disembodied and attenuated to a free-floating discoursing voice, Marlow's narrative also seems to shed his body, tearing itself loose in a moment of self-generation. Like Kurtz, the hollow man, whom the wilderness penetrates and petrifies, *Heart of Darkness* is also hollow at the core, an episode whose meaning is "not inside like a kernel but outside," an episode whose solid center cannot be located (5).

As he looks on at the dying Kurtz, Marlow thinks of Kurtz as desiring to engorge the world: "I saw him open his mouth wide—it gave him a weirdly voracious aspect as though he had wanted to swallow all the air, all the earth, all the men before him" (59); and later viewing the sickly and emaciated Kurtz, he exclaims, "I had a vision of him on the stretcher opening his mouth voraciously as if to devour all the earth with all its mankind" (73). We might think of this description of Kurtz as the figure of the text looping out of itself and deploying this dialectic of filling in and hollowing out, of embodiment and disembodiment, not only in terms of its intratextual bodies and voices but also in relation to the extratextual (extralinguistic) bodies of its future history. If Revelation is the apocalypse that is swallowed, then *Heart of Darkness* is the apocalypse as consuming cannibal. The incorporation of the African genocide into *Heart of Darkness* mirrors, on an apocalyptic scale, the process of mutilated embodiment already present in the text. The apocalyptic incorporation, it appears, was already prepared for in advance.

It is not, however, only through the retrospective vantage of

African genocide that we realize that the scene of the severed heads is caught up in a complex temporality. Ten years before Conrad's journey up the Congo River, Conrad's uncle and guardian, Tadeuz Bobrowski, suggested that he assist a certain Professor Kopernicki in the anthropological collection of skulls: "He earnestly requests you to collect during your voyages skulls of natives, writing on each one whose skull it is and the place of origin. When you have collected a dozen or so of such skulls, write to me and I will obtain from him information as to the best way of dispatching them from Crackow where there is a special Museum devoted to craniology."[51] Conrad did not oblige his uncle's request but the suggestion might have provided the inspiration for the company doctor who measures Marlow's skull with a pair of calipers: "I always ask leave, in the interests of science, to measure the crania of those going out there," he tells Marlow (11). But it was not out there, on his journey up the Congo, that Conrad came upon the collection of the severed heads. It appears, as Adam Hoschild has proposed, that this scene was suggested by events in Stanley Falls in 1895, when the station chief Captain Leon Rom led a punitive military expedition against some African rebels. A British journalist travelling through Stanley Falls (the original site of Kurtz's inner station) described the aftermath of the reprisal as follows: "Many women and children were taken, and twenty one heads were brought to the falls, and have been used by Captain Rom as a decoration round a flower bed in front of his house."[52] While it is not conclusively known, it is quite likely that Conrad and Rom met when Conrad was passing through Leopoldville in 1890 when Rom was station chief there. In any event, if he missed the report that appeared in the widely circulated *Century Magazine*, Conrad almost certainly read it in December 17, 1898, when it was reprinted by *The Saturday Review* (a magazine Conrad diligently perused) a few days before setting down to the writing of *Heart of Darkness*. From the outset, then, the severed heads were filled in from a textual future as *Heart of Darkness* retroactively produces its sources for Kurtz and his hut staked round with skulls.

We might start to think of this incorporation in terms of a radical inflation of the boundaries of the signifying gap inherent in the device of delayed decoding—a dehiscence of the text's textual field to include future material signifiers that would in turn require decoding. Conrad's delayed decoding presents the effect, in terms of immediate sense data, but withholds or delays the understanding of its cause. It is a technique then in which "effect" may be said to precede "cause." This device, however, is not only employed at the syntactic level of Conrad's prose, but is also a generalized feature of *Heart of Darkness* as a whole. Delayed decoding extends beyond the boundaries of the tale to the textual field of its future reception.

In its reversal of cause and effect, Conrad's delayed decoding involves Nietzsche's great insight that the assignment of meaning is retroactive. We recall that the role of punishment in *The Genealogy of Morals* consists in the making of man responsible for the future, capable of promising and keeping (since the body in pain is held as guarantor) to the promise. The scene is one of violence and of passional inscription, an inscriptional violence strong enough to overcome forgetfulness. We might conclude then that behind this machinery of punishment there lay a design, that punishment was purposive, but this Nietzsche tells us is to read backward, to impose a cause on what was only effect:

> Thus one also imagined that punishment was devised for punishing. But purposes and utilities are only *signs* that a will to power has become master of something less powerful and imposed upon it the character of a function; and the entire history of a "thing," an organ, a custom can in this way be a continuous sign-chain of ever new interpretations and adaptations whose causes do not even have to be related to one another but, on the contrary, in some cases succeed and alternate with one another in a purely chance fashion.[53]

What Nietzsche discerns here is that a marked or mutilated body amounts to an open text awaiting a future overcoding. Strictly speaking, since a body is always already coded, the marked or mutilated body is a palimpsest, always capable of taking on a future coding. Also concerned with the relationship between mutilation and meaning, Stephen Greenblatt makes the argument that "marks on a body, like marks on paper, may be distinguished from particular explanations, justifications, and claims of historical causality that led them to be made."[54] Local explanations are crucial to understanding the marks of propitiary rites, for example, but the "mark or mutilation is detachable from these accounts."[55] In a note on this claim, Greenblatt refers us to Derrida's analysis of iterability in "Signature, Event, Context." Greenblatt is less interested in "the indeterminacy that Derrida argues to be the condition of iterability but rather in the historical contest over meaning."[56] Derrida's analysis of the function of iterability, however, will prove useful in further grasping the superimposition of the severed heads onto the mutilated bodies of African holocaust.

Throughout his work, Derrida has developed the paradox that identity is founded upon the possibility of repetition, which in turn requires something like identity itself. It is this "structure of iterability" that underlies all possibility of articulation. In order for a sign or mark to function as a sign or mark, Derrida remarks, it has to be repeatable. It can never present itself as a singular instance. It requires comparison with earlier instances of itself in order to constitute itself as an identity—to be recognizable. This element of repetitive comparison that identity must pass through in order to constitute itself introduces an element of heterogeneity into the process of identification. Derrida goes on to claim that this alterity can never be erased or collapsed into the identification of the same with the same; a certain otherness always remains. The structure of iteration then implies both identity and difference.[57] It is not only that identity requires a differential relation to other elements in order to determine itself but also that even iteration in its "purest form" "contains *in itself* the discrepancy of a difference that constitutes it as iteration. . . . It is because this iterability is differential, within each individual 'element' as well as between the 'elements', because it splits each element while constituting it, because it marks with an articulatory break, that the remainder, although indispensable, is never that of a full or fulfilling presence."[58] This differential structure or remainder escapes "the logic of presence" because it does not only come after the element or mark that Derrida says it splits, but it also at the same time comes before it since it is precisely this difference of otherness that makes identification itself possible.

This splitting function of iterability might be related to the split between symbol and substance that Marlow imposes upon the mutilated heads of *Heart of Darkness*. Since the heads are simultaneously and irreducibly body and symbol, they are caught within the structure of iterability. The heads are identifiable through repeated instances as mutilated heads, yet because they are split, they are also symbolic and are capable of migrating out into the future and parasitically attaching to other mutilated bodies. This migratory quality of the mutilating mark is made more clear in the analysis Derrida has opened of the differential structure of the mark.

> The paradox here is the following: to be a mark and to mark its marking effect, a mark must be capable of being *identified*, recognized as the same, being precisely *re-markable* from one context to another. It must be capable of being repeated, re-marked in its essential trait as the same. This accounts for the apparent solidity of its structure, of its type, its *stereotypy*. . . . But more precisely, it is not simple since the identity of the mark is also its difference and its differential relation, varying each time according to its context, to the network of other marks. The ideal iterability that forms the structure of all marks is that which undoubtedly allows them to be released from any context, to be freed from all determined bonds to its origin, its meaning, or its referent, to emigrate in order to play elsewhere, in whole or in part, another role. I say "in whole or in part" because by means of this essential insignificance the ideality or ideal identity of each mark (which is only a differential function without an ontological basis) can continue to divide itself and to give

rise to proliferation of other identities. This iterability is that which allows a mark to be used more than once.[59]

As in Greenblatt's claim, but here under the auspices of a deconstructive analysis, the bodily mark is always capable of being sundered from its context along an indeterminate destinational axis. The future destination of the mark is always open, but I wish to claim that certain texts, by a kind of apocalyptic drive to power, are capable of capturing the mark, arresting for a moment its "destinerence" or wandering, and incorporating it into their textual field. Like the ritual mark of circumcision, the symbolic mutilation that marks the heads is capable of marking other mutilated bodies and coding them within its symbolism. But as with the differential relation of the mark that varies "each time according to its context, to the network of other marks," the bodies to which the heads symbolically attach recode the mutilated heads by situating them within another network of mutilated marks. The mutilated heads that come from the future of African genocide recode with their apocalyptic inscriptions the mutilated heads of *Heart of Darkness*, thereby transforming the book into a contemporary text of primitive African savagery. But since *Heart of Darkness* is endowed with a drive to power over the future catastrophic body, it is capable of overcoding even this genocidal absorption by pulling these dismembered bodies back into the gravitational well of its own dark apocalyptic trajectories.

It is by means of *Heart of Darkness*'s powers of overcoding and its capacity to inscribe or give meaning to these material wounds that African genocide thus becomes coded as *Heart of Darkness*, and these mutilated African bodies become part of the field of Conrad's text—they are entered into its horizon. The mutilated body in the text becomes the locus for this interrelation, establishing a homologous relation between violently inscribed textual bodies and material bodies inscribed with a signifying violence. *Heart of Darkness* spreads its textual field across these material bodies, coding or inscribing their wounds, and thereby literalizing or embodying itself.

As Watts surmises, in *A Personal Record*, Conrad makes Kurtz's problem that of the creative artist: "In that interior world where his thought and his emotions go seeking for the experience of imagined adventures there are no policeman, no law, no pressure of circumstance or dread of opinion to keep him within bounds. Who then is going to say Nay to his temptations if not his conscience?"[60] We may generalize this to claim Kurtz's problem is the problematic of the text of *Heart of Darkness* itself in relation to its future apocalyptic reception. The figure of the mutilated body in *Heart of Darkness* is always capable of being seized by a catastrophic event that then retroactively recodes this apocalyptic text. Since the figure of mutilated body in this text always has the potential to be "materialized," it can overwhelm any counter- or antiapocalyptic trajectory. The figure of the mutilated body has a potential material destiny that exceeds the control of the author; indeed this material future may well run against the grain of Conrad's intention. Thus, Marlow's ironic stance toward his own narrative becomes overrun by his apocalyptic text's potential to actualize itself, to become its own apocalypse. In the case of *Heart of Darkness*, the attaching of the mutilated African bodies to the mutilated textual bodies overwhelms in its fascinated horror the anticolonialist and counterapocalyptic trajectory of the text.

Thus, *Heart of Darkness* is, I claim, at one level self-consciously about its future destiny. In these terms, the agon between Marlow and Kurtz might be read as an allegorical struggle between the apocalyptic and antiapocalyptic trajectories of the text. Kurtz, in this allegory, would represent a textual will to apocalyptic power, Marlow a countervailing will to ethical restraint. The text is thus stationed in this continuing contest with the future. This split between Marlow and Kurtz is represented by the figure of the doppelgänger, which would also be the figure for the text's apocalyptic iterability.

While it is true that I am formulating *Heart of Darkness* in allegorical terms, I do not think that my reading simply imposes an allegorical mode on the text. An allegorical element, I believe, already pervades the text. Conrad, after all, seems to have bethought himself when he claimed in a letter: "What I distinctly admit is the fault of having made Kurtz too symbolic or rather symbolic at all."[61] In Conrad's maintaining that he made Kurtz "too symbolic," I take him to mean that Kurtz comes across not as a fully realized or individuated character but rather as one who stands as a symbol or type or one that is emblematic and open to an allegorical reading. I do not mean here to elide the distinction between allegory and symbol, which will be taken up in my next chapter, but I would note that Conrad's critique of Kurtz as "symbolic" resonates with Hegel's critique of the allegorical being. In his *Aesthetics* Hegel writes that "[a]n allegorical being, however much it may be given a human shape, does not attain the concrete individuality of a Greek god or of a saint or of some actual person, because in order that there may be congruity between subjectivity and the abstract meaning which it has, the allegorical being must make subjectivity so hollow that all specific individuality vanishes from it."[62] On the face of it, Conrad's claim of having made Kurtz "too symbolic" would seem to conform to Hegel's critique and Conrad seems to have decried leaving us with an emptied or hollowed-out allegorical being as opposed to a fully articulated persona. But Conrad's critique of Kurtz, I suspect, is not without its own hollowness or deception. Kurtz's hollowed-out subjectivity is precisely the point. Kurtz is the hollow man and it is as a hollow allegorical being that he becomes emblematic of the powers of textual consumption. And we should note that Kurtz himself does not evade consumption in his own text and is portrayed as belonging to the powers of darkness. The wilderness, we are told, "consumed his flesh," and "[t]he thing was to know what he belonged to, how many powers of darkness claimed him for their own" (48). If the wilderness consumes the flesh of Kurtz, taking him to its darkness, getting "into his veins" (48), in the same vein we might say that the textual wilderness of *Heart of Darkness* consumes into the event horizon of its black hole the mutilated bodies of contemporary African apocalypse.

MARLOW AND MESSIANISM

If Kurtz is emblematic of and represents an instance of the textual drive to the consumption of bodies, what recourse is offered us to summon Marlow's countervailing injunction to ethical restraint? If, like Kurtz, *Heart of Darkness* itself goes too far, what terms does the text offer us for redemption from its own extremity? And if Kurtz is made to "step over the edge" so that Marlow can be "permitted to draw back [his] hesitating foot" (70), if Kurtz, that is, goes out too far, so that Marlow can come back, or at least come back far enough to give us his report, what redemptive discourse might the text offer its readers to draw it back from the powers of its own incarnation? While I have focused thus far on the apocalyptic dimensions of the text, in this concluding section of this chapter, I will attempt to address these questions by analyzing *Heart of Darkness* with regard to the different registers of contemporary messianic discourse.

We might begin such an analysis by counterposing the phantom Kurtz who appears before Marlow on his visit to the Intended with a figure for the messianic drawn from Derrida's *Specters of Marx*. Marlow, we recall, has a vision of this apocalyptic phantom "opening his mouth voraciously as if to devour all the earth with all its mankind" (73). As opposed to this rapacious figure of the devouring open mouth, Derrida speaks of the messianic in terms of the "immensity, excessiveness, disproportion in the gaping hole of the open mouth—in the waiting or calling for what we have nicknamed here without knowing the messianic: the coming of the other, the absolute and unpredictable singularity of the *arrivant as justice*."[63] As with the open mouth of the phantom Kurtz, there is something unbounded and exorbitant in Derrida's figure of the "gaping hole of the open mouth," but unlike the cannibalistic rictus of the phantom Kurtz that would apocalyptically engorge or fill itself with human flesh, the gape or gap in Derrida's figure of the hollow mouth signifies an absolute openness before an incalculable and indeterminable future to come. In a certain sense, the cannibal phantom or spirit of Kurtz illustrates Derrida's claim that "[a]s soon as one no longer distinguishes spirit from specter, the former assumes a body, it incarnates itself, as spirit, in the specter."[64] Against this incarnating spirit, Derrida invokes the specter as a figure of radical alterity or exorbitant incalculability that lies at the heart of our asymmetrical ethical relation to the other. In contradistinction to the wilderness of *Heart of Darkness* and its powers of consumption, we might invoke Derrida's "desert-like messianism,"[65] by which he indicates an absolute openness and hospitality to the event or *arrivant* from the future to come that exceeds all forms of predestination or programming. Or as Derrida puts it in "Faith and Knowledge," "a certain desert in the desert that would make possible, open, hollow out or infinitize the other."[66]

Although he is not thinking of the "desert in the desert" in Derrida's incalculable terms, interestingly, Marlow does remark that "[y]ou lost your way on that river as you would in a desert" (33) and Marlow certainly comes very close to being lost (in all senses) on his journey to Kurtz. Having invoked this desert in the river, I do not, however, mean to read Marlow as *arrivant*. But there is at least one aspect of Marlow's relation to Kurtz that retains some element of the exorbitant and incalculable that makes possible the ethical relation to the other. Marlow tells us that he remained loyal to Kurtz to the end because having confronted death himself, he found no meaning in the contest, which far from conferring any romantic or singular authenticity upon his being left him reduced to the thought of life as a "mysterious arrangement of merciless logic for a futile purpose" (69). Kurtz, Marlow finds, however, proves a worthier agonist in the face of death. Kurtz still retains the purchase of some belief. He is able to judge, to sum up, or to summon up conviction before the moment of extinction. Marlow does not know the meaning of Kurtz's summation; he does not share in Kurtz's vision, but he remains exorbitantly loyal to the inordinate quality of Kurtz's conviction, which he calls an "affirmation," and even a "moral victory" (70). Perhaps this is partly what he means when he tells us "[i]t is his extremity that I seem to have lived through" (70). There is something incalculable and asymmetrical, then, in Marlow's loyalty to Kurtz. And according to Emmanuel Levinas and Derrida, it is precisely on this incalculable relation to the other that exceeds the calculus of the law or of the cycle of vengeance that the possibility of ethics and justice rest. Marlow does not believe that he has rendered Kurtz the justice he was due during his visit to the Intended. It would have been too dark to tell her the last of Kurtz's words. Kurtz had said that "he wanted only justice" (77) and if not in Marlow's lie, perhaps in the exorbitance of Marlow's loyalty, he may ultimately be given it. We might begin to think, then, in Derrida's terms, of Marlow's loyalty as a gesture that perhaps opens him up to the possibility of the messianic extremity, to the extremity he has lived through of Kurtz as *arrivant*. The thought of Kurtz as *arrivant* is certainly disquieting and frightful, but what Marlow is perhaps trying to tell us, what Marlow has come himself to have learned, is that there is that no assurance granted us that the *arrivant* will come, if he comes, in the form of a benign and guiding angel. In fact, as we shall now see it is not quite Kurtz himself but the deconstruction of the phantasm of Kurtz as imperial sovereign that functions for Marlow as the *arrivant*.

It is this Marlow whose destiny it is to encounter and live through Kurtz's extremity that Conrad leaves us with at the end of the text, but I want now to shift positions and situate Marlow not in relation to Kurtz's agonistic strength or power, but rather with regard to Walter Benjamin's invocation of a "*weak* messianic power" as a way of indicating a further degree of messianic repair or correction that Marlow may yet achieve. In his essay on Kafka, Benjamin indicates that the messianic correction can be thought of as an easing or unburdening of the backs of those oppressed before the law of the sovereign. The hunchback and other burdened "tenant[s] of the distorted world," Benjamin writes, "will disappear with the coming of the Messiah, who (a great Rabbi once said) will not wish to change the world by force but will merely make a slight adjustment in it."[67] As he enters the grove of death, or "circle of some Inferno" (16) as he calls it, Marlow comes across a host of dying African slaves crouched in "all the attitudes of pain, abandonment, and despair" (17). Abandoned to the law of the colonial sovereign, these crouched and starving, bent-over figures exceed even Benjamin's burdened tenants of the distorted world. In the grove, Marlow reports, two "bundles of acute angles sat with their legs drawn up. One, with his chin propped on his knees, stared at nothing in an intolerable and appalling manner. His brother phantom rested its forehead as if overcome with a great weariness; and all about others were scattered in every pose of contorted collapse, as in some picture of a massacre or a pestilence" (17). In this circle of the colonial Inferno, it is not difficult to see how the adjustment of unburdening the backs of these black bodies in extremis would amount to nothing less than a messianic act.

Reduced now to what Agamben calls bare life or that life that is exposed to death, these African bodies are also rendered creaturely. They are made into what Eric Santner has named "creaturely life," by which he refers to those captured and literally cringed by the juridico-political order.[68] Creaturely life refers, then, not to the reduction of human and animal life—although it does encompass the "peculiar proximity of human to animal at the very point of their radical difference"—but rather to the biopolitical submission of life crippled before the state of exception.[69] It is not simply in subjection to the sovereign that creaturely life emerges, but rather through exposure to the paradoxical topology that marks the state of exception—that impossible space that is simultaneously both immanent in and standing outside the law. As Agamben explains it: "*Being outside, and yet belonging*: this is the topological structure of the state of exception, and only because the sovereign, who decides on the exception, is, in truth, logically defined in his being by the exception, can he too be defined by the oxymoron *ecstasy-belonging*."[70] It is the sovereign who wields a decisive creative power that authors or suspends the law from the position that is and is not outside the law. "What I am calling creaturely life," Santner goes on to say, "is the life that is, so to speak, called into being, *ex-cited*, by exposure to the peculiar 'creativity' associated with this threshold of law and nonlaw; it is life that has been delivered over to the space of the sovereign's 'ecstasy-belonging,' or what we might simply call 'sovereign jouissance.'"[71] Creaturely life is summoned into being by the irresolvable trauma of those submitted to the enigmatic power of the sovereign who proclaims the law (or suspension of the law) from the place of nonlaw that is itself immanent in the law. Subject to this impossible contradiction, creaturely life is trapped in that unnatural realm of simultaneous agitation and constriction, of "petrified unrest," as Benjamin phrases it, and to which Santner speaks of as the space of "undeadness."[72]

It is through a number of German-Jewish writers that Santner traces the modern condition of creaturely life that he finds, for example, in Benjamin's reading of the stooped figure of melancholia in his *Origin of German Tragic Drama*, as well as in Kafka's hunchbacked figures literally cringed before the sovereign power that is dispersed through the labyrinth of the modern bureaucratic juridical order. Creaturely life emerges for these writers in direct relation to the Jew's traumatic exposure to the sovereign dimension of biopolitical power. While we should guard against an ahistorical conflation of two different orders of political power, it seems to me that certain aspects of Santner's analysis of creaturely life may readily apply to *Heart of Darkness*. As we have just seen, the Africans in the grove, as well as those working on roads, are similarly bent or cringed before the power of the colonial sovereign. Santner alludes briefly to Paul Celan's reference to "the angle of inclination" in Celan's own discourse on human creatureliness, and this surely resonates with Conrad's "bundles of acute angles" deposited in the grove. However, Santner also emphasizes that it is not simply in its subjection to the sovereign that creaturely life emerges, but rather through its very exposure to the irresolvable contradiction of the power of the sovereign to suspend the law from within the law, to mark out, that is, the paradoxical topology of the state of exception. It is precisely this sovereign power that is visited upon the Africans who are simply named as "enemies" in what Carl Schmitt defines as the fundamental political decision, and then enslaved as criminals in the "legality of time contracts"[73] whose enigmatic law must appear to them simultaneously as both utterly arbitrary and all powerful: "They were called criminals and the outraged law like the bursting shells had come to them, an insoluble mystery from the sea" (16). The sheer violence of the law is mixed here with its powers of enigmatic address. "They were not enemies," Marlow goes on to say of those dying Africans in the grove, "they were not criminals, they were nothing earthly now, nothing but black shadows of disease and starvation lying confusedly in the greenish gloom" (17). Here Marlow punctures the sovereign political logic of the friend/enemy distinction and replaces it with a poignant denunciation of the biopolitics of empire; and exposing this lie that empire tells itself must surely constitute Marlow's most efficacious political act. But if Marlow is quick to puncture the lie on which the politics of empire is founded, it is with the burden of Kurtz as colonial sovereign that he must still contend.

If there was ever a sovereign given over to his own "ecstasy-belonging" or jouissance, it was Kurtz. We recall Kurtz's argument in his report that given their advanced development, whites "must necessarily appear to them [savages] in the nature of supernatural beings—we approach them with the might as of a deity'" (50). And it was exactly this sovereign power that Kurtz seems to have exercised; all were rendered creaturely before him. The Africans, we are told, crawled before him, for Marlow the steamer "crawled towards Kurtz—exclusively" (35), and even Marlow himself "had, even like the niggers, to invoke him—himself—his own exalted and incredible degradation" (66). But what establishes Kurtz's exalted powers, what allows him to wield his decisive creative power, to subject and hold those in his enigmatic thrall, is that he himself embodies the state of exception. Kurtz is simultaneously both inside and outside colonial power, colonial *jurisdiction*.[74] The station manager laments that Kurtz's methods are "unsound," that he has gone too far, and that he has "ruined the *district*" (62) (my emphasis). Kurtz wields the powers of the law from the space of the outlaw, or even from the space of non-law, and it is over to this "ecstasy-belonging" or "sovereign jouissance" that Marlow finds himself delivered. "I had, even like the niggers, to invoke him—himself—his own exalted and incredible degradation. There was nothing either above or below him—and I knew it.... He had kicked the very earth to pieces. He was alone—and I before him did not know whether I stood on the ground or floated in the air" (66). Caught in Kurtz's "ecstasy-belonging," Marlow finds himself unmoored and drifting into the same impossible liminal space. That he is made creaturely before the enigma of the sovereign Kurtz is indicated by burden of the weight he feels on his back. Maneuvering Kurtz back to the boat, Marlow relates: "I wiped my forehead while my legs shook under me as though I had carried half a ton on my back down that hill. And yet I had only supported him, his bony arm clasped round my neck—and he was not much heavier than a child" (66). It is clearly, then, not Kurtz's actual weight that burdens Marlow as if he really were carrying half a ton back to the boat. Discomposed and psychically subject before this ghastly confoundment, Marlow finds himself struggling to throw off the burden of his captivation before the paradox of the sovereign Kurtz.

What is extraordinary about *Heart of Darkness*, however, is that Kurtz is both sovereign and later made creaturely. He is given over to his own "sovereign jouissance." We recall that Kurtz also crawls across the earth—"He can't walk—he is crawling on all-fours—I've got him," Marlow tells himself with exultation as he tracks Kurtz down (64). Emerging from the earth, as Marlow cuts him off, Kurtz takes on an undead, ghostly aspect: "He rose, unsteady, long, pale, indistinct like a vapour exhaled by the earth" (65). Kurtz's crawling through and rising from the earth bears an uncanny resemblance to the old mole or Ghost in Shakespeare's *Hamlet*, of whom Derrida remarks: "Every *revenant* seems here to come from and return to *the earth*, to come from it as from a buried clandestinity (humus and mold tomb and subterranean prison), to return to it as to the lowest, toward the humble, humid, humiliated."[75] And in confirmation of Kurtz's humiliating return to the earth or humus, we are told that Marlow sees that the "pilgrims buried something in a muddy hole" (69). But we know, too, that Kurtz will emerge again from this muddy hole in the form of the phantom with its all-consuming rapacious rictus.

In fact, from the start, Kurtz has appeared to Marlow in the aspect of the undead: he begins by coming to Marlow as a voice, a disembodied voice, but he also first appears to Marlow as a figure embodied in ivory. We recall Marlow's perception of the skeletal figure of Kurtz with his voracious mouth as "an animated image of death carved out of old ivory" (59) and it is this same image of Kurtz with his "phantom-bearers" (73) that visits Marlow on his approach to the Intended. If Kurtz sets himself up as a sovereign god or fetish, he is also transmuted into ivory as a commodity of late-nineteenth-century imperial capital. Simultaneously specter and idol, Kurtz, we might say, is emblematic of the fetishism of commodities. If the African woman covered in the trading commodities of brass wires and glass beads—"She must have had the value of several elephant tusks upon her" (60)—is excessively shot and killed off, Kurtz's return carries with it, and circulates, that fetish aspect of the commodity that is not readily evacuated. This is brought home to us in the object of the "grand piano [that] stood massively in a corner with dark gleams on the flat surfaces like a sombre and polished sarcophagus," in which are entombed keys carved out of old ivory (73). In his transubstantiation into both ivory and apparition, then, Kurtz also perfectly embodies Benjamin's condition of "petrified unrest": he literally embodies the impossible contradiction of an "animated image of death."

But if Kurtz is ultimately a figure of the undead, Marlow also begins to take on an aspect of undeadness. Upon his return to Brussels, he, too, finds himself wandering like the undead through the unnatural "sepulchral city." "No, they did not bury me," he tells us, "though there is a period of time which I remember mistily, with shuddering wonder, like a passage through some inconceivable world that had no hope in it and no desire" (70). While he is not buried in a muddy hole like Kurtz, Marlow does not escape being entombed in his own undead, gray, zombie-like world.

What is it that brings Marlow back from this undead realm? He is not very clear on this point, but he does inform us that it was not his body that needed tending but his "imagination that wanted soothing" (71). And are we truly sure that Marlow has indeed fully returned from his immurement in the undead realm? Or might we take his compulsion to tell his story again and again as evidence of an imagination that is still in want of soothing? Is there some way, then, in which Marlow's telling his tale is redemptive, or does it merely confirm his being caught in the agitated undead space of a repetition compulsion?

Having worked to read Marlow's encounter with Kurtz in terms of a Derridean conception of "messianicity," I want now to draw on Santner's reading of Benjamin to indicate a further aspect of messianic reparation that Marlow might still accomplish. Santner asserts:

> If I understand Benjamin correctly, the messianic dimension . . . cannot be understood on the model of an exchange, of a simple conversion of loss into gain, death into life. To use one of Benjamin's favorite formulations, the *awakening* at issue in the messianic advent should be understood not as a resurrection, an animation of the dead, but, as I have suggested, as *a deanimation of the undead*, an interruption of the "ban," the captivation at work in the spectral fixations—the petrified unrest—that cringes/curves the psychic space of human subjects.[76]

In what sense, then, might Marlow accomplish his own messianic awakening from the realm of the undead? How might he creatively deanimate the undead Kurtz that burdens his back? How, that is, might he attain release from implication in Kurtz's enigmatic address? I have already begun this analysis by indicating the way in which Marlow might turn the gape of Kurtz's harrowing rictus into the gaping hole of the open mouth that signals his awaiting the "unpredictable singularity of the *arrivant as justice*."[77] But how do we proceed further to the messianic deanimation of the undead? We might begin, perhaps, by returning once more to the scene of Marlow's lie to the Intended. In preparing us for this ending Marlow tells his listeners, "I laid the ghost of his gifts at last with a lie" (48). The issue of Marlow's lie to the Intended has received a great deal of critical scrutiny—lying is dying because it is upon a lie that Europe pursued its colonizing mission in Africa—but I want to take literally Marlow's claim that he laid the *ghost* of Kurtz's gifts at last with the lie as his deanimation of the ghost of Kurtz. Of all of Kurtz's gifts—and we should be cognizant here both of the economy of the gift and of Marlow's play on "gift" as meaning "poison" in German—it is Kurtz's voice, his gift for language, that Marlow singles out: "The point was in his being a gifted creature and that of all his gifts the one that stood out preeminently, that carried with it a sense of real presence, was his ability to talk, his words—the gift of expression" (47); and the Intended, too, speaks of Kurtz's voice as the "gift of the great" (75). When Marlow speaks, then, of laying the ghost of his gifts with a lie, he refers to his silencing of Kurtz's last words: "The horror! The horror!"—spoken with his last voice—as well as to his silencing or laying to rest of the atrocious phantom who speaks them as he stands before Kurtz's mourning Intended (76). As he stands before the threshold of the mahogany door, Marlow mentions that he had thought of Kurtz's memory like other memories of the dead as "a vague impress on the brain of shadows that had fallen on it in their swift and final passage" (72), but the vision that appears before him now, the same vision of Kurtz as an "animated image of death carved out of old ivory" is indeed literalized as Kurtz seems actually reanimated: "He lived then before me, he lived as much as he had ever lived—a shadow insatiable" (73). Yet before the Intended, Marlow is at least able to silence Kurtz's voice, to stop for a crucial moment the compulsion to repeat, to deanimate the undead, to keep back the invading voice "for the salvation of another soul" (73).

Of course, Marlow informs us that Kurtz's ghost is not so easily laid to rest: "I shall see this eloquent phantom as long as I live and I shall see her too, a tragic and familiar Shade resembling in this gesture another one, tragic also and bedecked with powerless charms, stretching bare brown arms over the glitter of the infernal stream, the stream of darkness" (76). If Marlow is ever to truly deanimate or defetishize the sovereign ghost of Kurtz as well as Kurtz as ivory commodity fetish, he must divest them of their spectral qualities and reduce them both to inanimate bones. We cannot entirely exculpate Marlow from complicity with the Company, as it is his navigational skill that allows the Station Manager to pick up the vast quantity of fossil ivory for which Kurtz has killed both man and elephant. I have spoken of Marlow's lie to the Intended—she shall never have Kurtz's last words and we shall never know her name—as laying to rest, if only for a moment, the ghost of his gifts. "There is a taint of death," Marlow tells us "a flavour of mortality in lies—which is exactly what I hate and detest in the world—what I want to forget. It makes me miserable and sick like biting something rotten would do" (27). Lying is tantamount to dying for Marlow, it makes him sick, but there is a sense in which the death and decay embodied in the lie is exactly what Marlow requires if he is to defetishize this undead Kurtz. In lying, in biting into something rotten, Marlow links himself to the restraint shown by the starving cannibals with their lumps of rotting hippo meat, and it is want of restraint that is the great danger in *Heart of Darkness*. When the danger is one of stepping over the edge, beyond the boundaries of any constraint and ultimately into the realm of undeadness, one must learn to "breathe dead hippo and not be contaminated" and salvation comes in the form of reliance on your faith in your "power of devotion not to yourself but to an obscure, back-breaking business" (49). In the jungle of Africa it is a steely focus on back-breaking work that removes the burden from the back. Or this, at least, is the case for Marlow. It is far different for those Africans enslaved before the enigma of the law.

The shade of the African woman "bedecked with powerless charms" recalls another shade wearing a similarly powerless charm. In order to escape the chain gang of slaves, Marlow turns to the left (traditionally the way out of a labyrinth) only to find himself in the grove of death. There he comes across one of the dying who has tied some white worsted around his neck. The wool strikes Marlow as a mystery: "Was it a badge—an ornament—a charm—a propitiatory act? Was there any idea at all connected with it. It looked startling round his black neck this bit of white thread from beyond the seas" (17). Whatever the reason, this white piece of wool, of animal hair from across the seas, fails in its apotropaic function. The thread of his life is about to be cut by the fates. As with his brother in the grove who crawls on all fours to drink in the river, the burden has not been lifted from his back.

But there is still one strand of white thread in the heart of darkness that does seem to hold redemptive powers, or at least hold together a book to which Marlow ascribes redemptive powers. This antique book has lost its covers and its pages are soft and grubby from use but the "back had been lovingly stitched afresh with white cotton thread, which looked clean yet" (37). Marlow holds the old book with great care "lest it should dissolve in my hands" (37), but the back of the book proves sturdy, and the content of the book on seamanship offers a further sturdiness to its reader. What this book offers Marlow is a kind of touchstone, a sense of coming upon something "unmistakably real" (38) in this back of beyond, this unreal realm. This book is as out of place in the jungle as the white worsted around the neck of the dying man; unlike that white thread, however, this book held together by a newly sown white thread still holds the power of a charm. "Not a very enthralling book," Marlow informs us, "but at the first glance you could see there a singleness of intention, an honest concern for the right way of going to work which made these humble pages thought out so many years ago luminous with another than a professional light" (38). It is precisely because of this book's lack of exoticism that it retains its powers that lie not in any fabled content, but in the craft of work, in its techne. It is this labor both congealed in, and expressed by, the book that makes it "luminous with another than a professional light" (38). It is this focused labor that Marlow fastens on, the same focus on labor that allows him to steer the boat, and that allows him to

Apocalyptic Futures

disenchant the approach to Kurtz "beset by as many dangers as though he had been an enchanted princess sleeping in a fabulous castle" (42).

And yet in another regard, this book is indeed enthralling and mysterious. It holds Marlow in its thrall. Or, at least, the enigmatic signs inscribed in its margins hold Marlow in their thrall: "Such a book being there was wonderful enough, but still more astounding were the notes penciled in the margin, and plainly referring to the text. I couldn't believe my eyes! They were in cipher.... Fancy a man lugging with him a book of that description into this nowhere and studying it—and making notes—in cipher at that! It was an extravagant mystery" (38). If the book's content—"inquiring earnestly into the breaking strain of ships' chains and tackle" (38)—is dryly technical, the notes inscribed in its margins, by contrast, appear to Marlow as hierophantic and enigmatical. What are we to make of this commentary, this study that takes place deep in the jungle? Or to approach this from another angle, how might this strange text lead us to a redemptive reading of *Heart of Darkness* itself? In order to help enlighten us, I want to turn to Benjamin's reading of Kafka's parable "The New Advocate" as well as to Agamben's analysis of Benjamin's essay on Kafka. Working to explicate Kafka's parable, Benjamin finds that it is study that opens the space that leads to redemption. Benjamin writes, "Reversal is the direction of study which transforms existence into script. Its teacher is Bucephalus, 'the new advocate,' who takes the road back without the powerful Alexander—which means rid of the onrushing conqueror. 'His flanks free and unhampered by the thighs of a rider, under a quiet lamp far from the din of Alexander's battles, he reads and turns the pages of our old books.'"[78] It is only once he is free of the colonizing violence of Alexander's wars that Bucephalus is able to take on the study of the old books. Lest we too easily transpose Bucephalus into the figure of the Talmudist, however, Benjamin warns that Kafka "doesn't dare attach to this study the promises which tradition has attached to the study of the Torah. His assistants are sextons who have lost their house of prayer; his students are pupils who have lost their Holy Writ [*Schrift*]. Now there is nothing to support them on their 'untrammeled, happy journey.'"[79]

The reader will already have guessed the analogy I am gesturing toward here between Bucephalus, or at least his assistants, and the Russsian harlequin figure that Marlow meets on his approach to Kurtz. Naturally, I do not mean to draw a strict parallel between them. The harlequin figure is no legal scholar and the old book that he studies is no legal text, but he does withdraw into the study of its rules as he turns the coded pages of his antique book, and he too has nothing underfoot, nothing to support him on his "untrammeled happy journey." If Marlow finds this book "luminous with another than professional light," this too seems the case for the Russian harlequin son of an archpriest. In the end, Benjamin tells us, "[t]he law which is studied but no longer practiced is the gate to justice."[80] I will return shortly to this crucial claim and its significance for my redemptive reading of Conrad's text, but for the moment, since we are on the theme of justice, I want to note that it is this harlequin who is conjoined to Marlow in his loyalty to Kurtz. In fact, the harlequin precedes Marlow in opening himself up to Kurtz as *arrivant*, "If the absolutely pure, uncalculating, unpractical spirit of adventure had ever ruled a human being, it ruled this be-patched youth," Marlow tells us (55). There is a strict difference, of course: Marlow wrestles with, and struggles deeply over, his inordinate loyalty to Kurtz, whereas for the harlequin, Kurtz is simply accepted as that which was destined him. "I did not envy him his devotion to Kurtz though," Marlow is compelled to assure us. "He had not meditated over it. It came to him and he accepted it with a sort of eager fatalism" (55). And indeed, Marlow is eager to set up this thoughtless harlequin as a foil for his own extravagant bond with Kurtz. Oddly, however, at least in terms of the "pure uncalculating spirit" of his acceptance of the *arrivant*, this harlequin appears closer than Marlow to approaching the possibility of justice in the Derridean sense. But together with his own lack of restraint, and in his going out so far that he is not sure that he will be able to come back, the harlequin is also in danger of the fate that befell Kurtz.

The mystery of the ciphered book is solved; the enigmatic signifiers in the margin no longer hold Marlow in their thrall—they are revealed simply to be the harlequin's notes written in Russian as Marlow finds out when he returns the book. Fearing the wrath and retribution of the Station Manager the Russian makes off into the bush. Before doing so, he asks Marlow for some Martini-Henry cartridges, which Marlow gives him, and as he watches the harlequin figure vanish into the night, he notes that "[o]ne of his pockets (bright red) was bulging with cartridges, from the other (dark blue) peeped 'Towson's Inquiry'" (63). We might read this, as Valentine Cunningham does, as bespeaking the violence of writing, and in a general sense I think this may be accurate. But unlike Kurtz or the pilgrims, the harlequin does not use his cartridges on the Africans, and we should recall that it is his advice to Marlow to use the steamer's whistle that allows Marlow to scatter the Africans before the pilgrims begin showering the jungle with their fusillade of bullets. Rather than simply acceding to this book as signifying the violence of the letter, then, I want to indicate a way in which we might read the harlequin and his book with its studious marginalia as deactivating the violence of the law.

In his *State of Exception*, Agamben offers us an interpretation of Benjamin that will prove crucial to this task. What Benjamin invokes with his enigmatic proclamation that "[t]he law which is studied but no longer practiced is the gate to justice," Agamben argues, is the remnant or still "possible figure of law after its nexus with violence and power has been deposed, but it is a law that no longer has force or application."[81] In some respects, this is the case for Marlow with regard to Towson's *An Inquiry into Some Points of Seamanship*. This old book with its dry technical rules and "illustrative diagrams and repulsive tables of figures" is of no use and has no application out in the jungle (37). It belongs to a different time and space, and even the vessels for which it provides the key to instruction are now outmoded. Its power has been deposed, and yet, for reasons I have addressed, Marlow still finds these "humble pages thought out so many years ago luminous with another than a professional light" (38).

Judging by the study he has given these pages, and the delight he proclaims upon recovering this book's pages, it is clear that for the harlequin these pages also hold a luminous power. In fact, as far as Marlow is concerned it is the study of these redemptive pages and finding in them the same focus and "honest concern for the right way of going to work" that holds the key to the harlequin's salvation and his coming back from the orbit of his enthrallment to Kurtz and the wilderness (38). But this harlequin who studies the pages of this old book might himself offer Marlow (together with ourselves as readers) one further lesson in his deanimation of the spectral sovereignty of Kurtz. When he first comes across the harlequin figure, Marlow expresses the same sense of astonishment as he does coming upon the book in the jungle: "There he was before me in motley as though he had absconded from a troupe of mimes, enthusiastic, fabulous. His very existence was improbable, inexplicable, and altogether bewildering. He was an insoluble problem" (54). What is especially important to note here, I think, is that this carnival figure represents a strange and even contradictory fusion of both Bucephalus and Kurtz: like Bucephalus he has withdrawn into his study of the old book, and like Kurtz he lacks restraint and is impelled to go ever further out beyond all boundaries. He even seems to take on some aspect of Kurtz's undeadness. But this carnival figure is also revealed to Marlow in the callowness of his unthinking youth as something of a child. In the very contradiction that he represents, the harlequin offers Marlow all that he needs to disenchant the phantom Kurtz. In one respect, his very aspect "carnivalizes," or holds up to ridicule, Kurtz's lack of restraint, Kurtz's erection of himself as imperial sovereign, and in another respect the harlequin's study points precisely the way to the deactivation of the spectral aspect of the law. Commenting on Benjamin's analysis of Bucephalus, Agamben writes:

> The decisive point here is that the law—no longer practiced, but studied—is not justice, but only the gate that leads to it. What opens a passage toward justice is not the erasure of law, but its deactivation and inactivity [*inoperosità*]—that is, another use of the law. This is precisely what the force-of-law (which keeps the law working [*in opera*] beyond its formal suspension) seeks to prevent. Kafka's characters—and this is why they interest us—have to do with the spectral figure of the law in the state of exception; they seek, each one following his or her strategy, to "study" and deactivate it, to "play" with it.[82]

Although the harlequin figure is by no means aware of it, he may function for Marlow (and for us) in the same way that Kafka's characters function to deactivate the spectral hold of the law in its state of exception. If Marlow might come to see it, the carnival figure of the harlequin offers the example of one who in his "play" and "study" unknowingly offers a path to the deactivation of the law of the sovereign.

After reading *Heart of Darkness*, and our encounter with the voracious undead figure of Kurtz, and then returning to the opening of the book, we might realize, without our having suspected it, that such play may already have been hinted at. The scene on the cruising yawl is one of imperial capital. The host and captain is the Director of Companies, who resembles a pilot, which ought to betoken the figure of trustworthiness itself. This pilot's work lies not in guiding his ship on the high seas, however, but in the directing of capital itself; as the frame narrator notes, the Director's work was not out "in the luminous estuary, but behind him, within the brooding gloom" (3). Along with the Director, we are also given the Lawyer and that functionary of capital, the Accountant. But, intriguingly, we are also told that "[t]he Accountant had brought out already a box of dominoes and was toying architecturally with the bones" (3). The dominoes are obviously made of ivory and their presence on the boat speaks to the global circulation of ivory as commodity, and they also foreshadow Kurtz as Marlow will see him as the figure of death embodied in ivory. But the accountant "toying architecturally with the bones" suggests not only a game played with this commodity but the defetishization of ivory as mere bone. The "whited sepulchre" city built out of the ivory trade may one day be doomed to come crashing down like a house built of dominoes. This toying with the bones, then, might also foreshadow that which emerges not before the law of the sovereign, but after the law has been deposed. For this deposed or deactivated law, Agamben indicates, is not extinguished but liberated and put to another use. "One day," he proclaims, "humanity will play with law just as children play with disused objects, not in order to restore them to their canonical use but to free them from it for good."[83] While the accountant toys like a child with the bones, we are reminded of that other childlike figure the harlequin, who studies by dim light the rules of his book. This book, we recall, inquires "earnestly into the breaking strain of ships' chains" (38). It is not too much to hope that in the full time of the law that is studied but no longer practiced, this messianic book made "luminous with another than a professional light" will also have taught us the breaking strain of the slave's chains.

I do not, of course, refer only to the literal enslavement or enchainment of those African bodies witnessed by Conrad and Marlow, "each [with] an iron collar on his neck and all . . . connected together with a chain whose bights swung between them, rhythmically clinking" (15). But also to the other sense in which these bodies remain enslaved or bound and chained to *Heart of Darkness*'s drive to incorporation. How, then, might we further deactivate or suspend this law of incorporation? We might begin again by returning to the narrator's remark that the accountant had begun toying with the bones, which uncannily foreshadows all the bones—the skeletons and skulls—that Marlow will encounter. The game of dominoes is not begun—play is deferred to make way for our story into the darkness, which Marlow assures us will be "uncanny and fateful" (11). It is not for nothing that he feels eerie before the "uncanny and fateful" women who guard the door into the darkness; and indeed, we have seen that the story has not disappointed in terms of its eerie prolepsis. Caryl Phillips, for example, has argued that "[m]odern descriptions of twentieth century famines, war, and genocide all seem to be eerily prefigured by Conrad, and *Heart of Darkness* abounds with passages that seem terrifyingly contemporary in their descriptive accuracy."[84] But it is precisely against this eerie prolepsis and its powers of incorporation that I want to invoke a counteraspect of the uncanny or the Freudian return of the repressed. Freud, we recall, maintains that contrary to the supposition that the uncanny constitutes that class of things utterly unfamiliar or unsuspected, "the uncanny is that class of the frightening which leads back to what is known of old and long familiar."[85] The uncanny, then, is that which was once secretly familiar, which has been repressed and now recurs. Among this class of the frightening, Freud includes "dismembered limbs, a severed head, a hand cut off at the wrist . . . feet which dance by themselves . . . all these have something peculiarly uncanny about them, especially when as in the last instance, they prove capable of independent activity in addition."[86] But here things get more complicated; for although dismembered limbs are certainly sometimes uncanny they are not always necessarily so. In fact, the severed skulls in *Heart of Darkness* are certainly grotesque and unnerving but they are not themselves uncanny. Indeed, as we shall see, it is not the proleptic powers of *Heart of Darkness* to incorporate contemporary African genocide that allows these bones to irrupt in all their uncanniness; quite the opposite, it is only when these bones return the text to the ruin of its political origins that their uncanny character becomes manifest.

I have argued for the deanimation of the phantom Kurtz, and the deactivation of *Heart of Darkness*'s drive to incorporation; my claim, however, is not that the bones and severed limbs of those victims of the genocide inflicted on the African peoples of the Congo in the 1890s (and later) should be reanimated or restored to a kind of plenitude, but rather that the incorporation of the genocidal bodies of the 1990s (and later) must be read against the accrual of contemporary apocalyptic power. The staked skulls around Kurtz's hut are not themselves particularly uncanny but simply grotesque. And yet when staked or read against the grain of their apocalyptic iterability, the skulls are revealed in all their uncanniness as the return of the repressed. For what *Heart of Darkness*'s incorporation of the genocidal bodies of the 1990s now calls up is not the horror of the mutilated corpses of contemporary African genocide but the repressed memory of colonial atrocity in the Congo of the 1890s, which was properly the political subject of Conrad's text, but one that has been overwhelmed or overwritten by the text's contradictory drive to accrual of apocalyptic powers. It is not simply that this colonial genocide once secretly familiar and long repressed now makes its return, but that the belated temporality of the skulls retrospectively inserted into the time of *Heart of Darkness* now display their uncanny powers. For it is not only the retrospective temporality of the skulls but the full extent of colonial atrocity in the Belgian Congo that has emerged along with them and which Hochschild has detailed in *King Leopold's Ghost*.[87] If the severed skulls were always already traumatically belated, introduced from an increasingly desperate future into an oppressive past, these skulls now call up the whole host of the mutilated dead, and this includes those whose hands were later cut from their bodies for failing to meet their rubber collection quotas. As the historian Peter Forbath has written, "The baskets of severed hands, set down at the feet of the European post commanders, became the symbol of the Congo Free State. The collection of hands became an end in itself.... They became a sort of currency. They came to be used to make up for shortfalls in rubber quotas, to replace ... the people who were demanded for the forced labour gangs."[88] While we do not know if Conrad had himself witnessed similar acts of mutilation on his journey up the Congo in 1890, we do know that he certainly came to be informed of these practices by his friend Roger Casement. In a letter to Cunningham Graham, Conrad wrote of Casement that "[h]e could tell you things! Things I've tried to forget; things I never did know."[89] As Alan Simmons has speculated, "The suggestion of events too painful to revisit leads one to wonder whether the 'unspeakable rites' in 'Heart of Darkness' have their source in the mutilations against which Casement inveighed."[90] Certainly the temporality of Conrad's assertion is ambiguous. Are these things Conrad has long known and tried to forget, or things that he never did know and is now trying to forget? It is, in any event, against this forgetting that the skulls from the future inserted into the text of the past make their traumatic return, and it is in this regard that the bones become properly fateful and uncanny.

I have used the figure of the textual black hole to describe *Heart of Darkness*'s powers of incorporation. And given that the text begins with the sun devolving from a "glowing white changed to a dull red without rays and without heat, as if about to go out suddenly, stricken to death" (4), this astronomical metaphor is not entirely out of place. But unlike two black holes drawn by their gravitational pull ineluctably together and colliding to form one massive black hole, the colonial genocide does have its powers of resisting its incorporation into the Rwandan genocide. If *Heart of Darkness* feeds off the trauma generated by the Rwandan genocide to draw mutilated bodies into the orbit of its reception, the traumatized mutilated bodies of the Belgian colonization mark the belated insistent return of the repressed pulling the text back, refusing to release it from the historical and political matrix from which it emerged.

In the sixth thesis of "On the Concept of History," Benjamin famously proclaims that "[t]he only historian capable of fanning the spark of hope in the past is the one who is firmly convinced that *even the dead* will not be safe from the enemy if he is victorious."[91] In turning *Heart of Darkness*'s incorporation of contemporary African genocide against itself, my hope has been to mark a space that allows for the ethical redemption of the Congolese dead. Or to put this another way, to demonstrate how the incorporation of contemporary genocide brings with it the necessary consequence of the uncanny return of the African dead. In the seventeenth of his messianic theses on history, Benjamin speaks of a "revolutionary chance in the fight for an oppressed past."[92] He means by this not only the redemption of the past but also the crucial work of thinking the relation of the oppressed past to a redemptive future. In working to counter the text's incorporation of the Rwandan genocide with the uncanny return of the Congolese dead, my analysis has been oriented not only toward the redemption of the oppressed past but in the hope of countering *Heart of Darkness*'s rampant drive to the further fullfilment of its apocalyptic future.

While this chapter has focused a messianic and ethical analysis against apocalyptic incorporation, in my next chapter I will turn to J. M. Coetzee's *Waiting for the Barbarians* to demonstrate how the marked body might function *politically* in a revolutionary fight for the oppressed past as well as for a more liberated future.

CHAPTER THREE

The Body in Ruins

Torture, Allegory, and Materiality in J. M. Coetzee's Waiting for the Barbarians

Allegories are, in the realm of thoughts, what ruins are in the realm of things.
—WALTER BENJAMIN, *The Origin of German Tragic Drama*

THE POLITICS OF THE ETERNAL PRESENT

Few authors are as deeply cognizant of the ethical responsibilities and dilemmas besetting the writer of torture as J. M. Coetzee. As I noted in my introduction, in *Diary of a Bad Year* (2007), Coetzee ascribes authorship of his novel *Waiting for the Barbarians* (1980) to his doppelgänger JC. JC goes on to remark a strict correspondence between new security legislation that effectively suspends the rule of law and which is put forth in the name of the struggle against terror and the old security apparatus of the apartheid state of South Africa. In the apartheid security state, the police, JC remarks, could "take you away to an unspecified site and do what they wanted to you." And they could do this "because special provisions of the legislation indemnified them in advance."[1] JC's "unspecified sites" clearly resonates with torture at the now-infamous CIA black sites and the legislation indemnifying military police in advance with the legal opinions rendered by lawyers working on behalf of the Bush administration. It is in this suspension of the law and in their effective enactment of a state of exception that those who operated the apartheid security apparatus were "just pioneers, ahead of their time."[2] What was universally decried as an outlaw practice of a dying regime at the end of the twentieth century is reborn anew at the beginning of the twenty-first. JC does not mince words in his indictment of the Bush administration, which "not only sanctions the torture of prisoners taken in the so-called war on terror but is active in every way to subvert laws and conventions proscribing torture. We may thus legitimately speak of an administration which, while legal in the sense of being legally elected, is illegal or anti-legal in the sense of operating beyond the bounds of the law, evading the law, and resisting the rule of law."[3] In his analysis of this extralegal apparatus subtending torture in both South Africa's apartheid prisons and in the torture chambers of Abu Ghraib Prison and the Guantánamo camp, JC recalls the J. M. Coetzee of "Into the Dark Chamber" (1986). In his essay that deals in the pitfalls surrounding the problem of the representation of torture in South Africa, Coetzee analyzes the same form of the suspension of the law, or what he calls a "twilight of legal illegality."[4] What happens in South African prisons, he asserts, is "nominally illegal. Articles of the law forbid the police from exercising violence upon the bodies of detainees except in self-defense. But other articles of the law, invoking reasons of state, place a protective ring around the activities of the security police. . . . [W]hat the prisoner in effect knows, what the police know he knows, is that he is helpless against whatever they choose to do to him."[5] If JC here clearly echoes J. M. Coetzee, it would be a mistake to collapse together their views on torture and resistance, and it is incumbent upon us to practice the same wariness with regard to the representation of torture that Coetzee himself does. Let me offer an example. Remarking on the fact that the administration will go to any lengths to eradicate all traces of its crimes, JC claims that "[t]he worst of their deeds we will never know: that we must be prepared to accept. To know the worst, we will have to extrapolate and use the imagination. The worst is likely to be whatever we think them capable of . . . and what they are capable of is, all too plainly, anything."[6] In order to ethically counter the erasure of the authorities' crimes, JC advocates that we imagine our way into the torture chamber and with it the full horror and spectacle of state torture. But it is precisely against just such untempered use of the imagination that J. M. Coetzee warns. "The dark, forbidden chamber," he writes, "is the origin of novelistic fantasy per se; in creating an obscenity, in enveloping it in mystery, the state unwittingly creates the preconditions for the novel to set about its work of representation." Yet, Coetzee goes on to say, "there is something tawdry about *following* the state in this way, making its vile mysteries the occasion of fantasy. . . . The true challenge is: how not to play the game by the rule of the state . . . how to imagine torture and death on one's own terms."[7] It would seem then that in his outrage at the Bush administration's wiping away of their crimes, JC falls into the trap of succumbing to an "occasion of fantasy" or the imaginative reconstruction or reanimation of the scene of torture.

And yet in light of Coetzee's focus on the ethics of the representation of torture, I am left with the question of what is at stake in Coetzee's ascription to JC of his *Waiting for the Barbarians*. For does *Barbarians* not confer a reality on JC that is purchased on the ethically ineradicable ground of the tortured bodies of the chambers of Abu Ghraib? Which *Barbarians* are we following: JC's or J. M Coetzee's? And in conferring a reality upon JC, does Coetzee's *Diary of a Bad Year* not risk fictionalizing the J. M. Coetzee of "Into the Dark Chamber" and diminishing his ethical critique? Furthermore, in placing *Barbarians* in the intemperate hands of JC, does Coetzee not risk *Barbarians*' accrual of an unalloyed spectacular horror? Or to put this another way, might the text not feed off the hooded figures and tortured bodies of Abu Ghraib and thereby gain a purchase on the future? For in situating *Barbarians* in relation to torture at Abu Graib, is JC not implicitly saying it was not only the legal state of exception of the apartheid state that was a forerunner of the new dispensation but my text *Waiting for the Barbarians* was equally a pioneer, ahead of its time? Why does Coetzee risk placing his *Waiting for the Barbarians* in the hands of an author who is less ethically canny with regard to the traps set by the representation of torture? The answer, I think, has something to do with the fact that this is a new twist on an old problem or on a problem that Coetzee faced from the inception of the composition of his text. In a certain sense, Coetzee's text is constituted around the problem of the incorporation of the tortured body, and in what follows I will attempt to address *Waiting for the Barbarians*' negotiation of this ethical dilemma.

In chapters 1 and 2 we saw how the modernist treatment of the inscribed or mutilated body as a floating or ungrounded sign left the text open to a future overcoding. We have also seen how mutilated bodies have been entered into the field of the text's future reception and how both *Heart of Darkness* and "In the Penal Colony" might be regarded as meditations on the relationship between an apocalyptic text and a future apocalyptic event. However, the retroactive linkage between the intratextually inscribed bodies and specific future genocides is necessarily brought out in the act of my retrospective interpretation of this conjunction. Although both Conrad and Kafka could anticipate the incorporation of future apocalypse into the ambit of their texts' later receptions, neither could foresee the specific event to which their texts would attach. In J. M. Coetzee's *Waiting for the Barbarians*, on the other hand, we are presented with the problem of the relationship of a text to the contemporaneous absorption of mutilated bodies and the consequent ethical dilemma of the author's responsibility for his or her text's accrual of a spectacular power.

Waiting for the Barbarians concerns the Magistrate of a remote colonial outpost and his encounter with an officer of the imperial police, Colonel Joll. Joll has come from the capital to investigate barbarian "disturbances" that he construes as preparations for a war on the Empire. Once at the fort, Joll engages in a series of systematic tortures designed to extract the "Truth." His tortures over, Joll returns to the capital, leaving behind a barbarian woman whose ankles have been broken and who is partially

The Body in Ruins

blinded and scarred with the marks of her torturers. Obsessed with knowing the intimate secrets of the barbarian woman's torture, the Magistrate engages in a ritualistic rubbing of her ankles with oil. These rituals continue until the Magistrate decides to return the barbarian woman to her people. After an arduous journey into the desert, the Magistrate succeeds in returning the woman to a nomadic clan of barbarians. Upon his return to the fort, the Magistrate is met by an officer of the imperial police and is accused of treasonously consorting with the enemy. The Magistrate is himself subjected to torture while Joll takes the army of the Empire on a campaign against the barbarians. Employing guerrilla tactics, the barbarians lure the army of the Empire farther and farther out into the desert. Together with the remnants of his scattered and defeated army, Colonel Joll abandons the outpost and makes for the capital. Resuming administration of the settlement, the Magistrate is left waiting for the barbarians.

While Conrad and Kafka both make use of the modernist ambiguities of the mutilated body, in *Waiting for the Barbarians*, Coetzee goes even further, placing the mutilated body under a postmodern hermeneutics of suspicion. Written in the wake of Michel Foucault's *Discipline and Punish* and strongly influenced by that work's coding of spectacular punishment as the law of the sovereign written on the body of the condemned, Coetzee's book engages in a more sustained and thoroughly reflexive reading of this figure. This reading begins, in fact, with *Waiting for the Barbarians*' intertextual relation to both *Heart of Darkness* and "In the Penal Colony." Like Kurtz before he goes upriver, the Magistrate is a believer in the Enlightenment narrative of progress. He believes in the administration of his juridical duties and in his responsibility toward a more benign governance. He, too, will become embroiled with a native lover and in an echo of the epithet applied to Kurtz, he will also imagine himself regarded by Empire as "unsound."[8] Further, as with both Marlow and Kurtz, his degradation will cause him to skeptically question the Enlightenment narrative upon which he constituted his earlier self. And in what I take to be an ironic echo of the staked skulls round

Kurtz's hut, the Magistrate fantasizes about his catastrophic end at the hands of the barbarians: "then my head could be hacked off and tossed on to the pile of heads on the square outside still wearing a look of hurt and guilty surprise at this irruption of history into the static time of the oasis" (143). Echoes of Kafka are even clearer. If the severed skull recalls *Heart of Darkness*, in its living expression it also recalls the undead spiked head of Kafka's "In the Penal Colony." While Kafka's novels display discernible traces in Coetzee's work, it is, as both David Attwell and Patricia Merivale point out, Kafka's short stories that have demonstrated the most profound influence. The Magistrate's statement, for example, that gossip "reaches us long out of date from the capital" (2) recalls the message, long out of date, sent by the emperor in "The Great Wall of China" and Kafka's figuring of hermeneutics as a problem of distance.[9] Both *Waiting for the Barbarians* and "The Great Wall of China" follow nomadic contours. They stage, in fact, a confrontation between what Gilles Deleuze and Félix Guattari describe as smooth and striated spaces. In Kafka's story, the people from the south go to great lengths to build the great wall to keep out the people from the north. But like the parable of the river that overflows its banks, the striated space of the wall has gaps through which the nomadic people of the north might easily flow. In Coetzee's narrative, the fixed walls and gates of the fortress outpost offer no protection to the soldiers of Empire who are lured out farther and farther into the labyrinth of the desert by the barbarians' cunning use of smooth space. Kafka's "In the Penal Colony" is even more directly alluded to. The sadistic overtones of Colonel Joll "with his tapering fingernails, his mauve handkerchiefs, his slender feet in soft shoes" (5) are strongly reminiscent of Kafka's sadomasochistic Officer and his immaculate uniform laden with epaulettes. The soft touch of Joll's mauve handkerchiefs ironically references the woman's handkerchiefs tucked into the Officer's uniform, and the Magistrate imagines Colonel Joll "back in the capital he is so obviously impatient for, murmuring to his friends in theatre corridors between the acts" (5). This delicate combination of culture and cruelty is replicated in the Officer's speaking French, the metropolitan language of culture, when regarding the Harrow in this colonial theater of torture. Both texts are, after all, narratives of empire, torture, and modern bureaucratic power. So obtrusive is this intertextual resonance that in the case of "In the Penal Colony," at least, Kafka's story should be regarded as Coetzee's strong urtext.

What is more intriguing about this intertext, however, is its metaleptic relation to its precursor. While it is not possible to specify the space in which *Waiting for the Barbarians* is located, the use of muskets, smoky-lensed sunglasses, and other details establish its chronology as earlier than the machine age of the penal colony. Although "In the Penal Colony" occupies a later epistemic regime than *Waiting for the Barbarians*, and while Colonel Joll owes a good deal to Kafka's Officer, thereby acknowledging "In the Penal Colony" as its urtext, *Waiting for the Barbarians* installs itself typologically as the primitive precursor to "In the Penal Colony." In a sense, then, *Waiting for the Barbarians* is constituted on the metaleptic reversal I have already determined to be at work in Kafka's story. The word "ENEMY" written in charcoal and beaten off the backs of the barbarian prisoners prefigures Kafka's writing machine and its lethal judgments written on the backs of the condemned.

There is, however, a further interrelation between Kafka's and Coetzee's treatment of time and narrative. In his technically demanding article "Time, Tense, and Aspect in Kafka's The Burrow," written around the same time as *Waiting for the Barbarians*, Coetzee explores how Kafka tries to utilize the resources of narrative to collapse the distance separating the time of events narrated in "The Burrow" from the time of narration itself. This attempt to congeal time into a frozen or iterative present is doomed to failure. Such a project, Coetzee argues, is syntactically or formally impossible but might be driven by Kafka the individual's psychological intuition of a possible breakdown in time or his mystical projection of a timeless present. (It is precisely this experience of the breakdown of time into static segments that the film *Memento* tries to portray.) The usual experience of reading "The Burrow" is that the form of "The Burrow" comes to emulate the paranoid content of its cunning and anxious passages. However, the narrator of "The Burrow," Coetzee argues, uses the ruses of narrative to collapse the movement of time into a cyclic or iterative present in an effort to still the anxiety provoked by a crisis forced by the drifting away or loss of time. The essay closes with Coetzee contrasting "eschatological" and "historical" modes of temporality. The eschatological consists of an "everlasting present" in which the narration or the narrative utterance is contained:

> Now that the narrator has failed time and again to domesticate time using strategies of narrative (i.e., strategies belonging to historical time), his structures of sequence, of cause and effect, collapsing each time at the "decisive moment" of rupture when the past fails to run smoothly into the present, that is, now that the construct of narrative time has collapsed, there is only the time of narration left, the shining *now* within which his narrative takes place, leaving behind it a wake (a text) of failure, fantasy, sterile speculation: the ramifications of a burrow whose fatal precariousness is signaled by the whistling that comes from its point(s) of rapture.[10]

As with the narrative remainder of "The Burrow," the narrative of *Waiting for the Barbarians* also seems subtended in a continuous present. Written in the present and present perfect tenses, *Waiting for the Barbarians* positions the Magistrate within the same *now* of narration that occupies Kafka's burrow builder. The Magistrate, in fact, is caught up in a similar struggle with time. During his ritualistic interludes with the barbarian woman, the Magistrate experiences spells of time out of time. Rubbing her feet he reports: "I lose myself in the rhythm of what I am doing. I lose awareness of the girl herself. There is a space of time which is blank to me: perhaps I am not even present" (28). Or falling into oblivion during his acts of caressing, he enters "dreamless spells [that] are like death to me, or enchantment, blank, outside time" (31). These eschatological or timeless spells seem in *Waiting for the Barbarians* to belong to the same order of time as the rhythmic cycle of the seasons against which the teleological or historical time of Empire contends. Toward the end of the novel, the Magistrate asks:

> What has made it impossible for us to live in time like fish in water, like birds in air, like children? It is the fault of Empire! Empire has created the time of history. Empire has located its existence not in the smooth recurrent spinning time of the cycle of the seasons but in the jagged time of rise and fall, of beginning and end, of catastrophe. Empire dooms itself to live in history and plot against history. (133)

The smooth recurrent spinning cycles of time, nomadic time, or the eschatological eternal present contrasts with the apocalyptic time of Empire. Since the eschatological and apocalyptic are usually considered to belong to the same order of time, their opposition in *Waiting for the Barbarians* seems fraught with contradiction. But it is precisely on images of the apocalypse that Empire feeds, that Empire sustains itself against last things, endings, or the closing of time: "One thought alone preoccupies the submerged mind of Empire: how not to end, how not to die, how to prolong its era. By day it pursues its enemies. It is cunning and ruthless, it sends its bloodhounds everywhere. By night it feeds on images of disaster: the sack of cities, the rape of populations, pyramids of bones, acres of desolation" (133).

But it is not only at the diegetic or narrative level that *Waiting for the Barbarians* is divided between historical time and a timeless present. For although *Waiting for the Barbarians* is set around one of the originary moments of the modern sciences of the humanities, it might be said to encode its own future in that it also constitutes a future or late twentieth-century critique of these origins. While the Magistrate's amateur pursuits of archeology or his early attempts at cryptography stand at the modern origins of these sciences, the Magistrate also foresees the future meaning and political critique of these practices. Meeting with the barbarians, on their own ground, and engaged in an act of barter to return the barbarian woman to her own people, the Magistrate thinks to himself:

> One day my successors will be making collections of the artifacts of these people, arrowheads, carved knife-handles, wooden dishes, to display beside my birds' eggs and calligraphic riddles. And here I am patching up relations between the men of the future and the men of the past, returning, with apologies, a body we have sucked dry—a go-between, a jackal of Empire in sheep's clothing. (72)

The men of the past (literally clothed in sheepskins) will soon be devoured by the jackal of Empire. The Magistrate as proto-archeologist also fits the figure of a jackal of Empire in sheep's clothing, for the ancient relics he collects are, he knows, proleptic of the artifacts to come: artifacts of an archeology that will someday stand as record of a vanished people. The Magistrate's cryptographic efforts also undergo the scrutiny of a critique of the future. Charged by Joll with decoding the ancient slips whose purpose, Joll surmises, is to pass messages onto the barbarians, the Magistrate produces a brilliant allegory of Joll's recent acts of torture. His translation of the techniques of cryptography in the service of a confessional politics of interpretation correlates with our contemporary critique of the political complicity of the ethnographer or cryptographer.

In its simultaneous compression of the future and the past, then, *Waiting for the Barbarians* partakes of what Richard Halpern has termed "historical allegory."[11] What historical allegory means for Halpern is elucidated by T. S. Eliot's concept of what he calls the "historical sense." The historical sense, Eliot states, "involves a perception, not only of the pastness of the past, but of its presence. . . . [It is] a sense of the timeless as well as of the temporal and of the timeless and of the temporal together."[12] The presence of the past derives from Eliot's conviction that the works of tradition form an atemporal or ideal order among themselves. "If from one perspective," Halpern comments, "they are products of a specific historical era, from another they participate in a timeless structure that is eternally present. It is in this sense that Eliot's 'historical sense' may be called allegorical."[13] What gives *Waiting for the Barbarians* its quality of historical allegory is not simply its fusion of past and future, but that it places its past within a continuous present. If Coetzee's text is situated in an unidentified past, that past is continuously shifted to critique the present. It is this capacity of Coetzee's text to make the future coterminous with the present, to shift future events and bodies into a continuous present, that will be one of our concerns in this chapter.

Near the end of the novel, the Magistrate thinks of himself as "swimming with even, untiring strokes through the medium of time, a medium more inert than water, without ripples, pervasive, colourless, odourless, dry as paper" (143). That the eternal present should be considered "dry as paper" speaks perhaps to Coetzee's claim for the powers of writing to halt and hold time. When asked once what claim he would make for the capabilities of narrative, Coetzee replied: "As for writing and the experience of writing, there is a definite thrill of mastery—perhaps even omnipotence—that comes from making time bend and buckle, and generally being present when signification, or the will to signification, takes control over time. You asked about claims for the capabilities of narrative, and this is one claim I make."[14]

If *Waiting for the Barbarians* takes on the mode of historical allegory, it also takes the form of a political allegory. Indeed it is as a political allegory that it has been most commonly read and critiqued. George Steiner, for example, reads Coetzee's novel as the transposition of Hegel's political allegory of the master and the servant onto the tragic facticity of apartheid.[15] In his review for the *New Yorker*, Steiner faults Coetzee for a lack of originality; his allegory is eclipsed by the long shadow of stronger predecessors. Curiously, however, Steiner's review suffers from its own lack of originality; it succumbs, in fact, to its own allegorizing impulse. In Steiner's reading, the particularity of *Waiting for the Barbarians* is abstracted as the novel takes its generalized place as another instance of the "master servant allegory [that] dominates South African writing."[16]

It is for a lack of particularity of another sort, though, that Coetzee's text is more frequently criticized. In her piece for the *New York Review of Books* on Coetzee's *Life and Times of Michael K*, Nadine Gordimer recapitulates the criticism that *Waiting for the Barbarians* evades the political obligation of engaging the historical and material circumstances of quotidian South Africa under apartheid:

> J. M Coetzee, a writer with an imagination that soars like a lark and sees from up there like an eagle, chose allegory for his first few novels. It seemed he did so out of a kind of opposing desire to hold himself clear of events and their daily, grubby, tragic consequences in which, like everybody else living in South Africa, he is up to the neck, and about which he had a inner compulsion to write. So here was allegory as stately fastidiousness; or a state of shock. He was able to deal with the horror he saw written on the sun only—if brilliantly—if this were projected into another time and plane. His *Waiting for the Barbarians* was the North Pole to which the agitprop of agonized black writers (and some white ones hitching a ride to the bookmart on the armored car) was the South Pole; a world to be dealt with lies in between.[17]

Gordimer's critique of Coetzee's abstracting his experience, of elevating it out of the muck of real history and onto the shining plane of allegory, was echoed by numerous critics for whom only an instrumental realism functioned as the appropriate mode for a revolutionary South African writing. The "horror written on the sun," when looked at through the eyes of allegory, only produced historical blind spots. Throughout the 1980s Coetzee was increasingly accused of a "dehistoricization" of the real. Paul Rich, for example, maintains that Coetzee's allegory of empire in *Waiting for the Barbarians* is devoid of "any understanding of the historical forces that produce actual imperial systems at particular phases of history."[18] The novel illustrates that "literary postmodernism in a postcolonial context as South Africa . . . is a moral dead end."[19] For Abdul JanMohamed, *Waiting for the*

The Body in Ruins

Barbarians' Manichean allegory epitomizes the "dehistoricising, desocializing tendency of colonialist fiction."[20] The text's "studied refusal to accept historical responsibility" renders it part of the mystificatory apparatus of imperialism.[21]

Coetzee's use of allegory in relation to the material history of South Africa has not, however, been universally condemned. In his essay "The Allegorical Text and History: J. M. Coetzee's *Waiting for the Barbarians*," Jean-Philippe Wade argues: "While the allegoric form acts as a critique of 'classic realist' writing, this does not signal the text's refusal of 'history'. Rather, it affirms its location as a signifying 'interpretation' of the real that recognizes its discursive specificity."[22] Situating Coetzee's allegory within recent South African history, Wade detects in Coetzee's novel an examination of the apartheid state's turn to the military option in the wake of the 1976 Soweto Uprising. Wade's essay, then, is exemplary of the emergence of a countervailing line of criticism that, cognizant of the poststructuralist reinterpretation of the function of allegory, is concerned to reevaluate *Waiting for the Barbarians*' allegorical relationship to the material history of apartheid. In its examination of a set of linkages between Coetzee's allegory and the future tortured bodies of apartheid, my chapter seeks to engage and extend this line. This chapter also marks a turn in my book. Whereas in the first two chapters my focus was on the power of a text to capture or incorporate catastrophic bodies into its field of reception, I now examine ways in which Coetzee's narrative offers a body and mode of writing that ultimately resists the apocalyptic powers of inscription and incorporation.

Countering the prescriptive demands of the Lukacsian novel of critical realism and the injunction to realist representation in South African fiction, Coetzee has claimed that the novel is now "after bigger game than that."[23] In the next section we shall examine the full consequence of what the pursuit of bigger game might entail.

TORTURE AND ALLEGORY

I want now to return to Coetzee's essay "Into the Dark Chamber: The Writer and the South African State," in relation to the historical context of South Africa. Here Coetzee poses the question of why so many South African writers (including himself) have been drawn to the "dark fascination" exerted by the torture chamber. He offers two reasons. The first is that the torture room reduces to its bare essentials relations between the authoritarian state and its victims. In doing so, it provides a powerful metaphor in the writer's arsenal. The second reason is subtler. The writer, Coetzee asserts, is a person standing outside a dark door waiting to enter but is barred from the dark room. He or she must imagine what takes place on the other side of the door. Precisely that tension becomes the source of his or her art. Forbidden to see into the room, the writer must create a representation of the prohibited scene. The torturer and the novelist share in common, then, the laying bare of the extremities of human experience. The novelist thus faces the danger of following the state, "of making its vile mysteries the occasion of fantasy."[24] Coetzee argues that, "for the writer, the deeper problem is *not* to allow himself to be impaled on the dilemma proposed by the state, namely, either to ignore its obscenities or else produce representations of them."[25] Ignoring the responsibility of representing torture, of leaving it in the dark chamber, merely facilitates the torturer's task of destroying all aspects of resistance; succumbing to a dark and voluptuous description risks an imaginative complicity or vicarious participation in the state's obscenities. Even worse, Coetzee laments, the writer risks drawing the population into acquiescence in the regime's disciplinary methods, of paralyzing the people with the spectacle of torture. The burden the writer faces is how to present torture on his or her own terms and how not to play into the traps set for representation by the state.

Coetzee's brief statement, in this essay, that *Waiting for the Barbarians* is "about the impact of the torture chamber on the life of a man of conscience" might induce us to seek in the novel a strategy for the confrontation of this problem.[26] In her piece "Torture and the Novel: J. M. Coetzee's *Waiting for the Barbarians*," Susan Van Zanten Gallagher argues, in fact, that Coetzee's novel "embodies his fictional solutions" to this dilemma. Gallagher, as others before her have done, points to Coetzee's poststructuralist repertoire of gaps, antonymic articulations, absences, and uncertainties as disrupting any fixed picture of torture. "Simultaneously," she asserts, "in his allusions to uncentered language and the death of the metaphysics of presence, Coetzee also points to the moral vacuum that allows torture to exist in the contemporary world."[27] But this, it seems to me, provides us with a rather generalized solution to the problems that beset the representation of torture. Coetzee's allusions to the death of the metaphysics of presence, she claims, simultaneously disrupt the articulation of torture and facilitate its existence in the contemporary world. (One notes that the metaphysics of presence, so worshiped during the Inquisition, hardly functioned as an apotropaic device against torture.) And further, it is, in fact, Coetzee's use of allegory as a transcendental signifier that Gallagher presents as the solution to Coetzee's problematic:

> The effect of this time displacement is to reveal truths about any oppressive society, any society that employs torture as a technique. By using this kind of setting, Coetzee solves his first moral dilemma. He does not ignore the obscene acts performed by the government under the guise of national security, yet neither does he produce representational depictions of these acts. . . . He does not identify the particular atrocities performed by the South African security police in Vorster Square . . . but nonetheless the maiming of the Barbarian woman and the Magistrate's own ill-treatment ineluctably point to the treatment of political prisoners in South Africa. In suggesting universal truths about torture and oppression, Coetzee also obliquely condemns his own country.[28]

In having Coetzee insist both on a deconstructive critique of presence and on the powers of transcendental or universal signification, Gallagher has recourse to a rather contradictory approach to the dilemma of a mode of representation that resists the lure of totalitarian torture. Although it lacks the specificity required more fully to engage the political use of allegory in Coetzee's text, Gallagher's piece does not simply fall into this difficulty unprompted. Her analysis is a symptom of the simultaneous elusion and precision of Coetzee's allegory. Coetzee himself has insisted on its unlocatable aspect: "[T]here is nothing about blackness or whiteness in *Waiting for the Barbarians*. The Magistrate and girl could as well be Russian and Kirgi, or Han and Mongol, or Turk and Arab, or Arab and Berber."[29] But at the same time, he has also acknowledged the effect that torture in South Africa has exerted upon him as a writer and he has, as we have seen, situated *Waiting for the Barbarians* in the context of a piece on the moral difficulties of representing torture in South Africa.

The specific history of the death and torture of Steven Biko has, in fact, become very much part of the critical reception of Coetzee's novel. Dominic Head, for example, observes "international concern for human rights was focused on the South African regime following the Soweto riots in 1976–7, and the death of Steve Biko in 1977. This is the immediate resonance of the torture scenes in the novel."[30] David Atwell remarks that "Biko's death in 1977 highlighted the role of torture and detention in the context of a security-dominated state, and the novel's response to these developments is in fact remarkably direct given Coetzee's nonreferential commitments."[31] So direct, in fact, that Jean-Philippe Wade has argued that the novel offers strong allusions to the inquest held after Biko's death: "At the Biko inquest," he reports, "the security police put forward the theory that Biko had sustained those injuries that would lead to his death during 'a violent struggle' in which he had hit his head against the wall."[32] The scuffle had irrupted, according to the security police, after Biko had been confronted with proof of his subversive activities. Major Harold Snyman describes the scene as follows: "I confronted him with these facts. He jumped up immediately like a man possessed. I ascribe that to the revelations that I made to

The Body in Ruins

him."[33] Wade compares this account with the account given by Joll's security police after the killing of an old barbarian man at the beginning of the novel: "During the course of the interrogation contradictions became apparent in the prisoner's testimony. Confronted with these contradictions, the prisoner became enraged and attacked the investigating officer. A scuffle ensued during which the prisoner fell heavily against the wall. Efforts to revive him were unsuccessful" (6).

The unmistakable correspondence between the content of the two accounts, combined with Coetzee's ironic iteration of the transparent semiotics of the official cover-up, demonstrate that it is not by accident that the event of Biko's torture and the speech act of governmental censorship become part of the critical reception of Coetzee's text. The scene of Biko's torture is not simply retrospectively read into the textual space of *Waiting for the Barbarians*. Rather, *Waiting for the Barbarians*, as the title reflexively notifies us, has already specified this reception. The barbarians' or Biko's tortures, the text knows in advance, will soon show up. Far from disarming the performative spectacle of South African torture, Coetzee's text accrues to itself a spectacular power. The tortured body, then, seems to set this trap for Coetzee's allegory. In order for his allegory to contest the spectacle of torture in South Africa, it must bear signifiers (tortured bodies) that identify or correspond to this spectacle. Yet in deploying these signifiers, his allegory runs the risk of being consumed or captured by the tortured body and conjoining itself to its exorbitant horror. The tortured body poses the danger of turning *Waiting for the Barbarians*' depiction of torture against itself and in the service of the apartheid state's regime of terror.

The novel becomes even further intertwined with the future history of torture in South Africa, even accruing to itself the aura of the prophetic in its unveiling of the secrets of state torture that were yet to be revealed. For it is not only Biko's mutilated body but also other scenes of torture and testimony that get incorporated into the moral orbit of the text's later reception. After looking into the shroud into which the tortured body of the old barbarian was sown, the Magistrate remonstrates to himself: "I know somewhat too much; and from this knowledge, once one has been infected, there seems to be no recovering. I ought never to have taken my lantern to see what was going on. . . . On the other hand, there was no way, once I had picked up the lantern, for me to put it down again. The knot loops in on itself; I cannot find the end" (21). This trope of the infectious nature of the act of witnessing torture was to become an inevitable part of the future national narrative of the new South Africa. In *Country of My Skull*, Antjie Krog's excruciating record and commentary on the South African Truth and Reconciliation hearings, she writes of the witnessing of torture: "the arteries of our past bleed their own peculiar rhythm, tone, and image. One cannot get rid of it. Ever."[34] "You will experience the same symptoms as the victims. You will find yourself powerless—without help, without words," one of the TRC counselors tells her. "I am shocked," Krog tells us, "to be a textbook case within a mere ten days."[35] *Waiting for the Barbarians* is caught in the same loop as Krog and the Magistrate; there is no entry into the forbidden knowledge of torture without the risk of replicating its structure. The knot loops in upon itself.

After his torture at the hands of Warrant Officer Mandel, the Magistrate wants some knowledge of his torturer: "I am terrified of you, I need not tell you that, I am sure you are aware of it" (126), he tells Mandel. "I am only trying to understand." The Magistrate pleads, "Trying to understand the zone in which you live. I am trying to imagine how you breathe and eat and live from day to day. But I cannot" (126). This scene of a desire for some form of compensatory knowledge in the face of the incomprehension of the tortured is replicated in *Country of My Skull*: "Never before had the double-edged relationship between the torturer and the tortured been depicted as graphically as it was that week . . . in the stuffy hall of the Truth Commission in Cape Town."[36] In what ought to be a reversal of the scene of interrogation and confession, infamous police captain Jeffery Benzien comes face to face with those he tortured. As a member of the

The Body in Ruins

new parliament, Tony Yengeni's voice has become recognizable for its strong tone of confidence. Facing Benzein this confidence is gone. His voice sounds choked. He is about to talk of a method of torture known as the "wet bag." A plastic bag doused in water is used to suffocate the victim. "Instead of seizing the moment to get back at Benzien," Krog reports: "Yengeni wants to know the man. 'What kind of man . . . uhm . . . that uses a method like this one with the wet bag to people . . . to other human beings . . . repeatedly . . .and listening to those moans and cries and groans . . . and taking each of those people very near to their deaths . . . what kind of man are you . . . I'm talking now about the man behind the wet bag.'"[37] Even in this scene of public accusation and confession, the structural relationship between torturer and tortured subtly duplicates itself. "A torturer's success depends on his intimate knowledge of the human psyche," Krog remarks. "Benzien is a connoisseur. Within the first few minutes, he manages to manipulate most of his victims back into the roles of their previous relationship—where he has the power and they the fragility."[38]

Is Coetzee's text not threatened by the same powers of reversal? Like the torturer, the writer faces the task of probing the extremity of human experience. Both share the secret knowledge of the intimate bond between tortured and torturer. Even as it takes on the ethical injunction of exposing torture, of bathing the dark chamber in white light, does Coetzee's text not risk reduplicating the structural relation between torturer and tortured? Might not the contest between Joll and the Magistrate, then, stand as Coetzee's allegory of the contest for his text's destiny or reception? Here, to follow the schema of my previous analysis, Joll would represent the apocalyptic trajectory and will to power over South Africa's tortured bodies and the Magistrate the countervailing, antiapocalyptic will to ethical critique. Joll and the Magistrate occupy the same positions as Kurtz and Marlow or the Officer and the Explorer, and yet in *Waiting for the Barbarians* the dialectical opposition between these two trajectories threatens to collapse. In both *Heart of Darkness* and "In the Penal Colony,"

Marlow and the Explorer face the danger of being lured over to the side of their counterparts. Marlow just resists falling into Kurtz's extremity and the Explorer flees the penal colony to avoid giving sanction to the graphic apparatus of spectacular execution. Even if, as I have tried to demonstrate, their texts engage the risk of a future apocalyptic literalization, Conrad and Kafka stage Marlow and the Explorer as figures of compromised opposition.

For Coetzee, the forces that hold open this dialectical split threaten to converge in a deeper complicity. Thinking back over the course of Joll's arrival, the Magistrate arrives at a bleak point of juncture with his double: "For I was not, as I liked to think, the indulgent pleasure-loving opposite of the cold rigid Colonel. I was the lie that Empire tells itself when times are easy, he the truth that Empire tells when harsh winds blow. Two sides of imperial rule, no more, no less" (135). The apparent antithesis of "the lie Empire tells itself when times are easy" and "the truth Empire tells itself when harsh winds blow" conceals an equivalence that is confirmed by the fluid parataxis of "no more, no less." Earlier the Magistrate had discerned that "an interrogator can wear two masks, speak with two voices, one harsh, one seductive" (7). Later he comes to understand that the "distance between [himself] and her torturers is negligible" (27); his erotic ministrations are simply the other side of the dialectic of torture. "The girl lies in my bed, but there is no good reason why it should be a bed. I behave in some ways like a lover—I undress her, I bathe her, I stroke her, I sleep beside her—but I might equally tie her to a chair and beat her, it would be no less intimate" (43). His correlation with Joll is sealed for the Magistrate, when after completion of a sexual act with the barbarian woman, he beholds himself "in the image of a face masked by two black glassy insect eyes from which there comes no reciprocal gaze but only my doubled image cast back at me" (44).

The Magistrate, himself the figure of liberal conscience, though aptly also of the failed writer, is emblematic of the dangers of the trap of collusion facing the writer of torture. The anachronism of the regime of the panopticon, alluded to in the glassy mirror of Joll's black lenses, is also indicative of the mirroring power of Coetzee's historical allegory. For Coetzee's text does not somehow bear an occult or prophetic relation to the future revelations of torture in South Africa. Its relation to the future history of torture in South Africa is not even properly uncanny since torture in South Africa, although buried, was never forgotten. *Waiting for the Barbarians*, rather, absorbs and reflects these revelations through the timeless shifting of its allegorical mirror.

In a piece entitled "The Novel Today," Coetzee took on the intractable dispute in apartheid South Africa between the novel and the demands of historical discourse: "In times of intense ideological pressure like the present, when the space in which the novel and history normally coexist like two cows on the same pasture, each minding its own business, is squeezed almost to nothing, the novel, it seems to me, has only two options: supplementarity or rivalry."[39] Supplementing historical discourse would involve the novel in providing the reader with vicarious experiences of living in particular historical times and of the contending historical pressures at work on characters located in those historical times. Rivalry with historical discourse, by contrast, amounts to "a novel that operates in terms of its own procedures and issues in its own conclusions, not one that operates in terms of the procedures of history and eventuates in conclusions that are checkable by history." A novel not subjected in advance to a delimited representational mode or the procedures of history would "evolv[e] its own paradigms and myths, in the process (and here is the point at which true rivalry, even enmity, perhaps enters the picture) perhaps going so far as to show up the mythic status of history—in other words, demythologizing history."[40] Coetzee's argument is not one of submitting the modalities of historical representation to the scrutiny of the literary or of attempting to dissolve the materiality of history into the efflux of an all-encompassing textuality. His claim is rather that history itself embodies codes of representation and that these should not be taken for naked or unmediated reality. Further, the "authority of history lies simply in the consensus it commands" and that even in a South Africa governed by the laws of apartheid, history should not be elevated to a "master-form of discourse."[41] The novel, in Coetzee's estimation, must resist being "colonized" by the discourse of history.

The novel, then, evolves its own strategies and maneuvers, its own codes of contention, but Coetzee's text is confronted by more than the demands of a realist instrumentalism or the claim to primacy of historical discourse; it is menaced by the prospective peril of being overcoded by the tortured body of history itself. In a text as self-reflexively canny about the traps set for representation by the problem of torture as *Waiting for the Barbarians*, what strategies of resistance might we detect in that work to counteract its being appropriated by the authoritarian spectacle of the tortured body? How might Coetzee's text be said to crack its allegorical mirror that functions to subject the future to its own panoptic regime of reflection? In the next section I will attempt an answer these questions by offering a reading of *Waiting for the Barbarians* that turns torture against itself.

THE BODY IN RUINS

An avatar of the Inquisition, Joll conceives of himself as an inexorable searcher after the truth. When asked by the Magistrate how he knows when a tortured prisoner is telling the truth, Joll answers, "There is a certain tone . . . a certain tone enters the voice of a man who is telling the truth" (5). Joll is certain of the tone of truth—for the tone of truth is not conveyed by the prisoner but *enters* ineluctably at the point of breaking. Upon, ironically, inferring that Joll must have a remarkably acute ear, perfectly attuned to the tone of the truth, the Magistrate then asks him if he can pick up this tone in quotidian speech. "No, you misunderstand me," Joll answers. "I am speaking only of a special situation now, I am speaking of a situation in which I am probing for the truth, in which I have to exert pressure to find it. First I get lies, you see—this is what happens—first lies, then pressure, then more lies, then more pressure, then the break, then more pressure, then the truth. That is how you get the truth" (5). The tone of truth does not register subtle inflections but sounds a uniform note. Trying to awaken a moment of conscience in the Colonel, the Magistrate has pressed him with regard to the moral responsibility of the torturer. What if the prisoner is telling the truth? What if he has divulged everything or had nothing to divulge in the first place? "Imagine," the Magistrate pleads, "to be prepared to yield, to yield, to have nothing more to yield, to be broken, yet to be pressed to yield more!" (5). How can the torturer ever be sure that the prisoner is telling the truth? Picking up on the rhetorical rhythm of the Magistrate's plea, Joll answers with his own percussive delineation of the "set procedures" (4) of torture, his delineation of the formula by which the truth is extracted. The percussive form of his answer is meant to drum out any question of the Magistrate's doubt. "Pain is truth; all else is subject to doubt" (5) is the message the Magistrate takes away from his conversation with Colonel Joll.

Joll's protocols for eliciting the truth, or what we might call a grammar of torture, coincide with Elaine Scarry's analysis of what she calls the "deconstruction" of the victim's voice.[42] Under the pressure of extreme pain the victim's body is made unremittingly present to itself. The victim's voice (or consciousness) is consumed or, as Scarry says is "unmade," by the presence of this pain, which constitutes a reality that is anterior to language. The sheer phenomenological experience of the victim's body in pain is translated or conducted into the reality of the torturer's truth. But if the torturer's truth is tautological, it is also paradoxical, for "[t]he goal of the torturer is to make the one, the body crushingly *present* by destroying it, and to make the other, the voice, *absent* by destroying it. It is in part this combination that makes torture, like any experience of great physical pain, mimetic of death; for in death the body is emphatically present while the more elusive part represented by the voice is so alarmingly absent that heavens are created to explain its whereabouts."[43] For Scarry, as for Joll, the crushing of the body amounts to the destruction of the voice as consciousness and the issuing forth of the voice as the body in pain or the tone of truth. Pain registers truth as the metaphysics of presence.

As Michael Valdez Moses points out, Empire's use of torture is caught in Heidegger's hermeneutic circle: for the truths Empire extracts from the barbarian body are the very truths it has projected on to it.[44] This is made explicit in a scene where a number of barbarian captives are tied to poles by means of loops of wire that are threaded through their mouths and are made to kneel before Colonel Joll. Standing at the edge of a throng of townspeople who have gathered to view the spectacle, the Magistrate stares at Joll:

> The Colonel steps forward. Stooping over each prisoner in turn he rubs a handful of dust onto his naked back and writes a word with a stick of charcoal. I read the words upside down: *ENEMY . . . ENEMY . . . ENEMY . . . ENEMY*. He steps back and folds his hands. At a distance of no more than twenty paces he and I contemplate one another.
>
> Then the beating begins. The soldiers use the stout green cane staves. . . . The black charcoal and ochre dust begin to run with sweat and blood. The game, I see, is to beat them till their backs are washed clean. (105)

Since the barbarians cannot read the foreign signs inscribed on their bodies the spectacle of punishment puts imperial power on display. The inscription and erasure of the sign *ENEMY* functions, in fact, as a kind of double performative. The sign *ENEMY* linguistically stages the barbarians as enemy while the erasure or beating off of the sign functions to expunge the signifying space between sign and referent, rending the barbarian body, literally rendering it as the material sign "ENEMY" (105). Coetzee's use of the word "enemy" here might well echo and register Marlow's critique in *Heart of Darkness* of the way in which the Africans were also performatively named "enemies" and those enslaved called "criminals," while the beheaded corpses were ironically marked as those of "rebels": "Rebels! What would be the next definition I was to hear. There had been enemies, criminals, workers—and these were—rebels."[45]

The Body in Ruins

While the Magistrate is able to read the semiotics of spectacular punishment and to grasp that Empire is engaged in its exhilarated projection and reading of its own signs, his own intimate relation to the marks of torture remains enigmatic to him. What has stirred both his hermeneutical and erotic desire, he finds, are the marks the woman's torturers have engraved on her body. "It has been growing more and more clear to me," he tells us, "that until the marks on this girl's body are deciphered and understood I cannot let go of her" (31). Obscurely, the Magistrate's cryptographic desire to decipher the ancient barbarian slips is infiltrated by his desire to decode the secret script her body bears. It is not only that the marks, like the archeological slips, should be deciphered as some form of hieratic hieroglyph; the Magistrate will remain captivated until the relation between the origin of his erotic desire and these marks is understood. In an effort to discern the difference the marks of torture have made, the Magistrate tries to recover his memory of her, unmarked by the instruments of torture. He finds, however, that, try, as he will, he cannot recover his memory of her unmarked form. Her pristine form remains blank to him. Later, in the desert, after consummating intercourse with the barbarian woman for the first time, the origins of his desire as obscure as ever, the Magistrate contemplates the generation of his desire in relation to the opposition of marked and unmarked:

> Except that it has not escaped me that in bed in the dark the marks her torturers have left upon her, the twisted feet, the half-blind eyes, are easily forgotten. Is it then the case that it is the whole woman I want, that my pleasure in her is spoiled until these marks on her are erased and she is restored to herself; or is it the case (I am not stupid, let me say these things) that it is the marks on her which drew me to her but which, to my disappointment, I find, do not go deep enough? Too much or too little: is it she I want or the traces of a history her body bears? (64)

Unable to locate the origin of his desire, the Magistrate oscillates between two antonymic and impossible poles: his will to undo the work of torture and restore the barbarian body to a pristine plenitude or to experience the deeper traces of the imprint of Empire. Curious that he can entertain such antonymic articulations of his desire, the Magistrate wonders if "perhaps whatever can be articulated is falsely put. . . . Or perhaps it is the case that only that which has not been articulated has to be lived through" (64, 65). With his thought of a somatic experience anterior to articulation, the Magistrate gestures toward a divorce of the fusion of body and sign that Empire is founded on. In his consideration of a realm of disarticulation between body and sign, the Magistrate moves toward the deconstruction of Empire's program of inflicting on the body the sign of truth. The body that is anterior to discourse, the body qua body, will remain impervious to Empire's projection of the body into the realm of signs. But the Magistrate's thought of a body that is, as Coetzee puts it elsewhere, its own sign or that remains unassimilable to the sign of Empire cannot be thought without itself suffering articulation or capture by language.[46] The projection of Empire's signs onto the subaltern body threatens to overpower such subtle disruptions.

The Magistrate's effort to think of the body in a realm that evades articulation reaches this impasse that has also engaged Judith Butler. As we saw in the introduction, Butler tempers the claims of the strong version of constructivism or the notion that the body is constructed by language. She proposes that while the body is always mediated or grasped within a set of linguistic coordinates this does not mean that the body is nothing other than the language by which it is known. Some bodily remainder, some materiality of the body, occupies an ontology that escapes linguistic determination, she writes:

> Although the body depends on language to be known, the body also exceeds every possible linguistic effort of capture. It would be tempting to conclude that this means that the body exists outside of language, that it has an ontology separable from a linguistic one, and that we might be able to describe this separable ontology. But this is where I would

> hesitate, perhaps permanently, for as we begin that description of what is outside of language, the chiasm reappears: we have already contaminated, though not contained, the very body we seek to establish in its ontological purity. The body escapes its linguistic grasp, but so too does it escape the subsequent effort to determine ontologically that very escape. The very description of the extralinguistic body allegorizes the problem of the chiasmic relation between language and body and so fails to supply the distinction it seeks to articulate.[47]

If the body always presents language with its inassimilable other, and if language always fails to provide a perfect model of adequation, the body is also known by way of language and as it passes into linguistic referentiality is always susceptible to being governed by the coordinates of language.

Biko's tortured body, for example, was always in the process of being allegorized by the medical discourse of the inquest. In her examination of medical reports of the inquest, Rebecca Saunders concludes that "the reading of Biko as allegorical sign extended, for example, to his physical symptoms, which were not read as literal signs of injury resulting from torture, but as allegorical signs of 'shamming.'"[48] Biko's symptoms were constantly interpreted by his torturers under the sign of deviousness or dissimulation. In explaining his response to Biko's slurred speech (the result of head injuries inflicted during interrogation) one of his torturers claimed: "I spoke to Biko as before and he mumbled incoherently. At this stage I was honestly of the opinion that Biko was playing the fool with us as neither the district surgeon nor I could detect any scars or signs of illness."[49] Yet even somatic signs of illness, such as hyperventilation, were interpreted as "deliberately breathing in an unnatural way" or Biko's unconsciousness as "a technique of putting up a veil between himself and interrogators."[50] Biko's subsequent wounds and scars were similarly placed under the allegorical sign of "scuffle." It is, in fact, exactly this allegorical body that gets entered into the textual field of *Waiting for the Barbarians*. Or to put it another way, it is precisely because Biko's body is already allegorized that it can be so readily assimilated into Coetzee's text.

What terms for differentiation does Coetzee offer us, then, between the allegorization of Biko's body under the sign of the apartheid narrative and his own Manichean allegory? One useful approach to this question is by way of Michael Hardt and Antonio Negri's analysis of the difference between modern and postmodern forms of racism in *Empire*. For Hardt and Negri modern racism is founded on the theory of immutable biological differences or racial markers that demarcate a boundary of otherness. The exclusionary practices of colonialism or the neocolonialism of apartheid are indicative of a modern as opposed to a postmodern paradigm of racism. The postmodern form of racism relies on the force of cultural difference to maintain a state of social separation: "In other words, racial hierarchy is viewed not as a cause but as an effect of social circumstances."[51] Situating apartheid within a modernist register has important implications for grasping the way in which apartheid allegorizes the black body. Since Biko's body, for example, is already branded or allegorized as other or duplicitous by the apartheid narrative, it is especially susceptible to the deployment of a modernist hermeneutics of ambiguous surface that discloses an undergirding depth. The cracked surface of the tortured body, as the medical narrative of Biko's inquest makes clear, is interpreted by Biko's interrogators as giving off an ambiguous set of signs. It is into the underlying depth of the body that the torturer must go to get beyond the signs of shamming.

Revealingly, it is by way of the tortured body of the old barbarian man, and not by way of the tortured body of the barbarian woman, that Biko's body is entered into Coetzee's allegory. Cutting open the shroud into which the old man has been sewn, the Magistrate examines the tortured head: "The gray beard is caked with blood. The lips are crushed and drawn back, the teeth are broken. One eye is rolled back, the other eye-socket is a bloody hole. 'Close it up,' I say. The guard bunches the opening together. It falls open. 'They say that he hit his head on the wall. What do

The Body in Ruins

you think?' He looks at me warily" (7). Behind the outer layer of the beard caked with blood the tortured face divulges the crushed organs of a body that has depth. The drawn back lips reveal broken teeth, the eye socket a bloody hole. The solidity of this body pushes up against the veil of its shroud. The very depth of this body's damage renders the explanation of the damage allegorical.

The barbarian woman, by contrast, is unreadable; she provides no means of entry for the Magistrate, presenting an impenetrable surface that is undecidable as opposed to ambiguous: "But with this woman it is as if there is no interior, only a surface across which I hunt back and forth seeking entry. Is this how her torturers felt hunting their secret, whatever they thought it was? For the first time I feel a dry pity for them: how natural a mistake to believe that you can burn or tear or hack your way into the secret body of the other!" (43). The torturers' efforts of cutting into the interior or secret depth of the barbarian woman's body, and of inscribing that interior with the sovereign law of torture, are met by the depthless surface on which signs will not fix in any legible or even ambiguous way. Coetzee's barbarian woman counters apartheid's allegorizing of the body as modernist—constituting a depth into which its torturers can hack and a surface open to the ambiguities of interpretation—with a postmodern smoothness of depthless surface. If her undecidable markings evade the striating powers of imperialist narrative, it remains an open question as to whether she also eludes the sovereignty of the decentered modalities of postmodern empire.

But for the moment it is important to relate *Waiting for the Barbarians* itself to Hardt and Negri's concept of *"Empire."* (I will use italics to denominate this concept of "empire.") According to Hardt and Negri, traditional forms of empire have declined and have been replaced by an emergent Empire. This form of *Empire* does not bear resemblance to the territorial empires of Rome or China, or the empire represented in *Waiting for the Barbarians* itself. Contemporary *Empire* is characterized by a fundamental lack of territorial boundaries; it "encompasses a spatial totality," effectively distributes power through networks, and "creates the very world it inhabits."[52] What links *Empire* to *Waiting for the Barbarians*, then, is the form and function of *Waiting for the Barbarians* as historical allegory. Hardt and Negri stipulate that "the concept of *Empire* presents itself not as a historical regime originating in conquest, but rather as an order that effectively suspends history and thereby fixes the existing state of affairs for eternity. From the perspective of *Empire*, this is the way things will always be and the way they were always meant to be."[53] We have arrived, it seems, at a complex and contradictory point of intersection: the static or smooth rhythmic time of the cycle within *Waiting for the Barbarians* itself runs counter to the jagged historically driven time of Empire. Yet the eternal present, or mirroring time of *Waiting for the Barbarians* as historical allegory, functions like *Empire* to suspend the movement of history and fix the events of time in the frozen orbit of its timeless allegory. Is *Waiting for the Barbarians* doomed then to collapse into its own contradiction, or is there some way in which the defeat of the Empire within the text might gesture toward the deconstruction of *Waiting for the Barbarians* as *Empire*?

I might begin by pointing out that although contemporary *Empire* and the territorial Empire of *Waiting for the Barbarians* function by way of very different modalities, they both aspire to reach the end of history. In locating its existence in the "jagged time of rise and fall, of beginning and end, of catastrophe," Empire pursues the Hegelian dialectic, driving toward the telos of the end of history. "Empire," Coetzee's Magistrate tells us, "dooms itself to live in history and plot against history" (133). *Empire*, though antiteleological, operates from the same Hegelian end point. *Empire*, according to Hardt and Negri, "presents its rule not as a transitory moment in history, but as a regime with no temporal boundaries and in this sense outside of history or at the end of history."[54] One thought preoccupies both Empires: how to extend the plenitude of existence on the other side of the end of history.

As opposed to the static time of Empire, it is possible, I think, to detect in *Waiting for the Barbarians* the difference of a subtle

The Body in Ruins 153

flow of time within the timelessness of the eternal present. In his ritualistic oiling of the barbarian woman, the Magistrate experiences a space of time that is blank to him. Unable to enter her, he experiences, instead, a kind of cosmological diffusion and eddying of the mass of their bodies: "These bodies of hers and mine are diffuse, gaseous, centreless, at one moment spinning about a vortex here, at another curdling, thickening elsewhere; but often also flat, blank" (34). This sense of galactic fusion and dissolution is contrasted with the Magistrate's regaining of his sexual powers and his penetrative entering of a young prostitute: "I felt again the power of the old sensual enchantment, swam out into her body and was transported to the old limits of pleasure. So I thought: 'It is nothing but a matter of age, of cycles of desire and apathy in a body that is slowly cooling and dying'" (46). The Magistrate links the sexual cycle, of rise and fall, of arousal and the fading of desire, to entropy and the frozen time of heat death. Like the teleological time of Empire whose terminus is the end of history, the sexual cycle also runs down to a phase of frozen stasis. (We might also catch here an echo of the heat death of the universe with which *Heart of Darkness* opens.)

The Magistrate's figuring of a gaseous cosmological body seems to indicate orders of emergence and an infusion of swirling energy that runs counter to the frozen time of heat death. While out hunting, in the time between his two meditations on the fusion of bodies, the Magistrate experiences an epiphany that conjoins the cosmic, the body, and the freezing of time. Holding a ram in the sights of his gun, the Magistrate stares at the ram gazing back at him: "With the buck before me suspended in immobility, there seems to be time for all things . . . the sense that this has become no longer a morning's hunting but an occasion on which either the proud ram bleeds to death on the ice or the old hunter misses his aim; that for the duration of this frozen moment the stars are locked in a configuration in which events are not themselves but stand for other things " (39–40). Time is frozen, but for the *duration* of this frozen moment, in the time within timelessness, events stand not for themselves but as allegories of other things. The frozen time of the Magistrate's allegory of the hunter and the ram serves not to bind signs to bodies but to sever events from themselves, and since events do not stand for themselves, or coincide with themselves, they are set apart by the differential spacing of time.

By means of its powers of doubling or reduplication and since the allegorical sign always refers to a previous or anterior sign, allegory is invested in what Paul de Man refers to as the "rhetoric of temporality." "The meaning constituted by the allegorical sign," de Man tells us, "can then consist only in the *repetition* . . . of a previous sign with which it can never coincide, since it is the essence of this sign to be pure anteriority."[55] In this unbridgeable distance in terms of its relation to its own origin, de Man says, "the prevalence of allegory always corresponds to the unveiling of an authentically temporal destiny. This unveiling takes place in a subject that has sought refuge against the impact of time in the natural world to which, in truth it bears no resemblance."[56] As Teresa Dovey has pointed out, de Man's critique of a subject who takes refuge against the impact of time by seeking transcendence in the natural cycles of time can be brought to bear on the Magistrate, who reflects that "I wanted to live outside of history. I wanted to live outside the history that Empire imposes on its subjects, even its lost subjects."[57] The Magistrate laments Empire's imposition of historical consciousness and the impossibility of living in the "smooth recurrent spinning time of the cycle of the seasons" (133), or time experienced as organic unity.

In its concern with temporality and the failure of the allegorical sign to coincide with its referent, de Man's reading of allegory exhibits close affinities with Walter Benjamin's reading of allegory as ruin:

> The word 'history' stands written on the countenance of nature in the character of transience. The allegorical physiognomy of the nature-history, which is put on stage in the *Trauerspiel*, is present in reality in the form of the ruin. In the ruin history has physically merged into the setting. And in this guise history does not assume the form of the

The Body in Ruins

process of an eternal life so much as that of irresistible decay.... Allegories are, in the realm of thoughts, what ruins are in the realm of things.[58]

Benjamin's figuration of history as a ruin runs counter to Hegel's notion of history's progress toward its apotheosis as absolute spirit: the ruin displays a retrograde movement of fragmentation and decay that opposes the forward teleology of history's movement toward its fulfillment as immanent meaning. Since allegory fragments the sign by dividing it from its referent, with which it will not precisely coincide, allegory bears, in the realm of signs or thoughts, an equivalence to ruin in its fragmentary relation to the realm of things. But what precisely does Benjamin mean by an "allegorical physiognomy that is present in reality in the form of a ruin"? J. Hillis Miller provides us with an incisive exegesis:

> History is in allegory, says Benjamin, written on nature in the characters of transience. History is in the *Trauerspiel* present in nature as script (*als Schrift*). This gives nature an "allegorical physiognomy" (*allegorishe Physiognomie*), as though it were a human face or body inscribed with the signs of a person's character. In Benjamin's formulations emerges the deep necessity for allegories to take the form of personification, *prosopopeia*, the giving of a human mask and a voice to what is dead or inanimate. The essence of allegory is the way in which this process exposes itself as an unsuccessful projection. In allegory, writing and personification reveal, bring out into the open as *Scheinen*, the eternal disjunction between the inscribed sign and its material embodiment. It is writing, the characters written on nature as features are written on a face, which devastates it. In this disjunction a disarticulation in time appears as a disarticulation in space.... The ruin alludes backward in time to the former glory of the building and so ruins that glory metaleptically in its difference from it. In allegory naked matter shines through. It shines through as the failure of the idea to transform nature or thought. In this sense allegories are, in the realm of thought what ruins are in the realm of things.[59]

Hillis Miller's exegesis will soon prove useful in helping us grasp the relation among ruin, inscription, and allegory in *Waiting for the Barbarians*. Indeed, given the correlation between the incidence of scenes of excavation or disinterment, fragments, ruins, and mutilation in both Benjamin and Coetzee, it is hardly surprising that critics should be drawn to read *Waiting for the Barbarians* in terms of Benjamin's thinking on allegory.[60]

Benjamin's theorizing of allegory as ruin is, in fact, literalized in *Waiting for the Barbarians*. Accused by Joll of using the inscribed slips to transmit messages to the barbarians, the Magistrate tells Joll that the slips were found in the ruins and that allegorical sets can be found buried all over the desert. "It is recommended," the Magistrate continues, "that you simply dig at random: perhaps at the very spot that you stand now you will come upon scraps, shards, reminders of the dead" (112). Like the scraps and shards of the dead, most sets of slips are ruined by the action of the sand, but even those that have survived duplicate the spatial fragmentation of the ruin:

> See, there is only a single character. It is the barbarian character *war*, but it has other senses too. It can stand for *vengeance*, and, if you turn it upside down like this, it can be made to read *justice*. There is no knowing which sense is intended. That is part of barbarian cunning. . . . They form an allegory. They can be read in many orders. Further, each slip can be read in many ways. Together they can be read as a domestic journal, or they can be read as a plan of war, or they can be turned on their sides and read as a history of the last years of the Empire—the old Empire, I mean. (112)

Even though he cannot actually read the characters on the slips, in fact precisely because he cannot read the characters on the slips, the Magistrate will prove himself a master allegorist in Benjamin's sense. The arrival of Joll's inquisitors (who partake of modern forms of power/knowledge) strips the Magistrate of belief in organic or immanent meaning. This traumatic dislocation places him in the same melancholy position as the baroque allegorist for whom "one and the same object can just as easily signify a virtue as a vice" and therefore "any person, any object, any relationship can mean absolutely anything else."[61] Or as Terry Eagleton puts it: "The immanent meaning that ebbs from the object under the transfixing gaze of melancholy leaves it a pure signifier, a rune or fragment retrieved from the clutches of a univocal sense and surrendered unconditionally into the allegorist's power."[62] If the signifier has thus been emptied of its plenitude, it has also been emancipated and functions, according to Benjamin, "for the Baroque allegorist as a means of imposing significance on a world bereft of its own language and thus of immanent meaning."[63]

While critics have read the allegory of the slips (in an abstract sense) as disrupting the traditional relation between allegory and history and thus functioning as a metonym for the novel's powers of destructuration, they have not, to my knowledge, grasped that the Magistrate's spatial manipulation of the slips is itself strategically motivated.[64] Tracing the origins of the Magistrate's manipulation of the slips will involve us in an intricate scene of the deconstruction of imperial inscription. Finding that the slips form the perfect number of 256, the Magistrate tries to decipher them by means of combinations that will reveal a graphic composition:

> I cleared the floor of my office and laid them out, first in one great square, then in sixteen smaller squares, then in other combinations, thinking that what I had hitherto taken to be characters in a syllabary might in fact be elements of a picture whose outline would leap at me if I struck on the right arrangement: a map of the land of the barbarians in olden times, or a representation of a lost pantheon. I have even found myself reading the slips in a mirror, or tracing one on top of another, or conflating half of one with half of another. (16)

The Magistrate's allegory of the slips has its origins in his early techniques of decipherment; permutations that will later become strategic elements in the composition of his allegory. His reading the slips in the mirror, for example, reverses and turns the characters upside down. Later, because the barbarians are bent over, the Magistrate reads the words *ENEMY . . . ENEMY . . . ENEMY* written on their backs upside down. This scene of spectacular punishment is referenced by the Magistrate moments after he has interceded against the beating of the barbarians. It is better that he himself was beaten down, he thinks to himself, for words might have failed him: "Would I have dared to face the crowd to demand justice for these ridiculous barbarian prisoners with their backsides in the air? *Justice*: once that word is uttered, where will it all end? Easier to shout *No*!" (108). Composing his allegory the Magistrate reads the barbarian character for *war* (which can also stand for *vengeance*) by turning it upside down and giving it the meaning *justice*. The Magistrate's translation of the character on the slip must thus be understood as "embodied" or intersected by fragments of the body. We recall that as he translates (he refers to his allegory as a translation) the slips, the Magistrate runs his finger across the line of characters from right to left. This reading of the characters as though a kind of brail is reminiscent of the Magistrate's tracing the marks of mutilation on the barbarian girl's body. In demonstrating how meaning is retroactively inscribed, the Magistrate dislocates the performative power of the inscription of the word *ENEMY* on the barbarian body: the body in ruins stands at the origin of the allegory of the slips. Echoing Benjamin, Derrida has also claimed that the origin is always a ruin.[65]

The Magistrate's attempt to read the slips in the reflection of a mirror adumbrates another scene of deterritorialization. On his trek to return the barbarian woman to her people, the Magistrate's guide sights three barbarians on the horizon. But as his party attempts to approach, the barbarians recede into the distance: "As we move they move too. . . . But when I call a halt the three specks seem to halt too; when we resume our march they begin to move. 'Are they reflections of us, is this a trick of the light?' I wonder" (68). In "mirroring" the approach of the emissaries of Empire, the barbarians do not so much set up a reflection as erect a repeating mirage that foreshadows the technique they will later employ to defeat Joll and the army of Empire.

The Body in Ruins

Fleeing back to the fort after his defeat in the desert, the gates are opened and Joll sits in the carriage; his face, framed by the carriage window, is ashen in the moonlight. In a reversal of the beginning of his foray into the territory of the barbarians, when he sat with his eyes averted and his head inscrutably inclined, his black lenses now gone, Joll is forced to look at the Magistrate, who imparts a message on which he has long meditated: "'The crime that is latent in us we must inflict on ourselves' I say. . . . 'Not on others,' I say: I repeat the words. . . . He watches my lips, his thin lips move in imitation, or perhaps in derision, I do not know" (146–47).

Whether in imitation or derision, Joll's miming is still a mirroring. The message that the Magistrate imparts is one that he has learned himself. After suffering the dislocations of profound torture at the hands of Joll and Mandel, the Magistrate is reduced to reading the signs of his own torture. While oiling her scalp one night, the Magistrate notices a puckering in the corner of the barbarian girl's eye which he refers to as a "caterpillar" (31), and which he then traces with his fingernail. A moment later he tells us that until the marks on the girl's body are deciphered he cannot let go of her. Now he refers to his own wound of torture as having a "crust like a fat caterpillar [that] has formed on it" (115). Tracing his own wounds, the Magistrate finds himself caught in the circulation or reflection of his own figure. "'What did they do to you?' the Magistrate asks the girl after tracing the caterpillar to the edge of her eyelid. The girl shakes her head. 'Tell me,' I want to say, 'don't make a mystery of it, pain is only pain'" (32). But pain, as Scarry points out, is resistant to linguistic objectification. To be in pain is to have certainty; to witness another's ineffable pain, however, is to be put in doubt. The Magistrate is himself soon forced into a phenomenological experience of the intimate mysteries of the body in pain, but in what sense, it remains to be asked, might the tortured body be said to function like Benjamin's ruin?

THE MATERIALITY OF THE LETTER

One way into this question is through Paul de Man's counterintuitive concept of *materiality* that emerges in his posthumous *Aesthetic Ideology* and most particularly in his essay "Phenomenality and Materiality in Kant." I should say from the outset that my exposition of de Man is indebted to and draws upon J. Hillis Miller's analysis of *Aesthetic Ideology*.[66] This investigation will require a brief excursus into de Man's thought on a materiality that eludes conversion into either cognition or figuration. Or to put this a little less obscurely, materiality is prefigural and precognitive. De Man articulates this "concept" in his analysis of what he calls "material vision," which he finds operative in Immanuel Kant's *Critique of Judgment*. Focusing on Kant's use of the word *Augenschein*, "in which the eye, tautologically, is named twice, as eye itself and as what appears to the eye," de Man discerns a modality of vision that is nonphenomenal.[67] The redundant use of *Augenschein* emulates a mode of vision in which the eye simply "sees" without that sensory perception being interpreted by the mind. It is as if the activity of the eye is detached or disarticulated from the thinking part of the mind.

Let me use a physiological example that, by literalizing *Augenschein*, might help illustrate de Man's elusive concept. In the First World War, soldiers who had been blinded by injuries to their heads but not to their eyes were observed to duck flying shrapnel that they swore they could somehow "see." It was later discovered that these soldiers possessed something neurologists now refer to as "blindsight." It turns out that an ancient ocular pathway leading to a primitive region of the brain was still operative and capable of sending images to which the reptilian brain could respond. But since the occipital lobe, the area of the brain responsible for processing these images, was damaged or severed from its ocular pathway, these images could not be consciously seen or recorded. (My example of blindsight to illustrate "material vision" also relates to the ubiquitous thematic of blindness and sight in *Waiting for the Barbarians*.) The idea of a mode of vision

The Body in Ruins

operated by the eye alone is, strictly speaking, unintelligible. Any sense that we give to this *Augenschein* is retrospective and an illegitimate ideological imposition: "To the extent that any mind," de Man says "that any judgment, intervenes, it is an error."[68] It is in this sense that material vision is nonphenomenal, since phenomenality automatically involves the cognitively processing or rendering sensible what we see.

Since it is prior to cognition, material vision is also prior to all figuration: "Kant's vision can therefore hardly be called literal," de Man tells us, as this "would imply its possible figuralization or symbolization by an act of judgment."[69] In a passage in which he describes the sublime, Kant requires that it be seen with a naked eye unmotivated by reason:

> If, then, we call the sight of the starry heaven *sublime*, we must not place at the foundation of judgment concepts of worlds inhabited by rational beings and regard the bright points . . . as their suns moving in circles . . . but we must regard it, just as we see it . . . as a distant all-embracing vault. . . . To find the ocean nevertheless sublime we must regard it . . . merely by what the eye reveals—if it is at rest, as a clear mirror of water only bounded by the heavens; if it is stormy, as an abyss threatening to overwhelm everything.[70]

Reading this passage with an eye to his uncovering a previously unseen material vision in Kant, de Man comments: "The 'mirror' of the sea surface is a mirror without depth, least of all the mirror in which the constellation would be reflected. In this mode of seeing, the eye is its own agent and not the specular echo of the sun. The sea is called a mirror, not because it is supposed to reflect anything, but to stress a flatness devoid of any suggestion of depth."[71] Tropes here fail to function performatively. The sea is called a mirror but it reflects nothing. The eye is its own agent and not the "specular echo of the sun." The effect of these figures is that they fail to perform their figural function and revert to a disarticulated materiality. "Realism," de Man says, "postulates a phenomenalism of experience which is here being denied or ignored."[72] The demands for instrumentalist realism made by South African critics of a materialist (Marxist) inclination might be rejected by de Man, but in a strange turn, as we shall soon see, de Man's *materiality* is put to political purpose in *Waiting for the Barbarians*.

De Man names this prefigural or disarticulated materiality the "materiality of the letter" or what he also calls the "materiality of inscription." In order to isolate this materiality of the letter in Kant, de Man begins by examining Kant's remarks on the sublime in terms of the human body. If we are to apprehend what is sublime in the human body, Kant admonishes, "we must not regard as the determining grounds of our judgment the concepts of the purposes which all our limbs serve . . . and we must not allow this unity of purpose to influence our aesthetic judgment."[73] Since regarding the body as useful or productive disrupts the aesthetic vision of the sublime, we must regard the limbs as severed from the organic unity or function of the body. "We must in other words," de Man writes, "disarticulate, mutilate the body . . . we must consider our limbs . . . severed from any purpose or use."[74] If the materiality of vision disarticulates both nature and the human body, it also has its equivalence in the order of language: "To the dismemberment of the body corresponds a dismemberment of language, as meaning-producing tropes are replaced by the fragmentation of sentences and propositions into discrete words, or the fragmentation of words into syllables or finally letters."[75]

De Man here pushes at a progressive disarticulation of language from its material base. Letters and syllables are, after all, merely material units that have no significance outside of human perception. Language, in a sense, is thus a retroactive imposition of meaning upon a fragment of material. It is, as we all know, extremely difficult to grasp letters in this way; our mind instantly projects meaning onto these material marks, investing them with a significance that resists the erosion of sheer materiality. The materiality of the letter, however, emerges in the play of language that runs against the grain of sense. De Man isolates that aspect of the text in which repeated fragments of language, the sounds of letters and syllables, for example, produce an (un)motivated echo that renders literal meaning senseless as in Lucky's regressive repetition of "quaquaquaqua outside time" in Samuel Beckett's *Waiting for Godot*.[76] Or, in an illustrative instance of his theme, de Man maintains that the "persuasiveness" of a passage in Kant concerning the recovery of the imagination through material vision depends on the homophonic proximity between the German words for surprise and admiration, *Verwuderung* and *Bewunderung*. Kant's reader is made to assent to the aporia in his account of the imagination's powers and failures in its encounter with the sublime, not by argument, but by the assault of "a constant, and finally bewildering alternation of the two terms, *Angemessen(heit)* and *Unangemessen(heit)* to the point where one can no longer tell them apart."[77]

We are now in a position to consider the relationship between de Man's formulation of materiality and *Waiting for the Barbarians*. We might begin with the slips, which, in disarticulating the Magistrate's architectonics of a mathematical sublime, conform to the materiality of the letter. (The slips resist perfect patterning and will not reveal any pictorial outline.) The characters on the slips are embalmed as pure signifiers forever severed from their signifieds. Still, in the course of his allegory, they function for the Magistrate not so much as dead signs, but as fragments of bodies that he registers by a kind of materiality of touch. The Magistrate's rhythmic rubbing of the girl functions as the tactile equivalent of de Man's material vision and becomes his way into the materiality of the letter. His rubbing (as we have seen) results in a trancelike fading or senseless crash of oblivion: "I lose myself in the rhythm of what I am doing. There is a space of time which is blank to me: perhaps I am not even present" (28). Language itself retreats before the edge of oblivion: "On the edge of oblivion it comes back to me that my fingers, running over her buttocks, have felt a phantom criss-cross of ridges under the skin.... [W]ords elude me.... I struggle to speak; then blackness falls" (31–32).

The girl's body is "flat, blank" she offers no organic unity, no reproductive utility. The Magistrate "know[s] what to do with her no more than one cloud in the sky knows what to do with another" (34). In drawing an analogy between the lack of utility of her body and the lack of utility of the sky, the Magistrate figures her body in terms of the Kantian sublime. To see the sky as the source of fertile rain or the sea as reservoir of nourishing fish is to see them cognitively in their utility, not in their sublimity: to see the ocean as sublime we must regard it, as the poets do, with an unthinking eye.[78] Here the girl's body is prefigural: blank and flat as the mirror of the Kantian sea, and like that mirror, her body will not admit of reflection (in all its senses) but presents a flatness devoid of any indication of depth. The material marks of torture on her body function as a materiality of the letter, not only in their disarticulation of the Magistrate's language but in their refusal to reflect or support any figuration.

Significantly, it is when the Magistrate is hooded and hanging near death that he becomes sublimely perceptive to the approach of the other. With the rope around his neck drawn tighter, the blood begins to "hammer" in his ears. The "drumbeat" becomes amplified until it is all he can hear. Induced by what, following de Man, we might call an aural materiality, the Magistrate waits for his vision of the old barbarian to speak: "I watch his lips. At any moment now he will speak: I must listen carefully to catch every syllable, so that later . . . I can discover the answer to a question which for the moment has flown like a bird from my recollection" (120). The Magistrate must first hear with only his ears the disarticulated materiality of syllables. Later, he thinks, he will recompose the syllables in answer to his forgotten question. The syllables, like the slips, which they recall, will resist articulation but, in contrast to his desire to read the girl's body, he listens holding himself open to the alterity of the other.

Commenting on de Man's materiality of aesthetic vision, Judith Butler asks why it is that de Man draws a correspondence between the mutilated body and the mutilation of language, which de Man speaks of as the materiality of the letter. The mutilated body, she asserts, returns to haunt materiality as the very figure of a figuration that has been banished: "Indeed, if the body in pieces is neither figurative nor literal, but material, then it would still follow that the only way to convey that materiality is precisely through catachresis, as de Man actually does, and so through a figure.... And if dismemberment is but a sign of a prefigural materiality, then that materiality has been converted into a trope through the very example that is said to illustrate that nonconvertibility."[79] For Butler the failure of a trope to function mimetically or to correspond to itself does not, in and of itself, bespeak the erasure of the figural. "A figure," she holds, "can function as a substitution for that which is fundamentally irrecoverable within or by the figure itself: indeed, this is perhaps where Benjamin on allegory would, if he could, if I would let him, make his eerie return.[80] Butler does not allow Benjamin his spectral return. Oddly, given what she has just claimed concerning the power of figures, she seems to emphasize Benjamin's return as being a matter of her agency or invocation. But in an emulative instance of her claim for figures, Benjamin's return might also argue for the materiality of the letter inscribed on *Waiting for the Barbarians'* tortured bodies or what, to employ a catachresis, I am calling the body in ruins.

If de Man figures the materiality of the letter by means of the mutilated body, Benjamin, we remember, also personifies allegory in terms of physiognomy, or as Hillis Miller says, "as though it were a human face or body inscribed with signs."[81] Allegory manifests the failure of these signs to transform or transfigure since by the act of inscription they ruin or devastate the very face they are inscribing. "In allegory," Miller argues, "writing and personification reveal, bring out into the open as *Scheinen,* the eternal disjunction between the inscribed sign and its material embodiment.... In allegory naked matter shines through."[82] Hillis Miller's "naked matter" is the very stuff of de Man's materiality. *Augenschein, Scheinen,* shine, sign: prefigural, naked matter shines through, supporting no reflection. If on the one hand figures fail to perform their figurative (mimetic) function, on the other hand they perform that very mutilation or disintegration of the figure. This mutilating figure, Butler contends, is "no less a figure than a mimetic one, or one whose terms can be related through means of adequation."[83] So is the materiality of the tortured body figurable or not? Is it bound to the realm of reflection or will it shine through? The answer is ultimately suspended in the aporia of what is taken for figuration itself.

"The body," Butler argues, "does not, then, imply the destruction of figurality if only because a figure can function as a substitution for that which is fundamentally irrecoverable within or by the figure itself."[84] The very inadequation, I take Butler as saying, that makes figuration itself possible eludes absorption by de Man's materiality. And yet she has also argued that the body resists all efforts of linguistic capture, of dissolution into textual figuration; an elusive, ineradicable reserve obtains to both figure and body. It is this very reserve that Coetzee mobilizes in *Waiting for the Barbarians*: "Is representation to be so robbed of power by the endlessly skeptical process of textualization," he asks, "that those represented in/by the text—the feminine subject, the colonial subject—are to have no power either?"[85] Against the trap of abyssal textualization, Coetzee has set the bulwark of the body in pain. "If I look back over my fiction," he has commented, "I see a simple . . . standard erected. That standard is the body. Whatever else, the body is not 'that which it is not,' and the proof that it *is* is the pain it feels."[86] The tortured body, the body in pain, does not merely present an obdurate or passive withdrawal from the process of textualization, it takes on a performative political power of its own: "Let me put this baldly: in South Africa it is not possible to deny the authority of suffering and therefore of the body. It is not possible, not for logical reasons, not for ethical reasons, . . . but for political reasons, for reasons of power. And let me again be unambiguous: it is not that one *grants* the authority of the suffering body: the suffering body *takes* this authority; that is its power."[87]

In light of what we have just read, in what sense can the suffering or tortured body in *Waiting for the Barbarians* be said to take its power? In what way is the taking of power of the South African body correlated to the taking of power of the tortured body in Coetzee's text? My way of addressing this question will take us through the final difficult and most obscure element of de Man's materiality—his conception of the materiality of history. For de Man, the materiality of history occurs when language or signs touch upon the world and make something happen. History as a material event is thus constituted by irreversible performative speech acts that leave their mark upon the world. Kant's move to a "formal materialism" in his *Critique of Judgment*, de Man argues, leaves just such an irreversible mark. This was "an *occurrence*, which has the materiality of something that actually happens, that actually occurs. And there, the thought of material occurrence, something that occurs materially, that leaves a trace on the world, that does something to the world as such—that notion of occurrence is not opposed in any sense to the notion of writing."[88] What is opposed to Kant's materialism, in de Man's view, is Schiller's misreading of Kant, which reinscribes Kant's materialism into a cognitive or tropological system. Schiller's ideological misprision of Kant is not, for de Man, an event of history, most definitely not an irreversible material event: "In the whole reception of Kant from then until now nothing has happened, only regression, nothing has happened at all. Which is another way of saying there is no history . . . that reception is not historical. . . . The event, the occurrence is resisted by reinscribing it in the cognition of tropes, and that is itself a tropological, cognitive, and not a historical move."[89] For de Man, then, there is a way in which the materiality of history will always exceed its ideological superscription. In order to understand this claim, it is crucial that we grasp that history is the result of an instantaneous speech act that is not itself within time, but which has an effect on what we conventionally think of as the temporality of history. "There is history," de Man argues, "from the moment words such as 'power' and 'battle' and so on emerge on the scene. At that moment things *happen*, there is *occurrence*, there is *event*. History is therefore not a temporal notion, it has nothing to do with temporality, but is the emergence of a language of power out of a language of cognition."[90] Commenting on de Man's formulation of history or what he calls "these sternly recalcitrant statements," Hillis Miller maintains that this conception

> may be more understandable and perhaps even more acceptable if we remember that Althusser, and de Man in his own way, following Marx, define ideology as having no history, as being outside history, as having no purchase on history, since ideology is precisely an illusory misunderstanding of the "real conditions of existence," as Althusser put it in 'Ideology and Ideological State Apparatuses,' or, as de Man puts this in 'The Resistance to Theory': "What we call ideology is precisely the confusion of linguistic with natural reality, of reference with phenomenalism."[91]

We are now in a position to draw a further and final correlation between de Man's materiality of history and the materiality of inscription in *Waiting for the Barbarians*. Coetzee's text presents the barbarian body as material history resisting ideological inscription into the tropology of Empire. While the materiality of history is posited on irreversibility it is still open to tropological reinscription. The performative function of language, de Man asserts, "will always be reinscribed within a cognitive system, it will always be *recuperated*, it will relapse, so to speak, by a kind of reinscription of the performative in a tropological system of cognition. That relapse, however, is not the same as reversal."[92] In this arrangement, the tortured body of the old man represents the lapse of reinscription into the ideological tropology of Empire, while the tortured body of the barbarian girl represents the irreversible perdurability of the materiality of history. But there is another sense in which *Waiting for the Barbarians* is itself a material event, itself part of the materiality of history. In deconstructing apartheid's inscription of Biko's tortured body into its cognitive and tropological regime, Coetzee's text functions as a speech act or material occurrence that touches on the world to make something happen. De Man, we recall, speaks of the material event that leaves a trace on the world as not being in any way opposed to writing. In demonstrating that the materiality of the tortured bodies that are incorporated into the field of its future reception always exceeds the forces of tropological inscription, *Waiting for the Barbarians* deconstructs the spectacular power that accrues to Coetzee's text. In demonstrating that this reception is not historical but ideological, the tortured bodies disrupt the ideological apparatus of apartheid. Apartheid is shown to rest precisely on "the confusion of linguistic with natural reality, of reference with phenomenalism." Apartheid, then, is not, in de Man's sense, historical. It is not a material but an ideological event, destined to disappear. The tortured body shines through, metaleptically ruining apartheid's ideological edifice. The tortured body *takes* its power.

As a speech act or material event, *Waiting for the Barbarians* is in a strange sense not within time. The event or its performative effects occur instantaneously as the "emergence of a language of power out of a language of cognition."[93] In its being not within time, Coetzee's text emulates the "shining now" of Kafka's "The Burrow." Coetzee's continuous present seems to ride on the edge of a beam of light, stopping time, in order to, as he once put it, "redeem time from chronicity." It is in these terms, then, and not in the sense of Empire's end of temporality, that Coetzee makes his claim for the will to power of signification over time.[94]

MOURNING THE BONES

Toward the end of the novel, the Magistrate returns to his decipherment of the ancient aboriginal slips charactered with enigmatic signs. Prompted by thoughts of his settlement in ruins, the Magistrate thinks of leaving to posterity his own record of the history of the settlement buried beneath the walls of the town. What he begins to write, however, is not the history of the imperial outpost, but a retreat into the time out of time of a pastoral account of the settlement as a paradise on earth. Musing on the slips he mentions that it would be disappointing to find that they "contain a message as devious, as equivocal, as reprehensible" (154) as the false history and plea for the settlement he has begun composing. However sophisticated the Magistrate's skepticism, he is still caught up in the belief that if he could only decipher the script, it would release a message whose nuances would be clear to him: he still believes that he would register the evasions of its allegorical form. He falls, at times, then, into the belief of an unmediated and restorative access to the ancient past. Relinquishing his attempts at writing his contemporary history, he falls back on a future archeology:

> I think: "When one day people come scratching around in the ruins, they will be more interested in the relics from the desert than in anything I may leave behind. And rightly so." (Thus I spend an evening coating the slips one by one in linseed oil and wrapping them in an oilcloth. When the wind lets up, I promise myself, I will go out and bury them where I found them.) (155)

The Magistrate's coating the slips with linseed oil recalls his rubbing of the barbarian woman with almond oil and the metonymic relation between the body and the slips.[95] It also recalls his experience of time out of time. But his promise to inter the slips in the ruin speaks, as well, to his sense of an archeological time. It recalls, in fact, his thoughts about the future archeological collections of his successors and his figuring of himself as the jackal of Empire in sheep's clothing.

It is not just the Magistrate's projection of a future archeology that renders the relic proleptic, but the relic in *Waiting for the Barbarians* is already fraught with uncanny or proleptic powers. Early in the novel, the Magistrate tells us that in the course of his excavation of the ruins that lie outside the walls of the settlement, he has not found any human remains. Interpreting the ruins as the remains of an ancient empire, he wonders: "Perhaps in my digging I have only scratched the surface. Perhaps ten feet below the floor lie the ruins of another fort, razed by the barbarians, peopled with the bones of folk who thought they would find

The Body in Ruins

safety behind high walls" (15). Now close to the end of the book, while a well is dug inside the walls of the fort, a pile of bones (the remains of a massacre) is found haphazardly lying one atop the other. The bones, like the relic, or like the ghosts with whom the Magistrate tries to commune, will not remain buried. If the relic is proleptic, it is also apocalyptic.

It is not only ancient bones or relics that have the spectral power of living on, or of coming back. In insisting on a proper burial for the corpses of two deserters who have been found, the Magistrate takes on the task of ontologizing the bones: "I repeat to myself that by insisting on correct treatment of the bones I am trying to show these young men that death is no annihilation, that we survive as filiations in the memory of those we knew" (54). In *Specters of Marx*, Derrida speaks with some disapproval of ontologizing the remains as one of the tasks of mourning. The work of mourning, he remarks, "consists always in attempting to ontologize remains, to make them present, in the first place by *identifying* the bodily remains and by *localizing* the dead."[96] The work of mourning requires that the object of mourning be fixed and that it stay in place. The Magistrate insists on a proper burial, however, not so much as a means of localizing the dead but of allowing them to live on, to wander through the memories of those who knew them. The task of identifying the bones so as to release them, rather than to ontologize them in a world of presence, is precisely the work of mourning in the TRC. The repeated requests by relatives for the bones of the victims of apartheid's torturers so they can be given proper burial is partly a matter of the state stabilizing the dead (documentation and closure), but it is also a matter of honoring or mourning for those bones (even those bones that cannot be identified) that reaches far beyond the protocols of identification or ontologization. And it is here that the Magistrate's allegory of the slips meets up with TRC testimonies recorded in *Country of My Skull*.

In his reading of the second and third slips the Magistrate composes an allegory out of the bodies Joll has tortured. The allegory fuses together the broken ankles of the barbarian girl and the broken body of the old man that has been sewn into a sheet. The figure that emerges, however, is that of a young man who had been taken into the fort. The Magistrate gives this allegory that turns Joll's scenes of torture back against himself the inflection of a barbarian perspective. The story he tells is of a barbarian who has gone repeatedly to the fort to plead for the young man's return and is finally given a body. Insisting on identifying the remains, the barbarian opens "the sheet and saw that it was indeed he. Through each eyelid, I saw, there was a stitch. 'Why have you done that?' I said. 'It is our custom,' he said. I tore the sheet wide open and saw bruises all over his body, and saw that his feet were swollen and broken. 'What happened to him?' I said. 'I do not know,' said the man, 'it is not on the paper; if you have any questions you must go to the sergeant, but he is very busy'" (111). This last line embeds Empire and apartheid within the abyssal folds of the Kafkaesque, but the allegory ends with the Magistrate translating: "We have had to bury your brother here, outside their fort, because he was beginning to stink" (111–12). The Magistrate's allegory proves uncanny since the barbarian bones refuse to remain buried, but, as the return of the repressed, proleptically indicate the massacred bones of a previous empire that lie buried within the walls of the fort.

To conclude this chapter of my book, I want to relate the uncanny effects attributed to allegory within Coetzee's text to the allegorical correlation I have been drawing between *Waiting for the Barbarians* and *Country of My Skull*. In his "The Allegorical Impulse: Toward a Theory of Postmodernism," Craig Owens comments:

> In order to recognize allegory in its contemporary manifestations, we first require a general idea of what in fact it is, or rather what it *represents*, since allegory is an attitude as well as a technique, a perception as well as a procedure. Let us say for the moment that allegory occurs whenever one text is doubled by another; the Old Testament, for example, becomes allegorical when it is read as a prefiguration of the New.[97]

The Body in Ruins

In its doubling of the Hebrew Bible, the New Testament retroactively confers an allegorical status upon the Old Testament and it would seem that in its doubling or mirroring of Coetzee's novel, Krog's text (or the TRC testimonies) similarly confers an anagogical aspect upon Coetzee's text. While this is true, Coetzee's text is, as we have seen, also interfused from the start with a knowledge of what would come to be its uncanny relation to the future of South African torture. The uncanny aspect of what I have been calling the allegory of the slips does not only concern the facts of torture but also involves the aspect of attitude and tone. The dissembling tone of the Magistrate's allegory meets its material complement in *Country of My Skull*, in the form of an allegorical testimony given to the TRC by a shepherd named Lekotse. The security police have come to his house because of his son's involvement with APLA (the armed wing of the Pan-Africanist Congress). The shepherd gives his account of the security police ransacking his house. Here is a brief excerpt:

> Now listen very carefully, because I am telling you the story now. . . .
> Three policemen were black and the rest were white and they referred to us as *kaffers*. Many of them were white. They were together with big dogs—two in number. . . . They said every door of the house should be opened. They pulled clothes from the wardrobes. I said, "When a jackal gets into the sheep it does not do this. . . ."[98]

Interpreting this particular moment of the shepherd's tale, Krog writes: "To appreciate the power of the image, we must bear in mind the kind of predator the jackal is. He's a quiet, neat, gourmet hunter. . . . If there are lambs, he'll kill one or two and devour nothing but the fourth stomach. . . . They were worse than jackals, says Lekotse. And since the jackal is the shepherd's greatest enemy, a threat to the flock night and day, he means that the security police exceeded his worst expectations of evil."[99] The shepherd's identification of the security police with the jackal recalls the Magistrate's claim that as Empire's agent, he is a jackal in sheep's clothing, "returning, with apologies, a body we have sucked dry" (72). Since he is about to begin his interpretation of the slips that will include the returning of another tortured body, the Magistrate's invocation of the lambing season in his reading of the first slip is not only the ironic summoning of a barbarian pastoral but a signal of his stripping off his sheep's clothing, of his refusal to function as the jackal of Empire and his invocation of the position of the other. It is precisely this dissembling tone of the other that allows the shepherd's testimony at the TRC to double the Magistrate's testimony in his allegory of the slips. In his testimony the shepherd deploys figures and questions that turn both the questioning of the police as well as the administrator of the TRC back against them. His speaking from the position of the other so allegorizes official discourse that it becomes impossible to register the tone of his testimony as one of authenticity or dissimulation. Allegory (from the Greek, *allos*: other and *agoreuin*: to speak in public) means literally to speak other or to speak otherwise publicly. In his allegory of the slips the Magistrate speaks from the position of the other and speaks publicly otherwise to Joll and the warrant officer who stands poised to transcribe his testimony. His speaking from the position of the other and publicly otherwise throws official discourse off course or turns it away from itself.[100]

The question of testimony and tone returns us rather precisely to the question of torture and the tone of truth. Interpreting the traumatized crying of one of the victims testifying at the TRC, the Xhosa intellectual Professor Kwandiwe Kondlo tells Krog: "For me, this crying is the beginning of the Truth Commission—the signature tune, the definitive moment, the ultimate sound of what the process is about."[101] It would seem that Kondlo's tone of trauma is the equivalent of Joll's tone of truth: both emerge from and issue forth, an irrevocable truth. But the professor goes on to say:

> The academics say pain destroys language and this brings about an immediate reversion to a prelinguistic state—and to witness that cry was to witness the destruction of lan-

guage . . . was to realize that to remember the past of this country is to be thrown back into a time before language. And to get that memory, to fix it in words, to capture it with the precise image, is to be present at the birth of language itself. But more practically, this particular memory at last captured in words can no longer haunt you, push you around, bewilder you, because you have taken control of it—you can move it wherever you want to. So maybe this is what the commission is all about—finding words for that cry.[102]

The cry, for Kondlo, bears witness to the collective trauma of the South African past and apartheid's annihilation of language. But the tone of trauma, unlike the tone of truth, also marks the re-emergence of language and the conversion of traumatic memory into the manipulability of linguistic narrative. For although the traumatic memory is "captured in words," the words themselves do not remain fixed, but are open to an array of spatial and psychic manipulations—"you can move it wherever you want to."

While he does not specifically mention her, Kondlo seems to be referring to Scarry's thinking in *The Body in Pain*. His reference to Scarry's thought on the relation between torture and language recalls to us her claim that torture is mimetic of death: "for in death the body is emphatically present while the more elusive part represented by the voice is so alarmingly absent that heavens are created to explain its whereabouts."[103] Scarry's claim resonates in uncanny sympathy with the Magistrate's discourse on barbarian allegory. After informing Joll that barbarian burial sites mark good places for the discovery of "allegorical sets" of slips (112), the Magistrate remarks: "Also the air: the air is full of sighs and cries. These are never lost: if you listen carefully, with a sympathetic ear, you can hear them echoing forever in the second sphere. The night is best: sometimes when you have difficulty in falling asleep it is because your ears have been reached by the cries of the dead which, like their writings, are open to many interpretations" (112). With this the Magistrate finishes his allegory. The cries of the dead, like the slips, do not record a single tone of truth; their inflections register manifold interpretations. They resonate, in fact, with what Derrida terms an "apocalyptic tone." The apocalyptic tone, like the generalized structure of writing and differential structure of the apocalypse itself, is always divided within itself and is haunted by the "pure[ly] differential vibration" that constitutes breath, accent, and timbre and that exceeds all closure or collapse into an adequation or pure identification with itself.[104] The apocalyptic tone, then, shatters Joll's tone of truth—a tone that "would be that of a plenitude without vibration, without difference," Derrida remarks, "seems to me to be both the myth of metaphysics—and death."[105] The cries of the dead are never lost, but resonate at the point of the spectral emergence of language itself. It is not in the form of the undead marked body but in this sense that the future, as Derrida says, belongs to ghosts.

CODA

The Time of Inscription

Maus *and the Apocalypse of Number*

He who does not understand number does not understand death.
—J. M. COETZEE, *Dusklands*

In my readings of Kafka, Conrad, and Coetzee, I have worked to illustrate the ways in which their texts might be said to have apocalyptic futures. I have tried to show how "In the Penal Colony," *Heart of Darkness*, and *Waiting for the Barbarians* are apocalyptic not only in the violence that they portray but also in the etymological sense of apocalypse and the unveiling of their hidden futures that are still to come. (Etymologically, the English "apocalypse" derives from the Latin *apocalypsis* meaning "revelation" and from the Greek *apokalyptein* meaning to "uncover" or "unveil.") I have attempted further to demonstrate how a text may be written so as to encode an apocalypse to come, which on the event of its arrival, of its disclosure, appears already to have been inscribed or forecast. Having provided a sustained analysis of the way in which these three primary texts inscribe the revelation of an apocalypse that will always have arrived in the figure of the marked body, as well as the degree to which these texts are open to the deanimation of this undead figure or entity, I now want to conclude this book with a reading of Art Spiegelman's graphic novel *Maus* that weaves together a number of threads that run through this book.

I choose this brilliant graphic novel as a means of concluding this book partly because it offers me a chance to look into Spiegelman's own self-reflexive meditation on the ethical relation between his text's literary reception and the dead bodies of the Holocaust that haunt it. While I hope to have shown how Kafka, Conrad, and Coetzee wrestle with the ethical futurity of their works and how their texts might be taken as allegories of their struggle with their apocalyptic futures, Spiegelman affords me the rare instance of analyzing a writer's taking ethical account of his own responsibility with regard to the encryption of the apocalyptic body into his own text. I hope to tease out some of the more hidden or subtle elements that subtend this aspect of *Maus*. To this end, I will again look into the way in which a text comes to embody a violent future, but I also want to shift ground and meditate on the ethics of representing the marked body in a postapocalyptic text, one in which the work is haunted from the start not by the apocalypse to come but by the already-encrypted bodies of the Holocaust itself. My second reason for writing this coda on *Maus* is that, as I hope to show at the end of this book, it allows me one further instance at least of offering a messianic counter to the apocalyptic cycle of incorporation that so besets or marks the representation of the marked body. My purpose in writing this coda, then, is not to replicate the critical form of my previous chapters but to closely read *Maus* in conjunction with and for the light it sheds on the concerns of this book.

Reading Spiegelman's graphic account of his parents surviving Auschwitz and of the aftermath of his mother's suicide returns us to my chapter on Kafka. Spiegelman has spoken of Kafka's story "Josephine the Mouse Singer" as one of the origins of his *Maus* project. He tells us that "Josephine the Singer began humming to me . . . and I began pursuing the logic and possibilities that that metaphoric device opened up."[1] I suspect, too, given the importance of the number tattooed onto Vladek's arm in *Maus*, that the relation between the inscriptional machine of Kafka's "In the Penal Colony" and the inscriptional machine of the Nazi death camps could not have been far from Speigelman's mind during the long and studied composition of his text. In what follows I shall offer some commentary on *Maus* and two of its particular scenes of inscription.[2] The first records Spiegelman's representation of his mother, Anja, taking her own life that appears in the interleaved comic "Prisoner on the Hell Planet." By way of contrast, the second portrays the priest's Judaic reading of the number inscribed on Vladek's arm that appears in *Maus II*, and which gives Vladek hope of living on. I will again and for the last time be concerned with the apocalyptic and messianic registers of the marked body, and I would like to end where I began this book with the possibility of hope, but this time to gesture to a way in which the liberatory potential of hope that Bloch proposes might be deployed in the reading of the marked body that would at least offer us one further possibility of deactivating the apocalyptic cycle of incorporation that I have charted through the course of this book.

But let me begin by returning to a theme that I pursued in the chapter on Kafka, namely the right of a private text to a literary survival or living on. In *Maus*, Art Spiegelman presents himself, or more precisely his comic double Artie, as coming up against crucial moments of ethical responsibility with regard not only to the artistic composition but also to the reception of his texts. Although Art cannot be conflated with Artie, as the author of the comic, he cannot be entirely disassociated from ethical concerns addressed by his double. Unless otherwise specified, when I speak of "Artie," I have in mind an Art/Artie composite. Artie comes to learn, then, a number of lessons with respect to the dangerous effects of his comics in the world. One of the most poignant and personal of these involves his father's hurt at the uncovering of a text that should have remained hidden to him. Artie has asked Vladek to find Anja's diaries—the record of his mother's story in her own words—which in offering a counterpoint to his father's narrative, he claims, "would give the book some balance" (134). The lost diaries offer anything but balance, however, and lead, in fact, to a number of traumatic encounters. Unbeknownst to Artie, in a fit of desperation Vladek has long ago burned the diaries in an effort to extinguish or literally burn away the memories they hold. To offer something in their place, and perhaps to console Artie, Vladek has been searching for family photographs that survived the war. While searching, Vladek unearths Art's underground comic "Prisoner on the Hell Planet." Art's expressionist graphic depiction of Anja's suicide must surely have appeared to Vladek as the return of the repressed. Indeed, something of the shock that must have struck Vladek is conveyed when we witness Artie's own shock at learning his father has read "Prisoner."

This moment of Artie's encounter with the damaging personal effect that his comic has on his father has been prepared for in a scene that ends the first chapter of *Maus I*. The scene is critically positioned to open a self-referential commentary on the place of the personal and the private in *Maus*. The scene concerns Vladek trying to expurgate his less-than-valorous conduct with his lover Lucia by refusing to allow Artie to include such "private things" in his book (25). The page ends with the silhouette of Artie breaking his promise to his father even as he promises that he will not expose this private story to public display. Artie justifies this betrayal by claiming that such personal stories grant the *Maus* project authenticity, that it makes things "more real—more human" (25), that Vladek gets fleshed out as an individual person and not simply as symbol of the Holocaust survivor. Given the artificial status of the comic characters, this claim also registers a slight irony that perhaps even slips by Artie at the time. This is not to doubt that Artie deploys artifice to demonstrate the very constructedness of the "real." But Artie's claim for the "real" of the personal itself takes a different and more exacting personal turn when he sees how depressed his father has become at finding Anja's suicide horribly conjured in the comic before him. Artie has surely begun to learn something of the dangerous "reality effect" that lies in wait for those who come upon his comics. This is further confirmed when Mala (Vladek's second wife) speaks of the "reality" of the expressionist comic, calling it "accurate" and "objective" and telling Artie that she thought she'd faint: "I was so shocked. It was so . . . so personal!" (106).

Given that the clear allusion to Freud in "Prisoner's" subtitle—"A Case History"—should alert us, we ought not to be surprised that the reality effect of "Prisoner" is also invested in its powers of uncanniness. As Artie comes to find out on the last page of *Maus I*, in order to, as he puts it, "make an order with everything," to try that is to order his past, to keep it in its place, Vladek says, "these papers had too many memories. So I burned them" (161). To this Artie angrily responds, "You murderer!" He means by this outrageous exclamation that in burning Anja's words to ash, Vladek has killed off the possibility of giving Anja's words new life, of reconfiguring her story anew. Anja was after all an inveterate writer, and rewriter, of her story. Her diaries, Vladek tells Artie, "didn't survive from the war.... She wrote after her whole story from the start" (86). While Anja survives the Holocaust, the words in which she recorded her life during that time do not. Ironically, after her death by suicide, the words in which she recomposed not only the story of her survival but also the story of her life are burned in a second holocaust of texts and this irony is compounded by her wish that her story be passed on to her son. Despite his mollifying apology to his father, Artie does not retract this judgment when he silently repeats the solitary word "murderer" to himself as *Maus I* ends.

The uncanny and cruel irony is that having burned Anja's diaries to rid himself of the memories they hold, and in looking for the batch of photographs—photographs that survived both the Holocaust and his later burning—as a means of compensating for the loss of Anja's diaries, Vladek is forced to confront the very scene that led him to burning the diaries in the first place. We recall that it was Vladek standing in a pool of blood who first found Anja with her wrists slashed, and in unearthing the comic finds himself looking at himself looking again at Anja's body with her slashed wrists. If Artie's father bleeds history, history bleeds again out of his undead mother's ghastly body. If the father is charged by the son with the murder of the living word, then the son must surely be charged by the father with the grim resurrection of the dead scene. And this economy is repeated when Vladek confesses that he did not finally "save" the letters exchanged between himself and the French inmate that he met in Dachau and confronts Artie with "rebuild[ing] me all this" (258). The word "rebuilding" is not simply a consequence of Vladek's immigrant-inflected English, I think, but rather Vladek's effort to convey the way in which Artie's questions excavate the life in the camps he has tried to bury and the way in which Artie's interrogations regarding missing papers have erected or resurrected before him the scene of the Holocaust.

It is no accident but another manifestation of the uncanny that Artie's calling his father a "murderer" at the end of *Maus I* also calls up his accusation that "you *murdered* me mommy," the line that ends the "Prisoner" comic (105). Here, he charges his mother with "committing the perfect crime" and literally represents himself as imprisoned in a cell of guilt, an unassailable guilt that cannot ever be assuaged because in killing herself his mother has left herself beyond address. She has not even left a note as Artie announces immediately after telling us in the first panel of "Prisoner" that his mother killed herself, and the sheer significance of this is reiterated as Vladek cries, "Why? Why! Such a tragedy! And not even a note!!!" (103). Anja, who composed and recomposed the story of her life even in the bleakest of circumstances, desperately hanging on in coal cellars that were literally cells, as if the very act of writing itself kept her going, kept her alive, leaves no note to account for her taking of her own life. But it is precisely with regard to this absent note that I want to propose a way in which the note or letter in *Maus* becomes itself inscribed in the contorted logic or illogic with which my book deals.

While in Auschwitz, Vladek manages to transmit a message that he is still alive to Anja in Birkenau. A few days later his go-between Mancie gives him the coded message that she has left some "garbage" under a rock. The letter from Anja is given to us in her own words: "I miss you . . . each day I think to run into the electric wires and finish everything. But to know you are still alive it gives me still to hope" (213). "Garbage" is the code for the unmentionable letter but it also speaks to the scarce economy of paper in the camps. (So scarce, in fact, inmates used pieces of their clothes or just their hands to wipe their excrement or waste.) The next letter Vladek manages to smuggle to Anja is written on a scrap of paper used to wrap a piece of a kapo's cheese (kapos were prisoner functionaries who were given power over the other camp inmates). Here the letter is literally the litter. The letter informs Anja of a new barracks in Auschwitz and Vladek's thoughts of bringing her closer to him. It is on the precarious passage of these scraps of paper that Vladek's and Anja's hope for life rested in the camps. So when Anja writes on the back of the letter how desperately she wants to be close to him, she not only responds to his message of hope but indicates in her very writing that she is still alive and thus offers him hope in return. The blank space on the back of the scrap of waste paper is the space left open to the possibility of giving the hope of life, of life itself, of living on. Vladek's and Anja's letters pass precariously, then, as a metonymy of their vulnerable bodies in extremis of the camps, and these scraps of wastepaper that Vladek has "saved" are pitted against Vladek's and Anja's absolute wasting away, of the reduction of their bodies to ash. When Françoise (Artie's wife) says that she'd bet that "Anja's notebooks were written on both sides of the page" and that "if there were any blank pages Vladek would never have burned them" (249), she is speaking facetiously, or perhaps not so facetiously, of his miserliness. But she also speaks more truly than she proposes, for the saved blank pages offer the space for more writing, for the hope of more life, of a life still to come, of a living on. Anja's letter is presented as her own writing in her own words, and yet we know that the letter is Vladek's translation, his reconstruction (his "rebuilding") of Anja's words. When Vladek tells Artie that he burnt Anja's notebooks to "make an order with everything," these words must necessarily resonate with, or run up against, his remembrance of Anja's note and her thought "to run into the electric wires and finish everything." No longer metonymic of her frail body, the notebooks have been reduced by Vladek to scraps of used-up wastepaper filled with notes and returned to its former status as mere waste, which, in failing

Figure 4. *Maus*: Hitler did it!

ultimately to save, now need not be saved. However, in a bitter irony and logic reminiscent of a letter forever in search of its victim or embodiment, the suicidal threat in Anja's note comes to be embodied, and the words of her note written in the camps now come to fill the place of her suicide note that cannot be written.

Anja does not, of course, commit suicide by running into the electric wires. But in a further uncanny turn in "Prisoner," Artie accuses her of electrocuting him: "You put me here . . . shorted all my circuits . . . cut my nerve endings . . . and crossed my wires!" He is referring to the breakdown of his psyche, but he also positions himself as a survivor wearing the stripes of the camps and his claim of electrocution calls up and, seems to me, bespeaks a knowledge of his mother's dark thoughts before the electric wires of the fence. The younger Spiegelman, author of "Prisoner," may or may not have known at the time of his mother's thoughts in the camps, but nonetheless the revelation of Anja's letter in *Maus II* brings out the uncanny and undead element in the warped frames of the interleaved prisoner comic. In "Prisoner," Artie represents himself as feeling guilty for having turned away from his mother's overbearing need for his love. But in the context of the revelation of Anja's letter in the camp, a far deeper and more terrible guilt seems to emerge. "You murdered me mommy," Artie charges, and out of the prison of his guilt he also accuses her of afflicting him with a fate that should have been hers. Burned circuits and crossed wires, indeed!

There is, however, a less circuitous and more direct way in which Anja's letter from the time of the camps is conjoined with her suicide. In struggling to come to terms with the causes of his mother's suicide in "Prisoner," Spiegelman draws a frame in which he lays out his thoughts as to the reasons for her taking her life and the consequences this act has for his. The frame conflates and condenses the space and time of the camps with Anja's life after the camps and the scene of her suicide. Artie cites menopausal depression as one cause and, indeed, we know that Anja did suffer depression even before the war. But more prominently the words "HITLER DID IT!" cut across the frame (figure 4). A pile of skeletal corpses forms a pyramid and tellingly the fence of the camp lingers malign in the black background. (As in *Barbarians*, the apocalypse of corpses takes on a pyramidal form.) Speaking to the way in which Hitler programmed his mother's future suicide, Spiegelman displays a scene of multiple incisions. Anja's undead severed hand itself incised with her number from the concentration camp slits the veins across the wrist of her other severed hand with a razor blade. The number incised into Anja's arm marks an ineluctable path to the incision of the razor blade. The Nazi accountant finally makes collection of his corpse.

I have previously addressed Freud's assertion of the uncanniness of severed limbs and drawn a relation to the marked body in my chapter on *Heart of Darkness*. *Maus* has offered us a chance to return to this theme. I have tried to demonstrate the ways in which the "Prisoner" comic exhibits elements of the animating uncanny that are brought out in relation to the framing context of *Maus* itself. I want now to open an analysis of the way in which *Maus* offers us the chance of countering or deanimating the captivating powers of the marked body. Such an analysis will lead us back to Artie and the question of reception and ethical responsibility.

After we learn that Vladek has recently read "Prisoner" and seeing Artie's alarm at the coming to light of a comic that he'd drawn years before and that he thought Vladek would never encounter, we are given a frame in which we see Artie holding open and looking at the underground "Prisoner" comic (figure 5). Here Artie's hand, which is cut off from his shoulder by the border of the frame, holds onto the opening frame of "Prisoner," in which a disembodied hand holds onto a photograph of Anja with her own hand resting on the boy Artie's head. The disembodied hand is not identified in "Prisoner" itself, but I am interested in the way in which the imbrication of hands and the surrounding context of the *Maus* comic seem to confer identity and responsibility. The overlapping of Artie's hand in relation to the disembodied hand is surely not accidental but confers a nested relation between the hand responsible for the drawing of the comic and the hand that encounters responsibility for the reception of the comic. As we turn the page we get a close-up view of Artie's severed hand holding open the first pages of the "Prisoner" comic. Artie's hand has shifted down the page, now marking the space between writer and reader that opens between the two hands. Paradoxically, Artie's severed hands connect to Anja's severed hands, indexing the complicated and conflicted ties that on the one hand bind them together and on the other cut them apart. Artie holds a photograph that displays the bond between mother and son. On the bottom of the photograph is written "Trojan Lake, N. Y. 1958," which matches up with "Rego Park, N. Y. 1958," which

Figure 5. *Maus*: Prisoner on the hell planet comic.

we find on the opening page of *Maus*. The opening sequence of *Maus* chronicles a moment between father and son that is emblematic of the fraught history that conditions their relationship. The photograph that opens "Prisoner" chronicles the seemingly closer bond between mother and son. The correlation of the dates marks these two moments of parent-child relation as emblematic of the history out of which both comics were drawn. Anja, we know, was the first chronicler, the parent of the writerly and autobiographical sensibility, and Artie seems to draw a line of descent between her and him. On first consideration, then, Artie's is the hand that holds to the photograph signifying their bond while Anja's hand holds the razor blade that severs that bond. So it is Artie's hand that now writes the story, that takes up the pen to give a kind of life after life, while Anja's hand abjures the pen to take up the razor blade cutting off life and the story of that life. She is the survivor who succumbs to the violence etched into her arm, while he is the survivor who etches out the life that remains. Yet we know that things do not fit so perfectly into this antonymical analysis. It is Artie who feels guilt for turning away from Anja, for his resentment, as he puts it, "of the way she tightened the umbilical cord." If Artie is murdered, he is also something of a murderer, and if the correlation of severed hands marks the difference between the pen and the blade, it also marks something of their violent linkage.[3] Although both Artie and Anja are signified by the metonym of their severed hands, Artie's does not, of course, display the mark of the concentration camp, but in conjuring history, the hand that holds the pen is not entirely free of the violent traces and effects that attend that history. It is perhaps a recognition of this responsibility that is now held in Artie's hand, which itself holds the other severed hands.

There is still, however, one other hand we need to take account of and that is our own hand holding open and overlapping with Artie's hand that holds open the "Prisoner" comic and that holds, in turn, the hand that holds the photograph of Artie and Anja. This nesting of hands draws our, the reader's, hand into the sequential or abyssal arrangement of hands. Abyssal because our hand seems to be pulled into the textual frame of *Maus*, or more precisely it is paradoxically both within and without this frame, and the border between our hands and the hands of *Maus* is less than secure. We have a hand in the text. These effects are part of the elaborate metafictional aspects of *Maus* itself. But to what end? In "Partial Magic of the Quixote," Borges considers the extraordinary capacity of the metaeffects of fiction to render us fictitious: "Why does it disturb us that Don Quixote be a reader of the *Quixote* and Hamlet a spectator of *Hamlet?* I believe I have found the reason: these inversions suggest that if the characters of a fictional work can be readers or spectators, we, its readers or spectators, can be fictitious. In 1833, Carlyle observed that the history of the universe is an infinite sacred book that all men write and read and try to understand, and in which they are also written."[4] We the readers of *Maus* are each of us inscribed in this strangely sacred comic book, or at least in the long shadow of the history it inscribes. But we readers and spectators of this book are not so much rendered fictitious, I believe; rather this fiction is itself inverted and freighted with the material weight of our hands. We do not, that is, escape ethical implication in the address of the text. Lest we imagine that we are wholly outside the ethical register and dangerous effects of this book we are literally brought to hand and reminded that we too have a responsible hand in the reception of this text.

If Artie encounters the troubling aftereffects of his early "Prisoner" comic in *Maus I*, it is at the beginning of the "Time Flies" chapter of *Maus II* that he again comes up against difficult questions of artistic responsibility and the reception of his comic, but this time his concern is with the aftereffects of *Maus I* itself, and not simply the particular anguished instance of Vladek's reading, but also of the generalized reception of his *Maus* project. "Time Flies" opens with Artie tallying up a number of crucial periods in the composition of *Maus I* that are drawn from his father's past and his contemporary present (201). The bottom frame of the first page presents us with Artie slumped over his drafting table wearing the mask of a mouse or what I would refer to as a meta-

Figure 6. *Maus*: Spiegelman at the drawing board.

mask (figure 6). I call this a metamask because unlike the mask in *Maus I*, which was predominantly used to indicate a moment of disguise, this mask does not so much conceal but reveals the way in which Artie himself has become captivated or conditioned by the *Maus* project. It is a mask that reflects on the powers of masks to capture identity. Heaped before his drafting table is piled a pyramid of skeletal corpses, some still frozen in their anguished rictus of death. Outside his studio window stands the guard tower and fence of the concentration camp.

What has captured and almost crushed Artie is the overwhelming critical and commercial success of the *Maus* project. In the frames that follow we see Artie gradually reduced in size to that of an infant. What appears to be particularly overwhelming is the guilt that he feels at profiting from the Holocaust. Ironically, when Artie proposes drawing the comic that will become *Maus*, Vladek cautions, "Better you should spend your time to make drawings that will bring you some money" (14). Now, Artie finds himself overwhelmed with guilt at the burgeoning commercialization of his comic. A caption at the top of the frame reads, "At least fifteen foreign editions are coming out. I've gotten 4 serious offers to turn my book into a T.V. special or movie (I don't wanna.)" (201). Floating above the pile of corpses a bubble caption reads, "Alright Mr. Spiegelman . . . We're ready to shoot!" The reference is to the television special or movie of course, but the caption also lies in the long shadow cast by the camp tower that intrudes through the window into Artie's studio. "Ready to shoot!" refers not only to the movie but also to the actual scene of execution in the camps and Artie's guilt at the way in which his art feeds or lives off the corpses of the Holocaust.

It is telling that Artie begins his ethical reflection on the reception of *Maus* with recourse to a verbal and visual citation from his "Prisoner" piece. In fact, his words "In May 1968 my mother killed herself. (She left no note.)" almost reiterate Artie's first words in "Prisoner": "In 1968, when I was 20, my mother killed herself . . . she left no note!" We have already seen what was at stake in Anja's refusal to write her note and Artie's guilt over her suicide. I want now to reflect further on the pyramid of corpses that Artie carries over from "Prisoner" and that he encrypts as the emblem of his self-reflection on the guilty debt and destiny of his text. The pyramid of corpses appears first in "Prisoner" and next appears in the frame in which Artie despairs over the popular reception of *Maus I*. These are the encrypted dead whose stories will not be told. The floating pile of corpses attends his ruminations on the costs entailed in bringing *Maus* to life and I use the word "debt" because the *Maus* project is entangled in a history of cruel economies.

At the opening of the "Time Flies" chapter of *Maus II*, we find Artie sitting at his drafting table and measuring out a set of timely counterpoints and correspondences between himself and his father. He is trying to keep track of the complex relays between moments of historical time and moments in the time of the composition and reception of *Maus*. I am particularly interested in the panel in which we see Artie drawing a page in which he remarks: "Vladek started working as a tinman in Auschwitz in the spring of 1944. . . . I started working on this page at the very end of February 1987" (201). An analysis of the implications of this panel offer us as a way into the complex set of historical and contemporary economies that mark the production of *Maus*. We remember that Artie maintains that he became an artist as a way of evading competition with his father and as a means of countering Vladek's mechanical prowess. He started drawing comics precisely because they were impractical, and as he puts it "a waste of time" (99). The commercial success of *Maus* seems to draw out a revised relation between himself and his father. Artie now marks a correlation not only between moments of historical time and the contemporary time in which he records that history but also between his "work," or the labor of his art, and his father's "work," or his labor as a tin man. Artie's comic, that is, is no longer simply a "waste of time" but has its own economic and material consequences. The irony, however, is not simply that Artie's comic is making money but that it has revised the *instrumental* relations between himself and his father. When Artie tells his shrink Pavel that he has lived with the psychological insufficiency of always being told by his father that he could not do anything as well as he could, Pavel wonders if with his success Artie feels "bad about proving your father wrong" (204). But the guilt that Artie feels is less, I think, that he has proven Vladek wrong and more that in the composition of *Maus* he finds that he is closer to Vladek than he supposed; or to put this more precisely, what the success of the *Maus* project reveals to Artie is that his comic is inscribed in and inscribes some of the same economies in which he discovers his father implicated.

There is obviously an immense distance between Vladek's slave labor as a tin man and Artie's labor on the composition of his page of *Maus*. But Artie's marking this heretofore unseen or perhaps unacknowledged correlation opens onto a complex set of transactions and transpositions involving texts and textiles that runs through *Maus*. The exposition of this conjunction will allow me to better demonstrate my contention. I shall not attempt to address the full range of this linkage in *Maus*; rather, I shall focus on a number of intersecting threads that I hope will better allow me to show what I mean. As we shall soon see, the linkage between text and textile is caught up in a further set of relays involving translation and transmission.

When Vladek begins work as a tin man he is placed under the dangerous supervision of a Russian Jew named Yidl who was a communist. Yidl is properly suspicious of his work as a tin man. He regards Vladek as a dirty capitalist and accuses him of exploiting his workers in his big textile factories. Yidl's accusation leads us back to an early episode in *Maus I* where we find Anja involved in radical politics translating important communist documents and messages into German. Warned about a police raid, she rushes to hide a batch of documents with the seamstress Miss Stefanska, who agrees because of her dependence upon Anja as a good customer. The seamstress is caught with the documents and imprisoned. When Vladek hears of the incident, he angrily warns Anja that she will have to choose between him and her communist sympathies. "She was a good girl," he reports, "and of course she stopped all such things" (31). Anja's nascent radical politics are subsumed in a moment of capitalist patriarchy. It is after this episode that Anja's father funds Vladek's opening of a textile factory. The seamstress is left to take the rap, spending three months in prison before she is released. The irony imposed by the bleak transpositions of the camp, then, is not simply that the capitalist Vladek has become a slave worker under the communist slave worker Yidl or that he is imprisoned like the seamstress for no good reason but that he now takes up Anja's dangerous role of transmitting messages. Vladek's messages are not, of course, political, to say nothing of radically political, in content but like Anja's they are also sent in the hope of a liberatory moment. If Anja takes on the dangerous task of translating and transmitting messages in the hope of a liberatory communist politics, Vladek too sends his messages in hope of liberation from the Nazi extinction.

But Vladek's deep loyalty to Anja, whom he loves, and the risks he takes for his friend Mandelbaum also bring into relief his capacity for exploitation of the vulnerability of others in the camps. After his incarceration in Auschwitz, Vladek manages to get in with a kapo whom he teaches English. His knowledge of other languages, his capacity to teach and translate, helps save his life in Auschwitz as it does through the course of the Holocaust. When the kapo takes him to a room filled with prison clothes, Vladek tells Artie that "I took myself clothes like tailored," and with his odd vanity he asserts in a phrase that he is particularly partial to, "I looked like a million" (193). For all his vanity, though, Vladek does not forget the terrible suffering of his friend Mandelbaum, for whom, at risk to himself, he secures a belt and shoes. This episode stands in strict contrast to the way in which Vladek secures a clean shirt for himself in Dachau. Since the camp guards would dole out soup only if the inmates had a shirt that was not infested with lice, a clean shirt was a matter of life or death. In the exiguous economies of Dachau, Vladek's knowledge of English again saves his life. He is fortunate to meet an isolated French prisoner desperate to talk to anyone in the camp and conversing in broken English they become friends. As the Frenchman is not Jewish he is allowed to receive Red Cross packages containing biscuits and chocolate that he shares with Vladek. Scheming, Vladek uses the chocolate to trade for the shirt of one of the other Jewish inmates. He then carefully cleans the shirt and keeps it wrapped in a piece of paper. Hiding his old lice-infested shirt in his pants, he presents the clean shirt in order to get his soup. We have seen how difficult it was to find scrap paper in Auschwitz; in the even further reduced circumstances of Dachau, finding a piece of paper large enough to wrap and keep a shirt clean would seem well nigh impossible, but somehow Vladek is lucky enough to find this piece of paper. This gambit he repeats in the service of the Frenchman, who calls him a genius. "I helped the Frenchman to also organize a shirt," he says, "so we both got always soup" (254). His claim of also helping others in the service of himself is repeated when he uses snow from the roof of the cattle-car transports to barter sugar from those dying of thirst: "So I ate also sugar and saved their life" (246). We might, given the utterly desperate conditions, wish to collude with Vladek by excusing his evasion of responsibility and avowing his claim that in helping himself he has helped others as well. But we can be under no illusions as to what having bartered away his shirt will cost his fellow in the camp. And I do not really think Vladek has any either.

Nor do I imagine that this has escaped Artie. Returning to the opening pages of the "Time Flies" chapter, we find a panel that deals again with Artie's anxiety over profiting from the Holocaust. The panel displays a shrunken Artie facing the caricatured figure of a shyster trying to con Artie into licensing spin-off products from *Maus*. The con artist holds a placard on which reads "MAUS You've Read The Book Now Buy The Vest." A picture of Artie's vest with diagonal stripes on the inside is printed in the middle of the placard. At the top of the panel, a caption reads "Artie baby. Check out this licensing deal. You get 50% of the profits. We'll make a million. Your dad would be proud!" (202). The panel represents Artie's humorous caricature of those who would glom onto his book in order to make a profit but it also subtly registers his anxiety over a certain complicity with his father. Given the context we quickly discern the play on "vest" and "investment," but what is also revealed by the fantasy caricature is Artie's own anxious "investment" in his father's story.

"We'll make a million" recalls Vladek's refrain of "looking like a million." It recalls too the earlier moment in which Vladek throws Artie's "shabby" coat into the garbage and makes him put on his jacket with his refrain, "Ah! It looks on you like a million dollars" (71). As we read further, we come to realize that this seemingly minor incident is not only indicative of the struggle between father and son or of Vladek's compulsion to save and dispose but that it is caught up in Vladek's history of the camps and clothes. This history includes Vladek's odd souvenir photograph of himself in a clean camp uniform that he keeps on his desk as well as his deadly barter for a clean camp shirt. And it is here that Artie, I think, subtly registers his deep anxiety of a particular complicity with his father in the composition of *Maus*. He registers a relation between the text (paper) and textile, a transmission or relay that runs through Vladek's history and his own text, a textile transmission or relay out of which *Maus* comes into production. The vest with its card background recalls the camp shirt with its background of paper. For does Artie not enter into a barter or gift economy, exchanging his time in the present for the story of the past? (I mean here to register a reference to Marcel Mauss on the gift economy that we might already hear in the very title *Maus*.) Does Artie not barter time with Vladek in exchange for his "rebuilding" his story? Is this not the price Artie pays for the story of *Maus*, for profiting, that is, off his father's story? Is this not what also lies behind Artie's cartoonish fantasy projection, "We'll make a million. Your dad will be proud!" Of course, Artie does not enter into so deadly a barter as Vladek does, but we should remember that the exchange that he makes is not only with his father but with those dead Holocaust bodies off which his text profits, and it is the debt to this more exorbitant economy that he cannot escape, and which is guiltily encrypted in the pyramid of corpses piled below his drafting table. These corpses are literally piled in the form of a pyramid-shaped crypt that is depicted as both there and not, ghostly corpses that haunt Artie's guilt-ridden conscience.

The focus of this book has been on the textual capture of the marked body and on the metaleptic embodiment of the apocalyptic text. Kafka, Conrad, and Coetzee, I have claimed, each wrestled with the ethical consequences of the future incorporation of undead marked bodies. In *Maus*, Spiegelman wrestles more, I think, with the ethical consequences of the encryption of undead Holocaust bodies. The problem is not that these bodies will come to enter or incarnate the field of *Maus*'s reception but that they are already encrypted into the graphic novel migrating from the "Prisoner" comic to their haunting irruption near the beginning of *Maus II*. This is not to say that the *Maus* text is closed to the future; on the contrary, in his more recent comic *In the Shadow of No Towers*, Spiegelman demonstrates how life with his father and the composition of *Maus* come to code his reception of the burning of the Twin Towers, the disaster of 9/11 through which

Coda

he himself lived.⁵ But in the end, it is *Maus* that overshadows the ghostly shadow of *In the Shadow of No Towers*. However, we have also seen how the note or letter in *Maus* comes to claim its marked body, how the severed hands of "Prisoner" imbue the comic with an undead aspect, and how encrypted pyramids of Holocaust bodies haunt the reception of *Maus I* and even trouble its future composition. No less than for Kafka, Conrad, and Coetzee, for Spiegelman, too, the marked undead body opens the problem of the ethics of future reception and the apocalyptic text.

As promised, I will conclude this book by turning now to a messianic reading of a scene of the marked body that gestures toward the deactivation of the cycle of apocalyptic embodiment. When Artie asks Vladek to describe his entrance into Auschwitz, he speaks of having come often to the town of Oswiecim (in which Auschwitz became situated) before the war to sell textiles, and now, ironically, he finds himself naked and forced to dress in torn, ill-fitting, prison clothes. Immediately after this, we get a further linkage of text and textile as Vladek speaks of being registered, literally inscribed, into the camp by means of a number tattooed on his arm. "They took from us our names and here they put me my number" (186). Vladek means that the Nazis matched his name with his number but his garbled English accurately captures the substitution of his name for a number and the reduction of his identity to an instrument of the camp. A short time later, we are offered an extraordinary scene. Near his nadir, slumped, crying, worn, shivering, with the smoking crematoria in his thoughts, and utterly reduced before the absolute sovereign power of the camps, Vladek is approached by a Polish priest who asks to see his number.

Utilizing Judaic principles of interpretation, the priest turns the Nazi arithmetic of death against itself by turning Vladek's number into a sacred text that prophesizes his salvation.⁶ He overcodes the machine of the number, offering Vladek the possibility of another destiny. The priest's reading gives Vladek hope (figure 7). "I started to believe," he tells Artie, "I tell you he put another life in me" (188). As opposed to the number on Anja's arm that

Figure 7. *Maus*: reading the number.

programs her death, the priest interprets Vladek's number so as to give him hope of life, literally to "put another life in him."

The inscription that kills (we are reminded of the sentence in Kafka's "In the Penal Colony") is now interpreted to give life! The program of the number plays out differently. In Dachau, Vladek cuts into his infected hand in order to prolong his life in the infirmary; Anja, we know, will come to cut her veins. Artie calls the priest a "saint" for offering Vladek hope, and this word is reserved for only one other person in *Maus*: Anja, who also once gave Vladek hope and the will to live on.

There is a way in which Artie also enacts the role of the priest. He puts another life into Vladek. When Artie proposes writing

Coda

a book about Vladek's life, Vladek replies, "It would take many books my life" (14). He means that it would take many books to cover his improbable and long-suffering life, but his odd phrasing gives the sense of the way in which a book "takes a life," takes the life out of his life, but takes a life too in the sense of preserving a life. I do not quite mean this in terms of the notion that Vladek's life is simply transcribed into Artie's comic art. Although it is true that Vladek's story is at least preserved and allowed to live on, his life cannot simply be passed into art without loss as if by means of some superconductive transmission, and *Maus*, which is above all a text on the nature of the transmission of texts, is imbued with and imbues this knowledge. For all its canny self-reference as to the nature and time of its composition, there is always a time of composition, the time that composition "takes" that is "outside" the text or that cannot be wholly recorded within the time of composition itself.

The focus of this book has been on the way in which a text may retroactively embody itself as an apocalyptic work, the means by which it may unfold or reveal itself as already inscribing the apocalypse that is always on its way. But as part of a final messianic counter or countertime to this retroactive apocalypse, I want to summon the "fabulous retroactivity" of *Maus* and its time of the composition of life. I borrow the phrase "fabulous retroactivity" from Derrida, who uses it to describe the way in which the signatories of the American Declaration of Independence retroactively invent or constitute the "We the people" with which the declaration begins, performatively establishing "We the people" before they properly exist as such an entity.[7] *Maus* is also composed according to this principle of "fabulous retroactivity," with the difference that it self-referentially displays both the "fabulous" and "retroactive" elements of its composition. At the opening of the first chapter of *Maus II*, we are confronted with a sketch pad containing a number of animal cartoon figures. Artie is composing animal cartoons, trying to figure out how to draw his wife, Françoise. The problem is that Françoise is not Jewish but French and Artie thus feels required to consider the history of French anti-Semitism. Should she be a mouse or a rabbit or a frog? Françoise makes the point that she converted and that if Artie is a mouse she should be one too. Artie settles on making her a mouse and the nearest contending rabbit figure is dropped from the book. There are lessons here with regard to the politics of representation and to the violence of writing in which a figure is brought into being only to be excised from the text. What is fabulously retroactive about this page, however, is that we have Françoise already composed as a mouse figure asking Artie what he is doing as Artie is himself composing the array of figures from which he will compose Françoise. In a warp of time Françoise looks on and even helps to fashion her own moment of composition. If the character of the rabbit is rubbed out, Françoise will *convert* herself into "becoming mouse." What particularly interests me here, then, is that for all its compulsion to draw everything into its frame, *Maus* also gestures to that time of composition that cannot be contained by or absorbed into the abyssal scene of composition. Or to put this differently, what is precisely indicated by this abyssal composition is the time of composition that slips away, that remains always "outside" the frame of the text. There is always a time, the time of composition itself, that cannot be completely absorbed into the nested structure of this book. Like the hand of the reader, this time of composition is both within and outside the frame of the book, even as this is a book, like other apocalyptic books, that is written on the inside and the outside.

Toward the end of *Maus*, we encounter a harrowing scene. Sick with typhus, and close to death himself, Vladek each night has to step down a corridor laden with corpses in order to get to the toilet. The accompanying graphics display a grotesque carpet of bodies lining the corridor of the camp barracks. While stepping on this pile of bodies, he thinks to himself, "'Now it's my time. Now I will be laying like this ones and somebody will step on me!" (255). Vladek here thinks himself into the impossible position of a corpse on which one of the dying will step. He thinks himself into that space that cannot be thought, that space that is literally dead to thought, the space of death itself. When he thinks of himself as a trodden corpse, then, he occupies the realm of the undead. His vision of his own dead body is outside of time. Like the time of composition, it cannot wholly exist within the frame of his mind. But as the priest had predicted, now was not Vladek's time, and he survives this undead ghostly vision. In their harrowing aspect, this carpet of corpses recalls the pyramid of corpses that attend Artie's guilty portrayal of the reception of *Maus I*. But while certainly harrowing, this carpet of corpses does not haunt in quite the same way as the crypt of copses that trails Artie. The corpses that line the corridors of the camp are grotesque but dead, inert in their anguished postures. The crypt of corpses that trail Artie is undead, hauntingly there and not there at the same time. The encrypted pyramids of the Holocaust dead that haunt Artie's project cannot be entirely stilled or deanimated. The insistent ethical questions they pose with regard to the production and reception of Artie's book cannot be dissolved or done away with. Nor should they be. But like the priest who deanimates the Nazi arithmetic of death, putting another life in Vladek, Artie too puts another life in Vladek. His project offers testimony of Vladek's survival of his own ghostly vision of his death, and in this respect must surely stand alongside of, and offer some ethical response to, the encrypted corpses that haunt his book.

When Vladek says to himself, "Now it's my time," his words betray a loss of faith in the priest's reading of his number. "And whenever it was very bad," he tells Artie. "I looked and said: Yes, the priest was right! It totals eighteen" (188). But stumbling along the dark corridor strewn with skulls that act like slippery stepping-stones, which literally give him the sensation of falling to his death, Vladek loses hope and believes his time has come. But the priest was right and by a felicitous resonance of words we can contrast Vladek's "Now it's my time" with Benjamin's messianic "now time"; as we shall see, however, what I am pointing to is more than simply a coincidence of words. When the priest interprets Vladek's number he deploys a Judaic mode of numerology or gematria in which Hebrew letters are assigned numerical values. Thus the priest adds together the numbers on Vladek's arm and finds that they total eighteen, which is the numerical value of the Hebrew word "chai" or "life." (We are reminded here of Kafka's Kabalistic interpretation of "The Judgment.") Part of the reason that Vladek is inclined to believe in the priest's reading is because of his own mystical experience in telling the future. We recall that while interned in a German prisoner of war camp, Vladek has an indelible dream that he will be released on the date in which the Parshas Truma portion of the Torah is to be read. Indeed, after almost three months of debilitating prison labor, he is released on the day of the reading of that portion of the Torah and is confirmed by a rabbi in the camp as a "'Roh-eh hanoled,' one who will see what the future will bring" (62). As his life unfolds, Vladek finds the date of the reading of this portion to be one of great significance for him. Besides being released from the camp on that date, he learns that he had married Anja in the week in which the reading of this portion fell, that it was the week of this parsha, too, in which Artie was born, and that this was also the Torah portion that Artie read on his bar mitzvah. Perhaps the number thirteen that the priest points to on Vladek's arm might be read, in this context, as a forecast not only of Vladek's but of Artie's future as well.

Without, myself, acceding to kabalistic modes of interpretation, however, I want to situate the priest's interpretation of Vladek's number according to another mode of Judaic interpretation, Benjamin's "now of legibility." I spoke in the introduction of this book of Benjamin's desperate efforts to ensure the survival of his last texts and of his hope, like Bloch's, of the power of a past text to condition a redemptive future. Honoring this hope, I would like to conclude this book by attempting to show how the priest's reading of Vladek's number actualizes a Benjaminian hermeneutic of time and inscription. Fleeing Paris and the Nazi persecution, Benjamin entrusted the notes and texts that would finally come to be published as his *Arcades Project* to his friend Georges Bataille. As we now know, Bataille hid them well in a secret archive of the National Library (a crypt, we might say) where they were later uncovered after the war. In one of the notes of the *Arcades Project*, Benjamin formulates his particular hermeneutic of a "now of knowability" or "now of legibility." "Each now," he contends, "is the now of a particular knowability. In it, truth is charged to the bursting point with time." He goes on to claim,

> It is not that what is past casts its light on what is present, or what is present its light on what is past; rather, image is that wherein what has been comes together in a flash with the now to form a constellation. In other words: image is dialectics at a standstill. For while the relation of the present to the past is purely temporal, the relation of what-has-been to the now is dialectical: not temporal in nature but figural [*bildich*]. Only dialectical images are genuinely historical—that is, not archaic—images. The image that is read—which is to say, the image in the now of its recognizability—bears to the highest degree the imprint of the perilous critical moment on which all reading is founded.[8]

This elliptical note requires some analysis and legibility of its own. Let me begin with his notion of the "now of legibility." Here Benjamin posits a particular "now time" upon which the possibility for any true reading rests. Far from remaining open to myriad possible future interpretations, Benjamin argues for a particular historical moment and perilous "now" in which the image comes to its particular moment of legibility. Perilous, because up until the time of its actualization, this "now of legibility" remains forever endangered because it may always be missed, never to arise again. Missing its moment of reading, the potential image from the still-unrealized past will not arrive in a flash to form a constellation with its "now of legibility"; it will be extinguished, never, in effect, to have been, and never, in effect, to be. And by "image," it remains to be said, Benjamin denotes not only texts in the narrow sense but also objects of inscription, documents or works of art that also require their "now of legibility" if they are to be redeemed for history. Moreover, this image contains within it the perilous historical index or moment by which it is made legible.

The priest's reading of Vladek's arm offers, it seems to me, an exemplary instance of Benjamin's "now of legibility." It offers, in fact, the perilous enactment or literalization of Benjamin's principle of legibility itself. With this in mind, it is worth closely looking at the scene again. We recall that just after Vladek is interned in Auschwitz the old-timers tell him the only way out is through the chimneys of the crematoria and sinking into utter despair he begins to give up on life. Worn and crying, he is pictured as hunched over, alone, abandoned. Nobody even bothered to look at him, he remarks. But it is at this precise moment of sheer desperation, when the priest's reading is most needed, and offers the most hope, that he approaches. His very approach is somewhat mysterious. Is it just by chance that he emerges from another room to find Valdek hunched over and crying, or was there some design, some redemptive sign for which the priest was especially on the lookout? We will never know. As the *arrivant* that he is, his arrival is unexpected. He first enters the frame of the panel as a sliver of striped camp uniform out of which his bare hand hangs at his side. What is sure, however, is that when he takes Vladek's arm in his own hand and begins his analysis, the moment constitutes a Benjaminian "now of legibility." It is at this precise moment of absolute crisis that Vladek's number becomes most legible, and at this precise moment that the priest's reading registers its full redemptive impact. Had he not been endowed with a seemingly unlikely knowledge of Hebrew gematria (for a Polish priest) and had he not come upon Vladek in his hunched moment of crisis, Vladek's number would have remained forever illegible and unredeemed. As a way into his reading of Vladek's number 175113, the priest begins with the number 17, which indicates a good sign or omen. He then remarks on the 13 with which Vladek's number ends as the age at which a Jewish boy becomes a man and totaling the number to the value of 18 spells out "chai," the number of life. In truth, Vladek's number affords a vast number of applications or combinatory readings, but what is truly circumscribed is the moment in which the image comes together in a flash with the now to form a redemptive constellation. As the priest gives his reading, Vladek emerges from his hunched and creaturely position and the priest begins ever so slightly to dispel the hellish and absolute sovereign powers of the camp. Vladek tells Artie that he never again saw the priest but that when things looked very bad he looked at his arm and said to himself: "Yes, the priest was right it totals eighteen" (188). The reading is given in a singular "now of legibility," but the message of life that it gives lives on and is repeatedly and doubly affirmed in Vladek's living on. This point is emphasized when we see Vladek holding his arm in his hand, reiterating the priest's reading, in the book's portrayal of the narrative present (188). The priest's prognosticatory powers, however, do not extend to himself. He does not know if he'll survive the hell of Auschwitz. No "now of legibility" is given him. We are not told why. Perhaps the priest's powers are given only in the service of the reading of others, but perhaps, too, this particular "now of legibility" is reserved only for Vladek, and opens only for him.

I mentioned Benjamin's messianic theses on history in the introduction and briefly deployed elements of two of these theses in the hope of formulating a redemptive reading of *Heart of Darkness* and the Congolese dead. I turn now to a number of Benjamin's theses in one last messianic reading that concludes this book. Facing a state of crises himself, Benjamin famously writes in his second thesis that

> The past carries with it a secret index by which it is referred to redemption. . . . In the voices that we hear, isn't there an echo of the silent ones? . . . If so, then there is a secret agreement between past generations and the present one. Then our coming was expected on earth. Then, like every generation that preceded us, we have been endowed with a *weak* messianic power, a power on which the past has a claim. Such a claim cannot be settled cheaply. The historical materialist is aware of this. [9]

This thesis will prove useful in allowing us to endow not only the priest but also Artie himself with a *weak* messianic power over Vladek's future. It is the unfulfilled or missed potentialities of the past, and not only the distant, but equally the immediate past, Benjamin maintains, that lay claim to their fulfillment in the future. It is in the very possibility of the future actualization of these missed possibilities that the past endows future generations with the *weak* messianic power of redeeming that which was previously failed and now lays claim to its particular fulfillment. This work of redeeming the past requires the new hermeneutic of the dialectical image which Benjamin also refers to as the "now of recognizability." "The true image of the past flits by," he warns in his fifth thesis: "The past can be seized only as an image that flashes up at the moment of its recognizability, and is never seen again. . . . For it is an irretrievable image of the past which threatens to disappear in any present that does not recognize itself as intended in that image."[10] This tenuous or *weak* messianic power that lays its claim to the restoration of the distorted and unrealized past of what might have been is weak precisely in that it can never in itself guarantee its future realization. This demand of the past is dialectical precisely in that it depends on the recognition of the future generation, on which it lays its particular claim, to seize that moment in which it flashes up as an image.

If the priest redeems Vladek's life by the reading of his number according to its moment of legibility, then might we not see Artie as endowed with a *weak* messianism of redeeming not only Vladek's past life but also the priest's making legible Vladek's number? Does Artie not access that secret index by which, Benjamin tells us, the past is referred to redemption? And is Artie not also that representative of the present generation by which the past stakes its claim? In a number of respects, *Maus* seems to enact the tenets of Benjamin's second thesis. There is something of a secret, albeit fraught, agreement between the past generation of the Holocaust and Artie as representative, as well as one who represents, the present generation. In the voices that he hears, not only of Vladek and Anja but of Mala and Pavel too, there is certainly an echo of the now-silent ones of the Holocaust dead. Both

Vladek and Artie are all too well aware that such a claim cannot be settled cheaply, and as we have seen, Artie is guiltily aware of the deep costs involved in settling this claim. Indeed, to speak of Artie as "redeeming" Vladek's past life is to invoke both the historical and economic registers of this term. It remains Artie's task to seize the true image of his father's past as it flits by before it is irretrievably lost and consigned to oblivion. He in conjunction with Vladek is that dialectical agent by which the present recognizes the significance of the past and the past reaches its fulfillment in the present.

Of all contemporary thinkers it is Agamben who has most absorbed Benjamin's principle of the particular time of legibility into his thought. For Agamben, as for Benjamin, texts are not equally legible across time. Agamben refers, in this regard, to a "historical index" that somehow apportions or conditions a text's legibility.[11] He does not mean, of course, that a text cannot be read at different times but, rather, that it becomes truly or fully legible only when it establishes a constellation with a particular historical moment. A text that has remained obscure for centuries might suddenly under the right historical conditions open to the particular reading that has awaited it. In contrast to what he takes to be contemporary notions of interpretability, Agamben asserts of the "now of legibility" that it "defines a genuinely Benjaminian hermeneutic principle, the absolute opposite of the current principle according to which each work may become the object of infinite interpretation at any given moment (doubly infinite, in the sense that interpretations are never exhaustive and function independently of any historical-temporal situation)."[12] In his *The Time That Remains*, Agamben offers a brilliant exegesis of Benjamin's theses in which he uncovers Paul as the hunchback theologian so cryptically hidden in Benjamin's first thesis. Agamben's commentary is not simply an exegesis on Benjamin's principle but functions itself as an exemplary instance. Remarking on his uncovering of the way in which Paul's messianic text is cryptically cited in Benjamin's theses, Agamben maintains "there is no reason to doubt that these two fundamental messianic texts of our tradition, separated by almost two thousand years, both written in a situation of radical crisis, form a constellation whose time of legibility has finally come today, for reasons that invite further reflection."[13] Agamben himself does not offer further reflection on why the legibility of this constellation has finally emerged today but what is at stake in this "now of legibility" is not only the exegetical uncovering of a particular citation but also the liberating of messianic energies that might function politically or ethically in our time.

In contrast to a number of German philosophers for whom the term *Jetztzeit* (contemporary time) denotes a shallow present time, Benjamin endows the term with messianic powers of blasting new *passages* "out of the continuum of history." In his fourteenth thesis, Benjamin writes that "[h]istory is the subject of a construction whose site is not homogeneous, empty time, but time filled full by now-time [*Jetztzeit*]."[14] Critiquing a narrow unthinking conception of the inevitability of historical progress with which he associates "homogeneous, empty time," Benjamin counterposes the radical possibilities that might be unfolded or seized in the revolutionary potential that each moment brings with it. For Benjamin the messianic potential of "now-time" is not directed toward some distant future in which the Messiah might still appear. Rather it is in the "now-time" of the present in which the radical potential that inheres in each moment might be liberated for the use of those in the suffering world. In his commentary on messianic time in Paul and Benjamin, Agamben remarks, "one must first distinguish messianic time from apocalyptic time, the time of the now from a time directed towards the future."[15] Agamben demarcates an absolute distinction between the eschatological time of apocalypse as the time of the end and messianic time that denotes the "time that remains between time and its end." He remarks further, "The most insidious misunderstanding of the messianic announcement does not consist in mistaking it for prophecy, which is turned toward the future, but for apocalypse, which contemplates the end of time."[16]

What I have endeavored to demonstrate throughout the course

of this book is that particular texts also have their moment of apocalyptic legibility and that this legibility takes place on the body in literature that is scored and branded with the future. It is my claim that these texts are always in danger of becoming apocalyptically legible or manifest, but I hope to have shown too how this cycle of apocalyptic incorporation might be ethically and politically resisted. This resistance, however, is fragile. It is fragile in relation to the immense pull of catastrophe and the text's compulsion to solicit its apocalyptic embodiment. It is fragile in relation to the text moving relentlessly toward its resolution in the catastrophic body. It is fragile in relation to the text always in search of its apocalyptically legible end of time. Benjamin asserts that "in reality there is not a single instant that does not bring *its* revolutionary opportunity with it. It wants only to be grasped as a specific one—namely as the opportunity for a completely new solution to a completely new task."[17] In his seventeenth thesis Benjamin speaks the work of messianic possibility congealed in now-time or what amounts to a "revolutionary chance in the fight for the oppressed past."[18] One of my tasks in this book has been to search for that countertime against the apocalyptic futures that oppress the libratory potential of past texts in the hope that that potential might be put to use now. Let me close by reciting the epigraph with which I began: Certeau's claim that "[t]here is no law that is not inscribed on bodies." In reading the priest's prophecy inscribed on Vladek's arm as an exemplary instance of the Benjaminian "now of legibility," I hope to have unlocked one more fragile moment of resistance to the law of apocalyptic incorporation. In the very furnace and ash of the apocalypse itself, the priest turned his prophecy of the number not toward the apocalyptic end of time, but toward a liberated future: it was in the very "now-time" of the then-present that his reading began its slow, fragile, messianic work against apocalyptic futures.

NOTES

INTRODUCTION

1. Qtd. in Fredric Jameson, *Marxism and Form* (Princeton: Princeton University Press, 1971), 149.
2. Gustav Janouch, *Conversations with Kafka*, trans. Goronwy Rees (Frankfurt: S. Fischer GmbH, 1971), 143.
3. Ibid., 150.
4. Max Brod, *Franz Kafka* (New York: Da Capo Press, 1995), 75. As it turned out, Janouch was perhaps more perceptive than Kafka allowed. Some few years later, John Richardson, Picasso's biographer, records that Picasso did indeed turn to a shamanic art that recalls Janouch's claim of "willful distortion" as he engaged in a series of exorcising portraits that sought to express his wife Olga's psychological decline and the deterioration of their marriage, and as Jeffrey Meyers remarks, Picasso "in works like *Large Nude in Red Arm Chair* (1929) portrays his still handsome wife—through malevolent distortions and drooping flesh—as a decrepit old woman." Meyers, "Creator and Destroyer," *Raritan* 28.1 (Summer 2008), 165.
5. Walter Benjamin, *Walter Benjamin: Selected Writings*, vol. 4, *1938–1940*, ed. Howard Eiland and Michael W. Jennings (Cambridge, MA: Harvard University Press, 2003), 430.
6. Ibid., 440.
7. Walter Benjamin, "On the Concept of History," in ibid., 389–400.
8. Joseph Conrad, *Notes on Life and Letters* (New York: Doubleday, Page, 1921), 74.
9. Thomas Mann, "The Making of *The Magic Mountain*," *The Magic Mountain*, trans. H. T. Lowe-Porter (New York: Vintage Books, 1969), 720.
10. Ibid.

11. James Joyce, *Ulysses* (New York: Random House, 1986), 154.
12. Joyce qtd. in Richard Ellmann, *James Joyce* (New York: Oxford University Press, 1982), 461.
13. Ellmann, *James Joyce*, 462.
14. Janouch, *Conversations*, 26.
15. J. M. Coetzee, *Diary of a Bad Year* (London: Harvill Secker, 2007), 171.
16. Percy B. Shelley, *Shelley's Poetry and Prose*, ed. Donald H. Reiman and Sharon B. Powers (New York: W. W. Norton, 1977), 482.
17. Ibid., 508.
18. Peter Brooks, *Body Work: Objects of Desire in Modern Narrative* (Cambridge, MA: Harvard University Press, 1993), 3.
19. Ibid., xii.
20. Ibid., 22.
21. Terence Cave, *Recognitions: A Study in Poetics* (Oxford: Oxford University Press, 1990), 23.
22. Franz Kafka, *The Complete Stories,* ed. Nahum N. Glatzer (New York: Schocken Books, 1971), 144, 161.
23. Michel Foucault, "Nietzsche, Genealogy, History," *The Foucault Reader*, ed. Paul Rabinow (New York: Pantheon Books, 1984), 83.
24. Judith Butler, "Foucault and the Paradox of Bodily Inscriptions," *The Journal of Philosophy* 86.11 (November 1989), 604.
25. Ibid., 603.
26. Ibid., 607.
27. Ibid.
28. Foucault, "Nietzsche, Genealogy, History," 83.
29. Jean-Luc Nancy, *Corpus*, trans. Richard A. Rand (New York: Fordham University Press, 2008), 119.
30. Jacques Derrida, *On Touching—Jean-Luc Nancy*, trans. Christine Irizarry (Stanford: Stanford University Press, 2005), 287.
31. J. M. Coetzee, *Foe* (New York: Penguin,1988), 131.
32. J. M. Coetzee, *Elizabeth Costello* (New York: Penguin Books, 2003), 210.
33. Judith Butler, "How Can I Deny That These Hands and This Body Are Mine?," *Material Events: Paul de Man and the Afterlife of Theory*, ed. Tom Cohen et al. (Minneapolis: University of Minnesota Press, 2001), 268.
34. Ibid., 257.
35. James Joyce, *Finnegans Wake* (New York: Penguin Books, 1999), 185–86.
36. Samuel Taylor Coleridge, *Poetical Works by Samuel Taylor*

Coleridge, ed. J. C. C. Mays (Princeton: Princeton University Press, 2001), 1133–34.

37. Butler, "How Can I Deny?," 257.

38. Peter Greenaway, *The Pillow Book* (Paris: Dis Voir, 1996).

39. Christopher Nolan, *Memento and Following* (London: Faber and Faber, 2001), 222.

40. Ibid., 224.

41. Russell Samolsky, "Metaleptic Machines: Kafka, Kaballah, Shoah," *Modern Judaism* 19.2 (May 1999): 173–94.

42. Jacques Rancière, *The Flesh of Words: The Politics of Writing*, trans. Charlotte Mandell (Stanford: Stanford University Press, 2004), 5.

43. Jacques Rancière, *The Politics of Aesthetics*, trans. Gabriel Rockhill (London: Continuum, 2004), 57.

44. Jacques Rancière, "The Politics of Literature," *Dissensus: On Politics and Aesthetics*, ed. and trans. Steven Corcoran (London: Continuum, 2010), 152.

45. Ibid.

46. Ibid., 163.

47. Ibid., 158.

48. Ibid., 165.

49. See "Sir Hiram Maxim," available at http://www.dartfordarchive.org.uk/technology/engin_maxim.shtml, and "No. 694: Hiram Maxim," available at http://www.uh.edu/engines/epi694.htm.

50. J. M. Coetzee, *Waiting for the Barbarians* (New York: Penguin Books, 1999), 31.

51. Kafka, *The Complete Stories*, 167.

1. METALEPTIC MACHINES

1. Walter Benjamin, *Illuminations: Essays and Reflections*, ed. Hannah Arendt (New York: Schocken Books, 1968), 143.

2. Ibid., 143.

3. George Steiner, introduction to *The Trial* by Franz Kafka (New York: Schocken Books, 1992), 50.

4. Bertold Brecht, "Challenges and Protests: Commentary by Bertold Brecht," *The World of Franz Kafka*, ed. J. P. Stern (New York: Holt, Rinehart and Winston, 1980), 180.

5. Theodor W. Adorno, *Prisms*, trans. Samuel and Sherry Weber (Cambridge, MA: MIT Press, 1983), 245.

6. Ibid., 251–52.

7. Ibid., 259.

8. Lawrence L. Langer, "Kafka as Holocaust Prophet: A Dissent-

ing View," *Admitting the Holocaust: Collected Essays* (New York: Oxford University Press, 1995), 109.

9. Ibid., 114, 116.
10. Ibid., 113, 121, 117.
11. John Updike, foreword to Kafka, *Franz Kafka*, xviii.
12. Steiner, introduction, xxi.
13. Langer, "Kafka as Holocaust Prophet," 117.
14. Janouch, *Conversations with Kafka*, 143.
15. Ibid., 150.
16. Franz Kafka, *Diaries 1910–1923*, ed. Max Brod (New York: Schocken Books, 1975), 399.
17. Steiner, introduction, xxi.
18. Janouch, *Conversations with Kafka*, 139.
19. Ibid., 46. The exchange with Janouch that I paraphrase runs as follows. Kafka has asked Janouch if he can read his writing, to which Janouch replies, "Your writing runs in a clearly flowing curve." Kafka responds: "It's the curve of a rope falling to the ground. My letters are nooses." My sense of this passage is that Kafka is referring not simply to the shape of his letters but also to the harrowing nature of his words.
20. Gershom Sholem, qtd. in Robert Alter, *Necessary Angels: Tradition and Modernity in Kafka, Benjamin, and Scholem* (Cambridge, MA: Harvard University Press, 1991), 69. For more on Scholem and Kafka's relation to the kabbalah, see Robert Alter, "Kafka as Kabbalist," *Salmagundi* 98–99 (1996): 86–99; David Biale, *Gershom Scholem: Kabbalah and Counter-History* (Cambridge, MA: Harvard University Press, 1979), 215; David Biale, "Ten Unhistorical Aphorisms on Kabbalah, Text and Commentary," in *Gershom Scholem, Modern Critical Views*, ed. Harold Bloom (New York: Chelsea House, 1987), 121; and Rivka Horwitz, "Kafka and the Crisis in Jewish Religious Thought," *Modern Judaism* 15.1 (1995): 21–33.
21. Alter, *Necessary Angels*, 76.
22. Kafka, *Diaries 1910–1923*, 214.
23. Ibid., 215.
24. Alter, *Necessary Angels*, 71.
25. Harold Bloom, *Kabbalah and Criticism* (New York: Continuum, 1993), 2.
26. Kafka, *Diaries 1910–1923*, 399.
27. Harold Bloom, *Franz Kafka* (New York: Chelsea House, 1986), 4.
28. Ibid., 2.

29. Jorge Luis Borges, "Kafka and His Precursors," *Labyrinths*, ed. Donald Yates and James Irby (New York: New Directions, 1964), 201.
30. Bloom, *Kabbalah and Criticism*, 32.
31. 30. Ibid., 66, 67.
32. Qtd. in Alter, *Necessary Angels*, 33.
33. Kafka, *The Complete Stories*, 472.
34. Susan Handelman, "Jacques Derrida and the Heretic Hermeneutic," *Displacement: Derrida and After*, ed. Mark Krupnick (Bloomington: Indiana University Press, 1983), 126.
35. Bloom, *Kabbalah and Criticism*, 70.
36. Martin Jay, *Fin de Siecle Socialism and Other Essays* (New York: Routledge, 1988), 33.
37. George Steiner, *No Passion Spent, Essays 1978–1995* (New Haven: Yale University Press, 1996), 310.
38. Ibid., 312, 314.
39. Ibid., 314.
40. Ibid., 313.
41. My brief exposition of Derrida's "Otobiographies" has benefited from my reading of Christopher Norris's fine chapter "Nietzsche, Freud, Levinas: On the Ethics of Deconstruction," *Derrida* (Cambridge, MA: Harvard University Press, 1988), as well as his chapter "Deconstruction against Itself: Derrida and Nietzsche," *Deconstruction and the Interests of Theory* (Norman: University of Oklahoma Press, 1992).
42. Jacques Derrida, *The Ear of the Other: Otobiography, Transference, Translation*, ed. Christie V. McDonald, trans. Peggy Kamuf (New York: Schoken Books, 1982), 20.
43. Ibid., 31.
44. Ibid., 30–31.
45. Ibid., 29.
46. Ibid., 32, 30.
47. Janouch, *Conversations with Kafka*, 150.
48. I am using the concept of performative language in the register that it has come to take on in the work of Jacques Derrida, Paul de Man, J. Hillis Miller, and Shoshana Felman, rather than in the strictly Austinian sense. That is, I am using the notion of the performative to denote the general capacity of words to enact, do, or perform something in the material world.
49. Kafka, *The Complete Stories*, 148–49. Following citations to "In the Penal Colony" in the text are given parenthetically.
50. Benjamin, *Illuminations*, 133.

51. Ernst Pawel, *The Nightmare of Reason: A Life of Franz Kafla* (New York: Farrar, Straus, Giroux, 1984), 445.

52. Kafka, *The Complete Stories*, 277.

53. The logic of this performative necessarily exceeds the question of the author's intentions and in fact operates in the space of his or her absence or death. As Miller has detailed, this point is aptly elaborated upon in Paul de Man's reading of Rousseau in his *Allegories of Reading*. Here de Man opens up a provocative hermeneutics in his assertion that words in themselves have a performative effect that may run against the intention of the author and do not depend on his or her presence for their final signification. Paul de Man, *Allegories of Reading* (New Haven: Yale University Press, 1979), 296, 299, 300.

The future performative effects of a text then, are never wholly predictable and cannot be referred back to, or contained by recourse to an author or author function as transcendental signified. On the contrary and ironically, the only effect guaranteed by the efficacy of the performative is precisely the death of the author and this not only in the sense of the author's being dispossessed of hermeneutical and political sanction over the text in favor of the "arbitrary power play of the signifier" but also in the sense that the author's text, like the author's proper name, always outlives its subject.

54. Pawel, *The Nightmare of Reason*, 322.

55. Jacques Derrida, *Acts of Religion*, ed. Gil Anidjar (New York: Routledge, 2002), 87.

56. Qtd. in Giovanna Borradori, *Philosophy in a Time of Terror: Dialogues with Jürgen Habermas and Jacques Derrida* (Chicago: University of Chicago Press, 2003), 97.

57. Derrida, *Acts of Religion*, 83.

58. Ibid.

59. Ibid.

2. APOCALYPTIC FUTURES

1. While the guiding rubric "heart of darkness" enfolds the Rwandan killings within the orienting narrative of *Heart of Darkness*, demonstrating, as one commentator has it, "that in Africa, as Joseph Conrad's *Heart of Darkness* made so terrifyingly clear, no depth of evil is unimaginable," the mass media also make this linkage explicit. Writing just before the onset of the one hundred days of slaughter that would cost close to a million lives, Victoria Brittain, veteran Africa correspondent, offered forewarning that "[a] process of unraveling of ancient customs and complex civilizations is underway. It threatens

vast areas of the continent with a future in which Joseph Conrad's *Heart of Darkness* will be read as straightforward description." Her apocalyptic pronouncement was given confirmation when the *World Press Review* reprinted her piece in July 1994, toward the end of the Rwandan genocide, accompanied by the explanatory statement that this essay was written "just before Rwanda descended into hell this spring, a horror that underscores her warning." And commenting on the dispatch of a small contingent of French troops late in the genocide, a Gannet News Service correspondent protested: "While the French—with their Jaguar aircraft—move into a post-colonial horror only dimly foreshadowed by Joseph Conrad's nightmarish novel, *Heart of Darkness*, the United States and the United Nations stand away paralyzed by fear, bureaucracy and self-righteousness." The Rwandan genocide, then, does not only retrospectively resonate with *Heart of Darkness*, but is already foreshadowed by it. Conrad's text is granted something like a prophetic power by the mass media.

2. Jean Baudrillard, *The Illusion of the End*, trans. Chris Turner (Stanford: Stanford University Press, 1994), 55.

3. Edward Barnes, "The Heart of Darkness," *Time*, Janurary 25, 1999, 46.

4. Sam Kiley, "In the Heart of Darkness," *London Times*, May 10, 2000, n.p.

5. Ian Bruce, "Africa's Dark Heart in Crisis Again," *Glasgow Herald*, August 27, 1998, 13.

6. To be sure, while most accounts leave largely uncontested the misguided homology produced by the media, in rare circumstances analysts do critique the pervasive slippage of African genocide into the "heart of darkness." In an essay from 1996 entitled "Heart of Prejudice," which tries more accurately to read the relation between African violence and Conrad's text, the *London Independent* comments: "A message is being sent when the phrase 'heart of darkness' is casually bandied about: that Africa is irredeemably savage, the dark continent, a place where light and civilization (a Western preserve) can never penetrate. Conrad's work, and the casual use of its title to refer to bloodshed and war, has become an icon of Western attitudes towards the Third World, and Africa in particular, a supporting argument from art for the thesis that parts of the Third World are mad, bad and dangerous to know, and irretrievably so." After giving a brief summary of the text, the piece points out that the subject of *Heart of Darkness* lies in the clash between the colonial project of enlightenment, the *mission civilisatrice*, and the enslavement, plunder, pillage, and murder it engendered. The topic is colonial hypocrisy, not prim-

itive African violence. See Andrew Marshall, "Heart of Prejudice," *The Independent*, November 20, 1996, 20.

7. Pursuing other rhetorical concerns, J. Hillis Miller has differently addressed a similar version of this question in his brilliant analysis of *Heart of Darkness* as an apocalypse. See "*Heart of Darkness* Revisited," *Heart of Darkness (Case Studies in Contemporary Criticism)*, ed. Ross C. Murfin (Boston: Bedford, 1996), 206.

8. Sven Lindqvist, *"Exterminate All the Brutes,"* trans. Joan Tate (New York: New Press, 1996), ix.

9. Philip Gourevitch, *We Wish to Inform You That Tomorrow We Will Be Killed with Our Families* (New York: Farrar, Straus and Giroux, 1998), 7.

10. Ibid., 19.

11. Cedric Watts, *The Deceptive Text: An Introduction to Covert Plots* (Brighton: Harvester Press, 1984), 45.

12. Ibid., 49.

13. Ibid., 50. In making *Heart of Darkness* proleptic of a future apocalyptic violence, Watts continues a critical tradition that is already adumbrated in Lionel Trilling's *Beyond Culture*. Trilling writes: "This very great work has never lacked the admiration it deserves. But no one, to my knowledge, has ever confronted in an explicit way its strange and terrible message of ambivalence toward the life of civilization" (19). This terrible element of ambivalence is found in the figure of Kurtz who, while a paragon of civilization and bearing the strong lineaments of culture, yet succumbs to the chthonic powers of primitive lusts and a mortal attraction to the jungle. In his descent into the savage life, and in his affirmative cry at the point of death, Kurtz becomes emblematic of the modern artist. Trilling asks: "Is this not the essence of the modern belief about the nature of the artist the man who goes into that hell which is the historical beginning of the human soul, a beginning not outgrown but established in humanity as we know it now, preferring the reality of this hell to the bland lies of the civilization that has overlaid it?" (20–21). Presaging this aspect of the artist, Kurtz marks a portent of the future, for "nothing is more characteristic of modern literature than its discovery and canonization of the primal non-ethical energies." Lionel Trilling, *Beyond Culture: Essays on Literature and Learning* (New York: Viking Press, 1955).

14. Ian Watt, *Conrad in the Nineteenth Century* (Berkeley: University of California Press, 1979), 148.

15. Kirby Farrell, *Post-traumatic Culture: Injury and Interpretation in the Nineties* (Baltimore: Johns Hopkins University Press, 1998), 255. In a note justifying this claim, Farrell remarks that "[t]he

Belgian commission of inquiry sent in 1904 to the Congo Free State confirmed the abuses that reformers had bitterly deplored, yet in deference to business, the commission accepted forced labor as the only possible means of exploiting the country's riches. The first twentieth-century concentration camps were probably the crude compounds the British constructed in the campaign against the Boers as Queen Victoria was dying. Interned Boer families died of disease in scandalous numbers, which caused an outcry in England and Europe."

16. Ibid., 256.

17. Jonathan Schell, *The Unfinished Twentieth Century: The Crisis of Weapons of Mass Destruction* (London: Verso, 2003), 13.

18. Schell notes: "That century, Conrad apparently understood, was about to open up new possibilities for evil. In *Heart of Darkness*, he seems to thumb through them prospectively, as if through a deck of horrific tarot cards. The concentration camps are there. The black men 'dying slowly,' 'in all the attitudes of pain, abandonment, and despair,' whom Marlow witnesses in a grove of trees immediately upon arriving at an outer station, are the unmistakable precursors of the millions of men and women who were to die in the concentration camps soon to be built in Europe. The monster Kurtz, the charismatic station chief who murders in the name of progress, and who, although 'hollow at the core,' was gifted with magnificent eloquence and 'electrified large meetings,' is a sort of prefiguration of Hitler" (ibid.). *Heart of Darkness* even offers us "by way of inexplicably refined forecasting" a kind of prophetic ventriloquism in which Kurtz offers discourse on the voice of Hitler. In an intriguing moment of analysis, Schell compares Marlow's commentary on Kurtz's voice to comments Hitler makes about himself in 1936. Noting that the basic element of Hitler's magnetism was his voice carried over radio to the German public, Schell quotes Hitler: "Long ago you heard the voice of a man, and it struck to your hearts, it awakened you and you followed this voice. You followed it for years without having so much as seen him whose voice it was; you heard only a voice, and you followed" (xiv). Marlow presents Kurtz's voice in similar terms; he too followed Kurtz's voice. "Kurtz discoursed. A voice! A voice! It rang deep to the very last" (67). And yet underlying this resonant voice was nothing but emptiness: "The voice was gone. What else had been there?" (69). Unless otherwise noted, *Heart of Darkness* quotations are from Joseph Conrad, *The Heart of Darkness*, Norton Critical Edition, ed. Paul B. Armstrong (New York: W. W. Norton, 2006). Subsequent citations from Conrad's text are given parenthetically in the text. Schell also detects a forerunner of Hannah Arendt's "banality of evil" in Conrad's

minor bureaucrat "papier-mache Mephistopheles" located at the center of the ivory collecting operation.

19. Miller, "*Heart of Darkness* Revisited," 9.

20. Miller explains: "I claim to have demonstrated that *Heart of Darkness* is not only parabolic but also apocalyptic. It fits that strange genre of the apocalyptic text, the sort of text that promises an ultimate revelation without giving it, and says always 'Come' and 'Wait.' But there is an extra twist given to the paradigmatic form of the apocalypse in *Heart of Darkness*. The *Aufklarung* or enlightenment in this case is of the fact that the darkness can never be enlightened. The darkness enters into every gesture of enlightenment to enfeeble it, to hollow it out, to corrupt it and thereby turn reason into unreason, its pretense of shedding more light into more darkness" ("*Heart of Darkness* Revisited," 222).

21. James Berger, "Ends and Means: Theorizing Apocalypse in the 1990s," *Postmodern Culture* 6.3 (May 1996).

22. F. R. Leavis, *The Great Tradition: George Eliot, Henry James, Joseph Conrad* (New York: New York University Press, 1963), 179.

23. Ibid., 177, 179.

24. Chinua Achebe, "An Image of Africa: Racism in Conrad's *Heart of Darkness*," *The Heart of Darkness*, Norton Critical Edition, ed. Robert Kimbrough (New York: W.W. Norton, 1988), 253.

25. Frances B. Singh, "The Colonialistic Bias of *Heart of Darkness*," Kimbrough, *The Heart of Darkness*, 271.

26. Conrad, *Heart of Darkness*, 14, 35.

27. Edward Said, *Culture and Imperialism* (New York: Vintage Books, 1993), 29.

28. Valentine Cunningham, *In the Reading Gaol: Postmodernity, Texts, and History* (Oxford: Blackwell, 1994), 257.

29. Ibid., 235.

30. Fredric Jameson, *The Political Unconscious: Narrative as a Socially Symbolic Act* (Ithaca: Cornell University Press, 1981), 208.

31. Patrick Brantlinger, *Rule of Darkness: British Literature and Imperialism, 1830–1914* (Ithaca: Cornell University Press, 1988), 257.

32. Ibid., 272.

33. Ibid., 264.

34. Jameson, *The Political Unconscious*, 206.

35. Achebe, "An Image of Africa," 253.

36. Interestingly, the split between *Heart of Darkness*'s aesthetics and politics has been reproduced throughout the recent history of the text's critical reception. Jameson, as we have seen, accuses Conrad of a "will to style" that empties the text of its political content. Troubled

Notes

by similar considerations, Raymond Williams charges not the text but its critics with a comparable evacuation of the material in *The English Novel from Dickens to Lawrence* (New York: Oxford University Press, 1970):

"It is ... astonishing that a whole school of criticism has succeeded in emptying *The Heart of Darkness* of its social and historical content, about which Conrad leaves us in no possible doubt. My quarrel with a whole tradition of criticism of fiction is about just this kind of endless reduction of deliberately created realities to analogues, symbolic circumstances, abstract situations. The Congo of Leopold follows the sea that Dombey and Son traded across, follows it into an endless substitution in which no object is itself, no social experience direct, but every thing is translated into what can be called a metaphysical language—the river is Evil; the sea is Love or Death. Yet only called metaphysical because there is not that much guts in it" (145).

The target of Williams's diatribe is those critics of the 1950s and 1960s who focus on the more "impressionistic" aspects of the novel. What disturbs Williams about the elaborately mythological treatment of *Heart of Darkness* as a descent into the underworld or with the symbolic rendering of the story as a fictive counterpart to Freud's investigations of the human psyche is the "sophisticated evasion of deliberately created, deliberately named places and people, situations and experiences" (145). Such a concentration on Conrad's impressionism leads to the deliberate abandonment of the social and material circumstances of Conrad's text, which results in a species of criticism that substitutes a rhetoric of imposition and critical game playing in place of a sustained engagement with an "imaginatively written reality"—a criticism, then, which "with all substance reduced or endlessly substituted can stand on [its] own as a detached methodology" (145).

Although this passage was written in the 1960s, Williams's displeasure with the critical abstraction attending *Heart of Darkness* adumbrates the current discontent with high theory. We can already hear in Williams the genealogical echoes of what, along very similar lines, was to become the contemporary critique of theory for its sequestering of material history within the abyss of textuality. In his epilogue on *Heart of Darkness*, Brantlinger, for example, argues that "in a good deal of contemporary criticism words themselves have ceased to have external referents" ("*Heart of Darkness*: Anti-Imperialism, Racism, or Impressionism?" Murfin, *Heart of Darkness*, 289). The point, however, is not so much to contest those critics who concentrate on Conrad's impressionism, but "to restore what their readings neglect" (289). By juxtaposing the gruesome account of the imperial slaughter of the African against the evasions of its critics, and against the impressionism of the text itself, Brantlinger strongly insists upon the restoration of *Heart of Darkness*'s occluded history.

37. Cunningham, *In the Reading Gaol*, 61.
38. Ibid., 227.
39. Ibid., 242.
40. Watt, *Conrad in the Nineteenth Century*, 175.
41. See, for example, Cunningham, *In the Reading Gaol*, 241.
42. Ibid., 242.
43. Homi K. Bhabha, "Signs Taken for Wonders: Questions of Ambivalence and Authority under a Tree outside Delhi, May 1817," *The Location of Culture* (New York: Routledge, 1994), 111.
44. Harold Bloom, *Poetry and Repression: Revisionism from Blake to Stevens* (New Haven: Yale University Press, 1980), 10.
45. A few pages later at the moment of his confronting the escaping Kurtz, Marlow will think of the old woman fatefully knitting black wool.
46. Here Bloom is thinking of the trope as defense in its mediating relations between strong poets, but the theme holds as well for Marlow's "reading" of the heads. See *Poetry and Repression*.
47. Jacques Lacan, *The Seminar of Jacques Lacan Book XI: The Four Fundamental Concepts of Psychoanalysis*, trans. Alan Sheridan (New York: W. W. Norton, 1998), 106.
48. Lacan's reversal of the agency of vision fits into a series of theoretical inversions that I have already begun to establish and will continue to perform throughout the remainder of this chapter. On first looking into *The Ambassadors*, the viewer's eye is drawn to the complex arrangement of signifying objects resting on a two-tiered table. The objects stand in representative relation to the Renaissance putting on display its knowledge of the sciences of measurement (thereby gesturing at a subtle commentary on the technical composition of the anamorphic skull and the magical meridians of perspective), as well as its accomplishments in the fine arts and literature. But even as the viewer is thus drawn by the intersecting planes into the picture, his or her gaze is troubled by a pale and blurred shape floating at an odd angle across the lower edge of the painting. It is only by blocking out the picture of the ambassadors, in a shifting of perspective by moving to the extreme right, that the contours of the skull come sharply into focus and we become aware of the ghostly gaze that has already fixed the viewer. Yet it is not with the anamorphic ghost that Lacan is strictly concerned. What he detects behind the empty sockets whose gaze holds the viewer captive is the very operation of vision itself: "But it is further still that we must seek the function of vision.

We shall then see emerging on the basis of vision, not the phallic symbol, the anamorphic ghost, but the gaze as such, in its pulsatile, dazzling and spread out function, as it is in this picture. This picture is simply what any picture is, a trap for the gaze" (89).

49. Ibid., 89.

50. Paul de Man, *The Rhetoric of Romanticism* (New York: Columbia University Press, 1984), 78.

51. Jeffrey Meyers, *Joseph Conrad: A Biography* (New York: Charles Scribner's Sons, 1991), 56.

52. Qtd. in Adam Hochschild, *King Leopold's Ghost: A Story of Greed, Terror, and Heroism in Colonial Africa* (Boston: Houghton Mifflin, 1999), 145.

53. Friedrich Nietzsche, *On the Genealogy of Morals*, trans. Walter Kaufmann and R. J. Hollingdale (New York: Vintage Books, 1967), 77.

54. Stephen Greenblatt, "Mutilation and Meaning," *The Body In Parts*, ed. David Hillman and Carla Mazzio (New York: Routledge, 1997), 222.

55. Ibid. In "Mutilation and Meaning," Greenblatt employs this insight in his reading of the beginnings of a vitiation, in the early modern period, of a belief in the universality of what he calls the "language of wounds" (222). "For Jews," Greenblatt asserts, "God manifested himself principally in a text, the Torah, but for Christians God's flesh was itself a text written upon with universal characters, inscribed with a language that all men could understand since it was a language in and of the body itself" (223). But in working through various travel accounts recording the practice of rites of wounding in India, for example, Greenblatt is able to demonstrate the interpretive pressure that began a decline in the sustained conception of the universal language of wounds.

56. Ibid., 238n.2

57. See Jacques Derrida, "Signature, Event, Context," *Margins of Philosophy*. trans. Alan Bass (Chicago: University of Chicago Press, 1982).

58. Jacques Derrida, *Limited Inc.* (Evanston, IL: Northwestern University Press, 1988), 53.

59. Jacques Derrida, "My Chances/*Mes Chances*: A Rendezvous with Some Epicurean Stereophonies," *Taking Chances: Derrida, Psychoanalysis, and Literature*, ed. Joseph H. Smith and William Kerrigan (Baltimore: Johns Hopkins University Press, 1984), 16.

60. Joseph Conrad, *A Personal Record*, ed. Zdzisław Najder and J. H. Stape (Cambridge: Cambridge University Press, 2008), 16. Watts, ibid.

61. Joseph Conrad, *The Collected Letters*, vol. 2,, ed. Frederick R. Karl and Laurence Davies (Cambridge: Cambridge University Press, 1990), 460.
62. G. W. F. Hegel, *Aesthetics: Lectures on Fine Art*, trans. T. M. Knox (Oxford: Clarendon, 1975), 399.
63. Jacques Derrida, *Specters of Marx: The State of the Debt, the Work of Mourning, and the New International*, trans. Peggy Kamuf (New York: Routledge, 1994), 28.
64. Ibid., 6.
65. Ibid., 28.
66. Cited in Robyn Horner, *Rethinking God as Gift: Marion, Derrida, and the Limits of Phenomenology* (New York: Fordham University Press, 2001), 235.
67. Walter Benjamin, "Franz Kafka: On the Tenth Anniversary of His Death," *Selected Writings*, vol. 2, 1927–1934 (Cambridge, MA: Belknap Press, 1999), 811.
68. Eric Santner, *On Creaturely Life: Rilke, Benjamin, Sebald* (Chicago: University of Chicago Press, 2006).
69. Ibid., 12.
70. Qtd. in ibid., 14.
71. Santner, *Creaturely Life*, 15.
72. Ibid., 27, 81; Benjamin qtd. in ibid., 81.
73. Schmitt qtd. in ibid., 17, 16.
74. In his account of creaturely life, Santner references Julia Lupton's analysis of the creature who "represents the flip side of the political theology of absolute sovereignty." She remarks that "in Schmitt's analysis the king is like God in the creative-destructive potential of his decisive word, his juris-diction." Qtd in ibid., 29.
75. Derrida, *Specters of Marx*, 93.
76. Santner, *Creaturely Life*, 88.
77. Derrida, *Specters of Marx*, 28.
78. Benjamin, "Franz Kafka," 815.
79. Ibid.
80. Ibid.
81. Giorgio Agamben, *State of Exception*, trans. Kevin Attell (Stanford: Stanford University Press, 2005), 63.
82. Ibid., 64.
83. Ibid.
84. Caryl Phillips, "Was Joseph Conrad Really a Racist?" *Things Fall Apart*, ed. Francis Abiola Irele (New York: W. W. Norton, 2009), 204.
85. Sigmund Freud, "The 'Uncanny,'" *Writings on Art and Literature* (Stanford: Stanford University Press, 1997), 195.

86. Ibid., 220.
87. Hochschild, *King Leopold's Ghost*.
88. Peter Forbath, *The River Congo: The Discovery, Exploration and Exploitation of the World's Most Dramatic River* (London: Secker & Warburg, 1978), 105.
89. Qtd. in Alan Simmons, "Conrad, Casement, and the Congo Atrocities," Armstrong, *Heart of Darkness*, 185.
90. Ibid.
91. Benjamin, *Walter Benjamin: Selected Writings*, . 4: 391.
92. Ibid., 396.

3. THE BODY IN RUINS

1. Coetzee, *Diary of a Bad Year*, 171.
2. Ibid.
3. Ibid., 39.
4. J. M. Coetzee, "Into the Dark Chamber: The Writer and the South African State," *Doubling the Point: Essays and Interviews*, ed. David Atwell (Cambridge, MA: Harvard University Press, 1992), 363.
5. Ibid.
6. Coetzee, *Diary of a Bad Year*, 42.
7. Coetzee, "Into the Dark Chamber," 364.
8. Conrad, *Heart of Darkness*, 62; Coetzee, *Waiting for the Barbarians*, 11. All citations in the text from *Waiting for the Barbarians* are from this edition and are subsequently given parenthetically in the text.
9. As Patricia Merivale points out, *Waiting for the Barbarians* may owe something of its oriental aspect to the influence of "The Great Wall of China." For more on Kafka's influence on Coetzee, see her "Audible Palimpsests: Coetzee's Kafka," *Critical Perspectives on J. M. Coetzee*, ed. Graham Huggan and Stephen Watson (London: Macmillan, 1996), 152–67.
10. J. M. Coetzee, "Time, Tense, and Aspect in Kafka's The Burrow," Atwell, *Doubling the Point*, , 579.
11. Richard Halpern, *Shakespeare Among the Moderns* (Ithaca: Cornell University Press, 1997), 1–14.
12. Qtd. in ibid., 3.
13. Halpern, *Shakespeare Among the Moderns*, 3.
14. J. M. Coetzee, "Autobiography and Confession," Atwell, *Doubling the Point*, 204.
15. Steiner also points to the influence of "In the Penal Colony," "the classic of all modern treatments of the obscene intimacies be-

tween torturer, victim and liberal witness," whose structure is reflected in the triangular desire (though Steiner does not use this Giradian term) exposed in Coetzee's text. George Steiner, "Master and Man," *New Yorker*, July 1982, 102–3.

16. Ibid., 103.

17. Nadine Gordimer, "The Idea of Gardening: *Life and Times of Michael K* by J. M. Coetzee," *Critical Essays on J. M. Coetzee*, ed. Sue Kossew (New York: G.K. Hall, 1998), 139.

18. Paul Rich, "Apartheid and the Decline of the Civilization Idea: An Essay on Nadine Gordimer's *July's People* and J. M. Coetzee's *Waiting for the Barbarians*," *Research in African Literatures* 15.3 (1984), 385.

19. Ibid., 389.

20. Abdul JanMohamed, "The Economy of Manichean Allegory: The Function of Racial Difference in Colonialist Literature,' *'Race,' Writing, and Difference*, ed. Henry Louis Gates, Jr. (Chicago: University of Chicago Press, 1985), 73.

21. Ibid., 73.

22. Jean-Phillipe Wade, "The Allegorical Text and History: J. M. Coetzee's *Waiting for the Barbarians*," *Journal of Literary Studies* 6.4 (1990), 275.

23. Qtd. in Dominic Head, *J. M. Coetzee* (Cambridge: Cambridge University Press, 1997), 9.

24. Ibid.

25. Ibid.

26. Ibid., 363.

27. Susan Van Zanten Gallagher, "Torture and the Novel: J. M. Coetzee's *Waiting for the Barbarians*," *Contemporary Literature* 29.2 (1988), 278.

28. Ibid., 281–82.

29. Coetzee, "Into the Dark Chamber," 324.

30. Head, *J. M. Coetzee*, 76.

31. David Atwell, *J. M. Coetzee: South Africa and the Politics of Writing* (Berkeley: University of California Press, 1993), 74.

32. Wade, "Allegorical Text," 281.

33. Ibid.

34. Antjie Krog, *Country of My Skull: Guilt, Sorrow, and the Limits of Forgiveness in the New South Africa* (New York: Random House, 1998), 51. Krog reports that "[a]fter four months, most of us who travel frequently become ill—lungs and airways. The chairperson has bronchitis; the deputy chairperson, pneumonia. It's the planes, someone says, they are germ incubators" (63).

35. Ibid., 51.
36. Ibid., 93.
37. Ibid., 93.
38. Ibid., 95.
39. J. M. Coetzee, "The Novel Today," *Upstream* 6 (1988), 3.
40. Ibid.
41. Ibid, 4.
42. For more on Elaine Scarry and *Waiting for the Barbarians*, see Barbara Eckstein, *The Language of Fiction in a World of Pain: Reading Politics as Paradox* (Philadelphia: University of Pennsylvania Press, 1990).
43. Elaine Scarry, *The Body in Pain* (Oxford: Oxford University Press, 1987), 49.
44. Michael Valdez Moses, "The Mark of Empire: Writing, History, and Torture in Coetzee's *Waiting for the Barbarians*," *Kenyon Review* 15.1 (1993): 115–27.
45. Conrad, *Heart of Darkness*, 14, 16, 58.
46. See Coetzee, *Foe*, 157.
47. Butler, "How Can I Deny?," 257.
48. Rebecca Saunders, "The Agony and the Allegory: The Concept of the Foreign, the Language of Apartheid, and the Fiction of J. M. Coetzee," *Cultural Critique* 47 (2001), 241.
49. Qtd. in ibid., 242.
50. Qtd. in ibid.
51. Michael Hardt and Antonio Negri, *Empire* (Cambridge, MA: Harvard University Press, 2000), 193.
52. Ibid., xiv, xv.
53. Ibid., xiv.
54. Ibid., xv.
55. Paul de Man, *Blindness and Insight: Essays in the Rhetoric of Contemporary Criticism*, trans. Wlad Godzich (Minneapolis: University of Minnesota Press, 1983), 190.
56. Ibid.
57. Teresa Dovey, "Allegory vs. Allegory: The Divorce of Different Modes of Allegorical Perception in Coetzee's *Waiting for the Barbarians*," *Journal of Literary Studies* 4.2 (1988), 154.
58. Walter Benjamin, *The Origin of German Tragic Drama*, trans. John Osborne (New York: Verso, 1977), 177–78.
59. J. Hillis Miller, "The Two Allegories," *Allegory, Myth, and Symbol*, ed. Morton W. Bloomfield (Cambridge, MA: Harvard University Press, 1981), 365.
60. Arguing in her "Allegory versus Allegory" that Coetzee's text

stages a sundering between Hegelian and Benjaminian modes of allegorical perception, Teresa Dovey reads the novel as subverting liberal humanist discourse in South Africa. In his desire to resurrect the fragments of the ruin to a condition of wholeness and in his correlative desire to restore the barbarian woman to her people, the Magistrate is representative of the "Hegelian view [that] approximates the liberal notion of the progressive amelioration of the human condition; the liberal impetus to transcend conflict and suffering through the production of a work of art which gives them 'total meaning'" (136). At particular moments in the novel, however, Dovey argues that the Magistrate is "made to articulate" a more Benjaminian perception of the nature of history and the relation of time to allegory. While I find Dovey's invocation of Coetzee's use of Benjamin apposite, it seems to me that the Magistrate is not so much "made to articulate" a Benjaminian construction of allegory (as if he were merely a mouthpiece for Coetzee's deconstruction of South African liberal humanist discourse) as that this perception emerges through his contest with Joll and his self-conscious interrogation of that contest. See, too, her "*Waiting for the Barbarians*: Allegory of Allegories," Huggan and Watson, *Critical Perspectives on J. M. Coetzee*, 138–51.

Although appreciative of Dovey's sophisticated deconstructionist account of the function of allegory in Coetzee's novel, in his "The Allegorical Text and History," Jean-Philippe Wade finds her analysis incapable of dealing with the specific historical conjuncture out of which the novel emerges: "An index of the problematic status of 'history' in Dovey's account is her rejection of the novel's interest in the 'extratextual reality' of 'the power relations between oppressor and oppressed'" (280). Situating Benjamin's theorizing of allegory within the catastrophic history of early twentieth-century Germany, Wade draws a parallel between Benjamin's forging a relation with the baroque *Trauerspiel* in order to produce a "knowledge" of the present and Coetzee's portrayal of the collapsing of a past colonial empire to produce a present "knowledge" of South African colonialism in ruins.

61. Benjamin, *The Origin of German Tragic Drama*, 174–75.

62. Terry Eagleton, *Walter Benjamin, or, Towards a Revolutionary Criticism* (New York: Verso, 1981), 175.

63. Benjamin, *The Origin of German Tragic Drama*, 107.

64. Stephen Slemon, for example, contends that "Coetzee's tactic in this novel is to portray imperial allegorical thinking in the thematic level of his novel and to juxtapose it with the allegorical mode in which the novel itself is written. This juxtaposition foregrounds the discontinuity between the two kinds of allegorical discourse, one

based on imperial codes of recognition and the other on resistance to totalitarian systems." "Post-Colonial Allegory and the Transformation of History," *Journal of Commonwealth Literature* 23.1 (1988), 163.

65. See Jacques Derrida, *Memoirs of the Blind: The Self-Portrait and Other Ruins*, trans. Pascale-Anne Brault and Michael Naas (Chicago: University of Chicago Press, 1993), 65, 69.

66. J. Hillis Miller, "Paul De Man as Allergen," Cohen et al., *Material Events*, 183–204.

67. Paul de Man, *Aesthetic Ideology* (Minneapolis: University of Minnesota Press, 1996), 82.

68. Ibid.

69. Ibid.

70. Kant qtd. in ibid., 80.

71. De Man, *Aesthetic Ideology*, 82–83.

72. Ibid., 128.

73. Kant qtd. in ibid., 88.

74. De Man, *Aesthetic Ideology*, 88.

75. Ibid., 89.

76. Samuel Beckett, *Waiting for Godot* (New York: Grove, 1954), 45.

77. De Man, *Aesthetic Ideology*, 89.

78. Kant maintains that poets see precisely with their eyes and not with the cognitive overlay of their minds (79). Butler, "How Can I Deny?," 271.

80. Ibid.

81. Miller, "Two Allegories," 365.

82. Ibid.

83. Butler, "How Can I Deny?," 271.

84. Ibid.

85. Coetzee, "Autobiography and Confession," 248.

86. Ibid. Coetzee remarks that "[o]ne can get away with such crudeness in fiction; one can't in philosophy, I'm sure" (248).

87. Ibid.

88. De Man, *Aesthetic Ideology*, 132.

89. Ibid., 134.

90. Ibid., 133.

91. Miller, "Paul de Man as Allergen," 189.

92. De Man, *Aesthetic Ideology*, 133.

93. Ibid.

94. It is outside the scope of this chapter to fully historicize the intriguing relation between these two ascetic writers. Coetzee wrote

Waiting for the Barbarians in 1979 while de Man's work for his critique of aesthetic ideology, out of which his concept of materiality emerges, took place from 1977 to 1983. While it is safe to assume that Coetzee is thoroughly familiar with de Man's work, it is difficult to determine what knowledge he had then of de Man's concept of materiality. While certain of the essays that now constitute *Aesthetic Ideology* were published in the early 1980s, the incomplete project was published in book form in 1996. However, elements of de Man's thought on materiality also appear in his earlier work.

While I have drawn various correlations between de Man's thought and Coetzee's text, I do not wish to imply that Coetzee would acquiesce in de Man's view of history. Although Coetzee has been criticized for not acknowledging the revolutionary power of the oppressed, the barbarian body is given agency. It is the barbarians, after all, who lure the army of Empire farther and farther out into the desert and mountains and pick off the stragglers. Similarly, while apartheid is not a material event in de Man's sense, this does not mean, of course, that it did not have immensely tragic effects in what is conventionally called history. Coetzee's comments on the suffering body in South Africa speak not only to the tortured but also to the millions of disposed and malnourished bodies that suffered under the specific historical condition of apartheid.

95. Dovey comments that the Magistrate is unaware that his coating of the slips "leaves its own traces upon the objects which it retrieves" ("Allegory vs. Allegory," 138).

96. Derrida, *Specters of Marx*, 9.

97. Craig Owens, "The Allegorical Impulse: Toward a Theory of Postmodernism," *Art After Modernism: Rethinking Representation*, ed. Brian Wallis (New York: New Museum of Contemporary Art, 1984), 204.

98. Krog, *Country of My Skull*, 279.

99. Ibid., 287.

100. Coetzee writes that "[o]ur craft is all in reading the other." J. M. Coetzee, *White Writing* (New Haven: Yale University Press, 1988), 81.

101. Krog, *Country of My Skull*, 57.

102. Ibid.

103. Scarry, *The Body in Pain*, 49.

104. Jacques Derrida, *Points... Interviews, 1974–1994*, trans. Peggy Kamuf (Stanford: Stanford University Press, 1995), 137.

105. Ibid.

CODA

1. Qtd. in Michael G. Levine, *The Belated Witness: Literature, Testimony, and the Question of Holocaust Survival* (Stanford: Stanford University Press, 2006), 22. For more on *Maus* and the relation of Jews to the German language (and much else besides), see Levine's fine study, 21–24.

2. All quotations are taken from Art Spiegelman, *The Complete Maus* (New York: Pantheon, 1996).

3. For more on Artie as a murderer, see Nancy K. Miller, "Cartoons of the Self: Portrait of the Artist as a Young Murderer," *Considering* Maus: *Approaches to Art Spiegelman's "Survivor's Tale" of the Holocaust*, ed. Deborah R. Geis (Tuscaloosa: University of Alabama Press, 2003), 44–59.

4. Borges, *Labyrinths*, 196.

5. Art Spiegelman, *In the Shadow of No Towers* (New York: Pantheon, 2004).

6. For a different reading of this moment, see Stephen E. Tabachnick, "The Religious Meaning of Art Spiegelman's *Maus*," *Shofar: An Interdisciplinary Journal of Jewish Studies* 22.4 (2004): 1–13.

7. Jacques Derrida, "Declarations of Independence," *New Political Science* 7.1 (Summer 1986): 7–15.

8. Walter Benjamin, *The Arcades Project*, trans. Howard Eiland and Kevin McLaughlin (Cambridge: Harvard University Press, 1999), 463.

9. Ibid., 390.

10. Ibid., 390–91.

11. Agamben, *The Time That Remains: A Commentary on the Letter to the Romans*, trans. Patricia Dailey (Stanford: Stanford University Press, 2005), 145.

12. Ibid.

13. Ibid.

14. Benjamin, *The Arcades Project*, 395.

15. Qtd. in Leland de la Durantaye, *Giorgio Agamben: A Critical Introduction* (Stanford: Stanford University Press, 2009), 120.

16. Agamben, *The Time That Remains*, 62.

17. Qtd. in Leland de la Durantaye, *Giorgio Agamben*, 114.

18. Benjamin, *The Arcades Project*, 396.

INDEX

Abraham, Nicholas, 10
Abu Ghraib Prison, 7, 124–25
Achebe, Chinua, 77, 83
adequation, 26–27, 149, 166, 176
Adorno, Theodor, 2, 34–36
Agamben, Giorgio, 30, 104, 113, 115–18, 207–8. *See also* state of exception
allegory, 123, 133–35, 137–38, 149–58, 165, 170, 172–74
Alter, Robert, 40–41
Althusser, Louis, 168
apartheid, 7–8, 31, 123–25, 133–35, 137, 139, 143–44, 150–51, 168–69, 171–72, 175, 230n94
apocalypse, 3–6, 8–10, 16, 26, 28–32, 34, 39, 48, 56, 60, 62–63, 67–68, 71–75, 82, 93, 98–101, 119–20, 122, 126, 131, 135, 141–42, 171, 176–79, 185, 196–97, 199–200, 208–9, 218n7, 218n13, 220n20
Apocalypse Now (dir. Francis Ford Coppola), 64–65
Arendt, Hannah, 68, 219n18
arrivant, 101–103, 109, 114, 204
Atropos, 89
Atwell, David, 128, 138
Auschwitz. *See* concentration camp
autoimmunity, 30, 59–63

Balzac, Honoré de, 27–28
barbarians (in *Waiting for the Barbarians*), 126–30, 132, 137, 139–40, 142, 146–48, 150, 153, 156–59, 164, 168, 170–72, 174–75
Bataille, Georges, 203
Baudrillard, Jean, 65
Beckett, Samuel, 163
Benjamin, Walter: allegory as ruin, 123, 154–59, 165, 227n60; *Arcades Project, The*, 201–8; aura, 90; on Kafka, 33–34, 36, 49, 56, 113–16; messianism, 10, 30–32, 103–5, 121, 201–8; now of legibility, 32, 202–9; *The Origin of German Tragic Drama*, 105, 123, 154–59; petrified unrest, 105, 108–9; preservation of writings, 2
Benzien, Jeffrey, 140–41
Berger, James, 74
Bhabha, Homi, 87
Bible: Daniel, 29; Genesis, 54; Hebrew Bible, 48, 173; New Testament, 172–73; Old Testament, 172–73; Revelation, 29, 75, 93
Biko, Steven, 138–39, 149–50, 168
black sites (CIA), 123
Blake, William, 43
blindsight, 160–61
Bloch, Ernst, 1, 9, 31, 179, 202
Bloom, Harold, 39, 42–47, 58, 89
Bobrowski, Tadeuz, 94
Book of the Dead, 21
Borges, Jorge Luis, 44, 189
Brantlinger, Patrick, 80–82, 84
Brecht, Bertolt, 34

Brod, Max, 2, 6, 38
Brooks, Peter, 10–11
Bruce, Sir James, 67
Burroughs, William, 64
Burton, Sir Richard, 67
Bush, George W. (administration of), 123–24
Butler, Judith, 13–18, 20, 25, 148–49, 164–66

Cain, 10, 12
cannibalism, 65–66, 101–2, 111
Casement, Roger, 120–21
Catholicism, 75
Cave, Terence, 12
Celan, Paul, 105
Certeau, Michel de, 1, 209
circumcision, 98
Coetzee, J.M., 7–8, 15, 133, 196–97; *Diary of a Bad Year*, 7, 123–25; *Dusklands*, 177; *Elizabeth Costello*, 17; *Foe*, 17; "Into the Dark Chamber," 124–25, 136; *Life and Times of Michael K*, 134; "The Novel Today," 143–44; "Time, Tense, and Aspect in Kafka's The Burrow," 129–30; *Waiting for the Barbarians*, 7, 9, 16, 21, 28–31, 90, 122, 123, 125–34, 136–54, 156–60, 162–78, 185, 227n60. *See also* barbarians; Empire; Magistrate
Coleridge, Samuel Taylor, 19
colonialism, 7, 65, 67, 72, 78, 84, 87, 89, 99, 104, 106, 110, 120–21, 129, 150, 166. *See also* imperialism
Commandant, the (character in "In the Penal Colony"), 30, 55–56, 58, 60
concentration camp, 3–4, 25, 34, 49, 185, 188, 190, 218n15, 219n18; Auschwitz, 15, 48, 178, 182–83, 192–94, 197, 204–5; Birkenau, 182; Dachau, 182, 194, 198
Congo, 67–68, 75, 84, 92, 120–21, 205
Conrad, Joseph, 3, 196–97; *Heart of Darkness*, 5, 8–9, 15, 21, 28–29, 31, 53, 63–114, 126–28, 141–42, 146, 153, 177–78, 186, 205, 216n1, 217n6, 218n13, 219n18, 220n20, 220n36 (*see also* Director of Companies; the Intended); letters, 100, 120; *A Personal Record*, 99
Cordovero, Moses, 46–47
creaturely life, 104–7, 205, 224n74
Cunningham, Valentine, 79, 83–84, 87, 115

delayed decoding, 85, 95
Deleuze, Gilles, 55, 128
de Man, Paul, 31, 55, 91, 154, 160–68, 216n53, 229n94
Derrida, Jacques, 31, 39, 58, 86–87, 176; *Acts of Religion*, 59–63; *arrivant*, 101–3, 109, 114, 204; autoimmunity, 30, 59–63; *The Ear of the Other*, 50–55; fabulous retroactivity, 199; iterability, 53, 60–63, 96–98; *Memoirs of the Blind*, 158; mourning, 171; on Nietzsche, 50–55; *On Touching—Jean-Luc Nancy*, 16; "Signature, Event, Context," 96; *Specters of Marx*, 101–3, 107, 171
Diamant, Dora, 6
Diary of a Bad Year (J.M. Coetzee), 7, 123–25
Director of Companies (character in *Heart of Darkness*), 117
Dovey, Teresa, 154, 227n60, 230n95

Eagleton, Terry, 157
Eliot, T.S., 132–33
Empire, the (in *Waiting for the Barbarians*), 127–28, 131–32, 142, 146–48, 152–54, 156, 158, 168–70, 172–74
Empire (in Michael Hardt and Antonio Negri), 151–52
ethicopolitical, 9, 28–32, 62, 71, 209
exile, 45–46
Explorer, the (character in "In the Penal Colony"), 25, 55–56, 60–61

Farrell, Kirby, 72–73
Forbath, Peter, 120
Foucault, Michel, 13–17, 32, 89, 127
French Revolution, 27
Freud, Sigmund, 5–6, 44, 55, 58, 119, 181, 185–86

Gallagher, Susan Van Zanten, 137–38
gaze, the, 90–92
gematria, 29, 41, 202, 204
genocide, 6, 68–69, 119–20, 126; African, 5, 8, 15, 64, 66–68, 71, 74, 76, 78, 83, 90, 92–94, 98, 100, 119–22, 217n6; European, 68–69; Rwandan, 5, 8, 65, 67, 69–70, 75, 77–78, 80, 121–22, 216n1
German (language), 46
gift, the, 110–11, 196
Gordimer, Nadine, 134
gothic, 81, 83, 88
Gourevitch, Phillip, 69–71
Greenaway, Peter, *The Pillow Book*, 19–20
Greenblatt, Stephen, 96, 98, 223n55
Guantánamo camp, 7, 124
Guattari, Félix, 128

Halpern, Richard, 132–33
Hamlet (William Shakespeare), 3–4, 107, 189
Handelman, Susan, 46
Hardt, Michael, 150–52
Head, Dominic, 138
Heart of Darkness (Joseph Conrad), 5, 8–9, 15, 21, 28–29, 31, 53, 63–114, 126–28, 141–42, 146, 153, 177–78, 186, 205, 216n1, 217n6, 218n13, 219n18, 220n20, 220n36. *See also* Director of Companies; the Intended
"heart of darkness" (metaphor), 5, 8, 64–69, 92, 216n1, 217n6
Hebrew Bible. *See* Bible; Torah
Hegel, G. W. F., 52–53, 100, 133, 152, 154, 227n60
Heidegger, Martin, 146
Hitler, Adolph, 73, 185

Hochschild, Adam, 94, 120
Holbein, Hans, *The Ambassadors*, 90–91
Holocaust, 6, 8, 10, 15, 25, 34–39, 47, 49, 54, 56–58, 60, 67, 178, 180–85, 190–91, 194–96, 201, 206–7

imperialism, 78–81, 83, 85, 106, 116–17, 134–35, 146, 151. *See also* colonialism
impressionism, 80–85, 220n36
incorporation, 5–6, 8–10, 15, 25–26, 30–32, 47, 54, 71, 74, 80, 83, 93, 95, 98, 118–22, 126–27, 135, 139, 169, 178–79, 196, 209
inscribed body, 1, 10–25, 29–31, 55–56, 87, 89, 98–99, 126, 146, 155, 158, 165, 179, 197, 209, 223n55. *See also* marked body
Intended, the (*character in* Heart of Darkness), 101, 103, 108, 110–11
"In the Penal Colony" (Franz Kafka), 6, 9, 12–15, 25, 28–31, 37–39, 49, 54–63, 126–29, 141–42, 177–78, 197, 225n15. *See also* Commandant; Explorer; Officer
ivory, 67, 92–93, 108, 110–11, 117–18

Jameson, Frederic, 80–83, 220n36
JanMohamed, Abdul, 134–35
Janouch, Gustav, 1–2, 6, 37–38, 211n4, 214n19
Jay, Martin, 47–48
Jesus, 10
Jetztzeit, 208
Jewish Holocaust. *See* Holocaust
Joyce, James, 3–5, 18–19
Judaic modes of interpretation, 45, 48, 55, 179, 197, 202

kabbalah, 38–39, 41–47, 202
Kafka, Franz, 1–8, 21, 33–36, 42–47, 50, 53–54, 71, 105, 117, 172, 196–97, 214n19; "Before the Law," 40; "The Burrow," 129–30, 169; *The Castle*, 35,

49; destruction of manuscripts, 6, 38, 53, 61–63, 179; "The Great Wall of China," 128, 225n9; "A Hunger Artist," 39, 57; "In the Penal Colony," 6, 9, 12–15, 25, 28–31, 37–39, 49, 54–63, 126–29, 141–42, 177–78, 197, 225n15 (see also Commandant; Explorer; Officer); "Josephine the Mouse Singer," 178; "The Judgment," 40–41, 202; "Leopards in the Temple," 46–47, 54, 57; "The Metamorphosis," 37, 49; "The New Advocate," 113–14; The Trial, 37, 49, 58
Kant, Immanuel, 160–64, 167, 229n78
Klotho, 89
Kondlo, Kwandiwe, 174–75
Kopernicki, Professor, 94
Krog, Antjie, 140–41, 171–72, 226n34

Lacan, Jacques, 90–91, 222n48
Lakhesis, 89
Langer, Lawrence, 35–38, 47, 58
Leavis, F.R., 76–77, 79, 88
Lekotse (shepherd), 173
Leopold of Belgium, 68
Levinas, Emmanuel, 103
Lindqvist, Sven, 68–69
Lukacs, Georg, 135
Lupton, Julia, 224n74
Luria, Isaac, 43, 46–47
Lyotard, Jean-François, 69

Magistrate, the (character in Waiting for the Barbarians), 15, 30, 126–28, 130–33, 137–38, 140–48, 151–54, 156–59, 163–64, 169–75
Mallarmé, Stéphane, 3, 27
Mann, Klaus, 35
Mann, Thomas, 3
marked body, 9–12, 15–16, 18, 20–21, 29–31, 95–99, 122, 146–47, 158, 164, 177–79, 186, 196–97, 209. See also inscribed body
Marx, Karl, 48, 162, 168

mass media, 5, 65, 66, 68, 77–78, 83, 92, 216n1, 217n6
materiality, 8, 19, 32, 98–99, 123, 160–69
Mauss, Marcel, 196
Memento (dir. Christopher Nolan), 19, 22–25, 129
Merivale, Patricia, 128, 225n9
messianism, 71, 101–4, 109, 118, 121, 178–79, 197, 199, 201, 205–9
metalepsis, 5, 25, 26, 33, 129, 169, 196
Meyers, Jeffrey, 211n4
Mill, John Stuart, 48
Miller, J. Hillis, 57–58, 73–74, 155–56, 158, 165, 168, 220n20
mimesis, 10
Morel, E.D., 67
Moses, Michael Valdez, 146
mourning, 20, 110, 171

Nancy, Jean-Luc, 16
Nazi, 50–52, 60, 72, 178, 185, 193, 197, 201–2
Negri, Antonio, 150–52
Nero (Roman emperor), 29
Nietzsche, Friedrich, 5, 13, 39, 46–47, 50–54, 95
Nolan, Christopher, 19, 22–25, 129
notarikon, 41
now of legibility. *See* Benjamin, Walter

Odysseus, 10, 12
Officer, the (character in "In the Penal Colony"), 12, 25, 55, 58–61, 128–29
Owens, Craig, 172–73

Paul, Saint, 207–8
Pawel, Ernst, 57–58
performative, 39, 54–58, 74, 139, 146, 161, 166, 168–69, 199, 215n48, 216n53
Phillips, Caryl, 119
Picasso, Pablo, 1–2, 211n4
Pillow Book, The (dir. Peter Greenaway), 19–20
Pillow Book, The (Sei Shonogan), 20

Index

poststructuralist, 3, 32, 39, 54, 135, 137
prolepsis, 4, 7, 31, 71, 84, 119, 132, 170–72, 218n13

Rancière, Jacques, 26–28
Rich, Paul, 134
Richardson, John, 211n4
Rimbaud, Arthur, 27
Robbe-Grillet, Alain, 40
Rom, Leon, 94
rubber, 67, 120

Said, Edward, 78–79
Sankoh, Foday, 66
Santner, Eric, 30, 104–5, 109
Saunders, Rebecca, 149
Scarry, Elaine, 145–46, 159, 175
Schell, Jonathan, 73, 219n18
Schiller, Friedrich, 167
Schmitt, Carl, 105–6
Scholem, Gershom, 2, 33, 39, 41, 43, 49
Shakespeare, William: *Hamlet*, 3–4, 107, 189
Shelley, Percy Bysshe, 7
Shoah. *See* Holocaust
Shonogan, Sei, 20
Sierra Leone civil war, 65–66
Simmons, Alan, 120–21
Singh, Frances B., 77, 79
Slemon, Stephen, 228n64
Snyman, Major Harold, 138
Speke, John Hanning, 67
Spiegelman, Art, 9, 29, 31; *In the Shadow of No Towers*, 196–97; *Maus I*, 179–82, 184–99, 201–2, 204–7, 209; *Maus II*, 178–79, 182–83, 185, 189–92, 194–96, 199–201; *Maus* project, 10, 32, 177–82, 186, 188–93, 195–97, 199–201, 206–7
Stanley, Sir Henry Morton, 67
state of exception, 7, 104–6, 115, 117, 124–25. *See also* Agamben, Giorgio

Steiner, George, 34, 37–39, 48–50, 54, 133, 225n15

Talmud, Talmudist, 12, 41
tattoo, 22, 23, 178, 197. *See also* inscribed body; marked body
Tocqueville, Alexis de, 48
Torah, 55, 113, 202. *See also* Bible, Hebrew Bible
Torok, Maria, 10
torture, 7–8, 13, 15, 28, 30, 35, 49, 59, 61, 123–27, 129, 132, 135–51, 158, 164–69, 171–74, 225n15, 229n94
Trilling, Lionel, 218n13
Truth and Reconciliation Commission, 8, 140, 171, 173–74

uncanny, the, 30, 36, 39, 46, 53, 56, 58, 65, 118–22, 143, 170, 172–73, 175, 181–82, 185
undead, 30, 59–60, 105, 108–11, 117, 176–77, 181, 185, 196–97, 201
Updike, John, 36–37

Vietnam War, 73
Virgil, 70
voodoo, 65–66

Wade, Jean-Philippe, 135, 138–39, 227n60
Waiting for the Barbarians (J.M. Coetzee), 7, 9, 16, 21, 28–31, 90, 122, 123, 125–34, 136–54, 156–60, 162–78, 185, 227n60. *See also* barbarians; Empire, the; Magistrate, the
Watt, Ian, 72, 85
Watts, Cedric, 71–72, 99, 223n60
Western culture, 5, 10, 34, 66, 71, 75, 217n6
Williams, Raymond, 221n36

Yengeni, Tony, 141

Zionism 42–43, 48